Evariste Régis Huc

Christianity in China, Tartary and Thibet
Volume 2

ISBN/EAN: 9783337168308

Printed in Europe, USA, Canada, Australia, Japan

Cover: Foto ©Lupo / pixelio.de

More available books at **www.hansebooks.com**

CHRISTIANITY

IN

CHINA, TARTARY AND THIBET

BY

M. L'ABBÉ HUC,

FORMERLY MISSIONARY APOSTOLIC IN CHINA;
AUTHOR OF "THE CHINESE EMPIRE," ETC.

IN TWO VOLUMES.

VOL. II.

FROM THE DISCOVERY OF THE CAPE OF GOOD HOPE TO THE ESTABLISHMENT OF THE MANTCHOO-TARTAR DYNASTY IN CHINA.

NEW YORK:
P. J. KENEDY,
PUBLISHER TO THE HOLY APOSTOLIC SEE,
EXCELSIOR CATHOLIC PUBLISHING HOUSE,
3 AND 5 BARCLAY STREET.
1897.

CONTENTS OF VOL. II.

CHAPTER I.

Influence of the Catholic Missions of the Middle Ages upon European Civilisation.—Origin of the Lama Hierarchy and the Ceremonies of the Buddhist Faith.—Vasco de Gama doubles the Cape of Good Hope.—Portuguese Establishment on the Coast of Malabar.—First Conquests of the Portuguese as related by a Syrian Monk.—The Portuguese undertake the Discovery of the Cathay of Marco Polo.—They land at Canton.—Embassy of Thomas Pirès to Pekin.—Deplorable issue of the undertaking.—François Xavier resolves to convert the Chinese to Christianity.—After many adverse Accidents he reaches the Isle of Sancian.—Death of St. François Xavier in sight of China.—Gaspard de la Croix, the first Missionary who penetrated into the Celestial Empire.—Commercial Relations of the Portuguese and Chinese.—Establishment of Macao.—Father Roger.—Father Mathieu Ricci.—First Mission in the Province of Kouang-si 7

CHAPTER II.

The Missionaries are forced to abandon Tchao-King.—Return to Macao.—New and fruitless efforts to re-enter the Empire.—The Viceroy recalls Fathers Roger and Ricci to Tchao-King.—Grant of Land to Build a House and Church.—Buddhist Towers.—Pagodas.—Success and Hopes of the Missionaries.—Erection of a Chapel.—Preludes to Preaching the Gospel.—A Dying Man Baptized.—Interpretation of Christian Charity by Letters.—Success and Persecution.—Ricci applies himself to the Sciences and Letters.—Singular Map of the World in the Chinese Taste.—Completion of the Church.—Attempt at a Spanish Embassy to Pekin.—Two more Missionaries in the Interior.—Journey of Father Roger to Han-Tcheou-Fou.—Chinese Alchemists.—Rascality of the Neophyte Martin.—His Judgment.—Fresh Persecution.—Peace Returns.—Fête of Old Men.—Memorial against the Europeans.—Defence of Father Ricci.—His Popularity.—Solemn Visit of the Imperial Commissioner to the Mission of Tchao-King 44

CHAPTER III.

The Missionaries expelled from Tchao-King. — Farewell of the Christians. — Refusal of Indemnity. — Establishment at Tchao-T'cheou. — Monastery of the Flower of the South. — Founder of this Monastery. — Father Ricci refuses to lodge in it. — He founds an establishment not far from Tchao-Tcheou. — First and singular Disciple of Father Ricci. — The Missionaries change the Costume of the Bonzes for that of the Lettered Class. — Father Ricci sets off for Pekin. — Accidents on the road. — Arrival at Nankin. — Returns to the Capital of Khiang-Si. — Scientific Labours and celebrity of Father Ricci in that City. — His relations with the Viceroy. — The Mission of Tchao-Tcheou besieged by the Bonzes. — Tranquillity restored. — Father Ricci named Superior of all the Missions of China. — Father Ricci sets off for Pekin with the President of the Supreme Court. — Agitation in the City of Nankin. — Imperial Canal. — The Yellow River. — Arrival at Pekin. — The Missionaries deceived. — Forced to quit Pekin. — Sufferings on their Return. — Beautiful Chinese Town. — Fêtes of the New Year. — Father Ricci's Dream. — Preaching on Mathematics and the Sciences. — Observatory of Nankin. — Chinese Explanations of Eclipses. — Literary Solemnity. — Philosophical Discussion. — Palace haunted by Evil Spirits.... 84

CHAPTER IV.

Mode of Instruction adopted by Father Ricci. — Zeal of the Portuguese for the Missions. — Father Ricci sets out for Pekin. — Influence of Eunuchs in the Government. — Journey from Nankin to Pekin. — The Eunuch Ma-Tang. — The Missionaries taken prisoners at a sea-port. — Arrival of Ricci at Pekin. — The Court of Rites. — Rivalry between the Mandarins and Eunuchs. — Palace of the Ambassadors. — Homage to the Son of Heaven. — Various petitions to the Emperor. — Relations between the Missionaries and the Magistrates. — Conversion of a member of the Academy of Han-Lin. — Great success of the Clocks at Court. — Missions of the Provinces. — Fraternal feeling among the Christians of China. — Chinese Superstitions. — Procession in honour of the Idol of the Eyes. — The Missionaries mimicked by the mountebanks. — Success of the Christian preaching. — Profession of Faith of a Christian. — Native Clergy. — Academy of Han-Lin. — Conversion in the Imperial Family. — Insurrection of the Chinese at Macao. — Father Cataneo accused of seeking to get himself proclaimed Emperor. — Formidable armament at Canton. — Martyrdom of a Chinese Seminarist — Peace is restored. 126

CHAPTER V.

Cathay and China. — Father Goës travels by land from India to Pekin. — Cowardice of the Indian Soldiers. — The Robbers of the Desert. — Battle between the Caravan and the Tartar Robbers. — Difficulties of the ourney. — Town of Yarkand. — Jade Stone. — Goès visits the Jade Quarries. — The Mussulmen of Yarkand endeavour to Assassinate him. — Encounter of two Caravans in the middle of the Steppe. — News of the Pekin Mission. — Goès' courageous profession of Faith. — Journey through the Steppes. — Desert of Gobi. — Arrival at the frontiers of China. — The Great Wall. — Combination among the Merchants to deceive the Emperor. — Father Goès fails to reach Pekin. — He writes to Father Ricci. — He is sent for. — Death of Father Goès. — His companion arrives at Pekin, and then returns to the Indies. — Death of Father Soerius. — Peculiarity of the Chinese Letters. — Doctor Paul. — Mission of Schang-Hai. — The Influence and Labours of Father Ricci. — Death of Matthew Ricci. — His Funeral. — Grant of a piece of land for his Tomb. — Opposition of the Bonzes. — Virtues of Father Ricci . 163

CHAPTER VI.

Question of Rites. — The two Schools. — Consequences of these Discussions. — Important Conversions among the Educated Classes. — Doctors Léon and Michel. — Mission of Han-Tcheou-Fou. — Violent Persecution. — Memorial against the Christians. — Apologies from the Christian Doctors. — Edict against Christianity. — Courage of the Neophytes. — Poisoning, Flagellation, and Torture. — Death of two Neophytes. — The Missionaries shut up in Cages. — New Establishment. — The old Missions to Tartary and Thibet. — Father d'Andrada sets out for Thibet in 1624. — Mountains. — Avalanches. — Pagoda of Badid. — Fables of the Lamas. — Halt in the Valley of Mana. — The King of Sirinagar endeavours to arrest d'Andrada. — Terrible Journey of d'Andrada. — Immense Glaciers. — D'Andrada returns. — Reunion of the Caravan. — Arrival in Thibet. — The King of Caparangua. — Decree in favour of the Missionaries. — d'Andrada sets out for the Indies. — Return to Thibet. — Accounts of the Thibetans. — The King desires to turn Christian. — Opposition of the Lamas. — Religious Discussions. — Scarcity of information relating to this Mission. — Conjectures of the Tartar Historians 196

CHAPTER VII.

Revolutionary character of the Chinese.—Secret Societies.—Insurrection of the Sect of the White Lily.—Edict against Secret Societies.—Persecution of Christians.—Memorial in their favour.—Fall of the First Minister.—Doctor Paul.—The Mantchoo Tartars attack the Empire.—Their Chief swears to exterminate the Dynasty of Ming.—First successes of the Tartars.—Death of the Emperor Wang-Lié.—Curious Petition of the Christians.—Jesuits summoned to Pekin to make Cannon.—Discovery of the Monument of Si-Ngan-Fou.—Testimony of Father Semedo.—

Progress of Conversions.—Sincere Piety of the Neophytes.—Admirable Conduct of a Christian General.—Death of Dr. Léon.—Biographical details concerning that illustrious Christian.—Dr. Paul First Minister.—He favours the Christians.—Commissions the Jesuits to Reform the Calendar.—Fathers Schall and Rho arrive at Pekin.—They are placed at the head of the Board of Celestial Literature.—Death of Dr. Paul.—Abject condition of his descendants 235

CHAPTER VIII.

Father Schall fabricates a Harpsichord for the Emperor.—Christianity in the Imperial Harem.—The Tartars summoned to the Assistance of the Empire.—Father Schall establishes a Cannon Foundery.—Gratitude of the Emperor.—Progress of the Insurrection.—Ly-Koung the Chief of the Rebels.—He attacks Pekin.—Tragic Death of the Emperor.—Character of this Prince.—The Insurgents at Pekin.—Adam Schall before the Revolutionary Tribunal.—First Act of the Government of Ly-Koung.—Submission of the Lettered and the Magistrates.—Heroism of General Ou-San Koui and his Father.—Ou-San-Koui swears to exterminate Ly-Koung.—He invokes the Tartars.—Rout of the Insurgents.—Terrible Conflagration at Pekin.—The Catholic Mission is saved.—The Mantchoos Masters of the Capital.—Character of their policy.—Memorial of Father Schall.—He is appointed President of the Board of Mathematics.—The Government Astronomers.—The Mantchoos favour the Missionaries.—Father Martini and a Tartar Chief.—The Tyrant Tchang-Kien ravages and depopulates Sse-Tchouen.—Adventures of Fathers Buglio and Magalhans.—Father Schall at Pekin 269

CHAPTER IX.

Legend respecting the origin of the Mantchoo Tartars. — Father Schall and the King of the Coreans. — Rash Enterprise of the Regent of the Empire. — Ama-Wang listens to the advice of Father Schall. — Influence of that celebrated Missionary. — The Claimants of the Ancient Dynasty. — Their Friendliness to Christianity. — Dissensions among the Chinese Claimants. — They are Destroyed by Ama-Wang. — Death of that Illustrious Tartar.—Majority of the Young Emperor.—Application of Father Schall. — His Advice to the Emperor. — Intimacy between Father Schall and the Emperor. — Chun-Tché loves and favours Christianity. — Progress of the Missionaries. — Construction of a beautiful Church at Pekin. — Zeal of the Christians. — Religious Associations. — Titles conferred by the Emperor on Father Schall and his Ancestors. — Sickness of Chun-Tché. — Exhortations of Father Schall. — Death of the Emperor --- His Funeral 302

CHRISTIANITY

IN

CHINA, TARTARY AND THIBET

CHAPTER I.

Influence of the Catholic Missions of the Middle Ages upon European Civilisation.—Origin of the Lama Hierarchy and the Ceremonies of the Buddhist Faith.—Vasco de Gama doubles the Cape of Good Hope.—Portuguese Establishment on the Coast of Malabar.—First Conquests of the Portuguese as related by a Syrian Monk.—The Portuguese undertake the Discovery of the Cathay of Marco Polo.—They land at Canton.—Embassy of Thomas Pirès to Pekin.—Deplorable issue of the undertaking.—François Xavier resolves to convert the Chinese to Christianity.—After many adverse Accidents he reaches the Isle of Sancian.—Death of St. François Xavier in sight of China.—Gaspard de la Croix, the first Missionary who penetrated into the Celestial Empire.—Commercial Relations of the Portuguese and Chinese.—Establishment of Macao.—Father Roger.—Father Mathieu Ricci.—First Mission in the Province of Kouang-si.

THE Catholic missions of the middle ages, which we have endeavoured to sketch, were not followed by the results which might have been expected from the persevering efforts of numerous missionaries, who never ceased at that epoch to labour for the conversion of the nations of the East. The Christian communities, founded at the cost of immense sacrifices, by monks of the orders of St. Francis and St. Dominic, though flourishing in the commencement, never became deeply rooted enough in this ungrateful soil to withstand the tempest of persecution.

The people, before whose eyes the light of the Gospel had shone for a moment in all its brilliancy, soon relapsed into darkness, and wandered far from the path which leads to God, that is, to truth and life. It must be acknowledged, however, that the constant efforts of the Church to convert and civilise the Pagan nations produced results which have been perhaps too little noticed. The labours of the missionaries contributed greatly to the prodigious development of European civilisation, and they left in the extreme East curious recollections of the Catholic preaching.

The nations of Northern Asia had remained for many centuries completely unknown to the West. The Roman world did not even suspect that, far in the remotest parts of the mysterious East, there existed an immense empire, with great and wealthy cities, filled with numberless inhabitants, far advanced in the arts, industry, agriculture, and commerce. Thus, two systems of civilisation had established themselves at the two extremities of the ancient continent, and for centuries, their growth and development had gone on, without any communication or mutual influence, each working and depending on its own resources. But suddenly we find wars of unheard of magnitude bringing these two great powers into contact. The prodigious expansion of the Tartar races inundated the West at the same time that the Crusades were carrying into the East the new ideas fermenting in Europe.

Then began an extraordinary mingling of races, and the descendants of Shem and Japhet, children of one family so long parted, once more held communication with each other.

Numerous efforts at alliance and fusion were made on both sides. Twenty embassies were sent by the Tartars into Italy, Spain, France, and England, and on the other side the Christian Princes, especially the Popes, despatched legations and missions to the states of the grand Khan. The communications were long and active, and, what was singular, it was certainly not the fault of the Tartars that a coalition was not formed between them and the Crusaders which would have destroyed for ever the power of Islamism, both in Europe and Asia.

Official reports and solemn interviews were not, however, the only occasions on which the two races, hitherto strangers to one another, were put into communication. A more obscure, but more efficacious, intercourse was established by the travels of private persons, drawn to the opposite extremities of the world in the train of envoys and armies. Mongols were to be seen at Rome, Paris, Avignon, London, Barcelona, and many other important European towns. The Franks, as they were then called, were to be found in all directions, at immense distances from their native lands. They traversed all Asia to acquit themselves of the diplomatic missions confided to them, and to preach the Gospel to the heathen. The envoys of the sovereign pontiff were ordered, in remission of their sins, to observe the manners and customs of the distant nations they visited, and such an injunction could not fail to call forth many observations favourable to the progress of European civilisation; and in the middle ages industry and the arts had much to gain from intercourse with Oriental nations.

We have cited and analysed the travels of Rubruk, Plano Carpini, Marco Polo, Oderic de Friuli, and some others. But at that period it was an easier task to execute long journeys than to write an account of them; and the majority of these intrepid travellers have fallen into oblivion, from having left no connected account of their wonderful peregrinations. Their observations of foreign lands were not entirely lost, nevertheless. On returning to their native countries, they narrated the marvellous things they had seen, enriching their recitals, no doubt, with some exaggerations, in spite of which the narratives afforded much useful information. In France, in Italy, in Germany, they deposited in castles, monasteries, and in all ranks of society, the precious seeds destined in after times to bring forth much fruit. Thus, while the arts and ideas of Europe were astonishing Asia, the products and the knowledge of the East were exciting the admiration and imitation of Europe.

The mariner's compass, gunpowder, and the art of printing, those three grand discoveries, which gave such an impulse to European civilization, were the result of the narratives of missionaries, sent from the West to Asia. The polarity of the magnet was known, and turned to use among the Chinese from the earliest times. The missionaries who coasted the Celestial Empire, or traversed its great lakes, remarked on board the Chinese junks a little box containing a magnetised needle, which they callud *Ting-nan-Tchen*, or "needle which points to the south," and which sailors used to guide their vessels. Chinese books say that, 4456 years ago, a hero had recourse to it, to guide him out of a dark cloud with which an evil genius had surrounded him. It is true this is only a fable, but in such cases, an ancient fable is often an excellent authority. The same missionaries saw used by the Chinese and Tartar armies certain terrible machines called ho-pao, or fire-guns, from which, by means of inflammable powder, were ejected stones and missiles against the fortifications of towns. The learned Father Gaubil, describing the siege of Kai-Tong-Fou, in the beginning of the thirteenth century, as narrated by Chinese historians, says, "There were in the town some fire *paos*,* which projected pieces of iron in the form of a cupping glass. These were filled with powder, and when they were fired there was produced a noise like thunder, which was heard for twenty-five miles around, and the place where they fell was burnt. If this missile struck on iron cuirasses, it shattered them to pieces. When the Mongols were sapping

---

* Gaubil, "Histoire de la Dynastie des Mongols, tirée de l'Histoire Chinoise," Paris, 1739, p. 71.

a wall, they sheltered themselves in holes dug in the ground, so that from the walls they could not be injured, and the besieged, to dislodge them, used to attach some of these shells to iron chains, and let them down from the walls into their pits. When they reached the ditches or caves, they took fire by means of a match, and spread devastation among the besiegers. These missiles were more feared by the Mongols than anything."*

The Europeans who penetrated into China were no less struck with the libraries of the Chinese than with their artillery. They were astonished at the sight of the elegant books printed rapidly upon pliant, silky paper, by means of wooden blocks. The first edition of the classical works printed in China, appeared in 958, 500 years before the invention of Guttenburg. The missionaries had, doubtless, often been busied in their convents with the laborious work of copying manuscript books, and the simple Chinese method of printing must have particularly attracted their attention. Many other marvellous productions were noticed, such as silk, porcelain, playing cards, spectacles, and numerous other products of art and industry, unknown in Europe. They brought back these new ideas to Europe; "and from that time," says Abel Remusat,† "the West began to hold in due esteem the most beautiful, the most populous, and the most anciently civilized of all the four quarters of the world. The arts, the religious faiths, and the languages of its people were studied, and it was even proposed to establish a professorship for the Tartar language in the university of Paris. The world seemed to open towards the East; geography made immense strides; and

---

* I have not ventured, says Father Gaubil, to translate *pao*, gun. It is joined to the word *ho*, fire; and I do not know whether it was similar in construction to our cannon. I do not even feel assured that the balls were projected in the same manner as now, nor have I ventured to call the missiles *bombs*. It is well known that the Chinese have used gunpowder for more than 1600 years, yet up to this time it does not appear what use they made of it in sieges —*Note of Father Gaubil.*

† Mélanges Asiatiques.

ardour for discovery became the new vent for the adventurous spirit of the Europeans. As our own hemisphere became better known, the idea of another ceased to appear a wholly improbable paradox; and in seeking the Zipangou* of Marco Polo, Christopher Columbus discovered the New World.

The use of the compass, of stereotype printing, of engraving on wood, and of fire-arms, were, therefore, it appears, at the command of the Asiatics long before they were introduced into Europe; and measures for the propagation of the Christian faith now began to be organised. Numbers of missionaries were despatched into Asia: their communications lasted for a century and a half; and before another century had elapsed, all the inventions they spoke of were in use in Europe. Their origin, however, is enveloped in mystery. The countries where they first appeared, the men who produced them, are equally subjects of doubt; but they are not ascribed to the most enlightened countries, nor to the most learned men. It was men of the people, obscure artisans, who dazzled the civilized world with these unexpected lights.

Most of these inventions first appeared in Europe in the crude form in which the Asiatics possessed them; some were at once taken into use, others remained for some time lost in an obscurity which conceals from us their progress towards perfection; all were considered as new discoveries; and when improved, and as it were fertilised by European genius, their combined influence communicated an immense impulse to human intelligence.†

These great discoveries, of which modern civilization reaps the fruits, ought in justice to be attributed for the most part to the monks of the middle ages.

---

* The *Zipangou* of Marco Polo was Japan, called by the Chinese Je-Pan Kouo, or the kingdom of Je-Pan.

† The famous English monk, Roger Bacon, said to be the inventor of gunpowder, lived at the same time as Rubruk. He speaks of him in his books, and may very likely have seen him. As gunpowder was then in use among the Tartars, is it not probable that Rubruk may have given Bacon the clue to the discovery?

The Catholic loves above everything to regard missionaries as apostles going, crucifix in hand, to preach the Gospel to the heathen, and cheerfully bearing the privations and sufferings incident to their laborious task, provided they could but win souls to Jesus Christ. This ardent zeal for the propagation of the faith inspires little sympathy in men accustomed to count the interests of religion as nothing; but even these must acknowledge that missionaries have been in the past, as they are in the present, most useful agents of civilisation, and, however devoid of Christian sympathy for the preachers of the Gospel, might regard with some little admiration and gratitude, those who, by diffusing new ideas, so materially aid in human progress.

We have said that the missionaries of the middle ages left profound traces of their apostleship in the heart of Asia; and the reformed Buddhism established in Thibet, under the supreme direction of the Grand Lama, excited much curiosity in Europe.

The first missionaries who became acquainted with it in the seventeenth century, were not a little surprised to discover in the centre of Asia numerous monasteries, solemn processions, religious *fêtes*, a pontifical court, colleges of superior Lamas electing their ecclesiastical sovereign, and the spiritual father of Thibet and Tartary,—in a word, an organisation closely resembling that of the Catholic Church.

These missionary monks, full of good faith and sincerity, did not think of endeavouring to conceal this singular resemblance. On the contrary, they described it simply, and limited themselves to regarding Buddhism as a kind of degenerate Christianity, and the features which had particularly struck them as traces of the former sojourn of the Syrian sects in those countries.

But the anti-Christian philosophers, Voltaire, Volney, Baill and others, seized upon these analogies with eagerness, as a valuable discovery. They pretended at first, in the name of science, that mankind, with all their languages, their arts, and religious beliefs, descended originally from the mountains of Thibet; there was the cradle of science and faith, whence they had flowed successively through China, India and Egypt, and spread at last into Europe.*

This first point established, by means of a good deal of audacity and a little superficial and mistaken erudition, they talked of Buddhism and the Grand Lama with an affectation of mystery; they published a number of dissertations on the Lama hierarchy, with some apparently indulgent, but in reality treacherous, reservations; and as in that enlightened age it could not be permitted to hide the light of truth under a bushel, they then asserted boldly that Christianity was the offspring of Buddhism, and that the Catholic worship was founded on the practices of the Lamas. It is now easy to prove, however, that the real state of the case is precisely the contrary.

Voltaire and his partisans forgot in their dissertations one rather important point, which was to establish the date of the foundation of Reformed Buddhism.

According to Voltaire, it is *certain* that that part of Thibet over which the Grand Lama reigns formed a portion of the Mongol empire, and that the pontiff was therefore not disturbed by Tchinguiz-Khan. This assertion is either made ignorantly or falsely, for the office of Grand Lama did not exist in the days of Tchinguiz-Khan, and was only instituted by his successors. Kublai-Khan, after subduing China, adopted the Buddhist doctrines, which had made considerable progress among the Tartars. In the year 1261 he raised a Buddhist priest named Mati to the dignity of head of the Faith in the empire. This priest is better known under the name of Pakbo Lama, or supreme Lama: he was a native of Thibet, and had gained the good graces and confidence of Kublai, who,

---

* For the opinions o. the philosophers on these subjects, see "Les Voyages de Thunberg."

at the same time that he conferred on him the supreme sacerdotal office, invested him with the temporal power in Thibet, with the titles of "King of the Great and Precious Law" and "Institutor of the Empire." Such was the origin of the Grand Lamas of Thibet and it is not impossible that the Tartar Emperor, who had had frequent communications with the Christian missionaries, may have wished to create a religious organisation after the model of the Romish hierarchy, with which he was well acquainted. Thibet had not been a monarchy for many centuries, and the various tribes of the country obeyed each a different chief.

In order the better to establish his own dominion, Kublai divided it into provinces, governed each by an ecclesiastic, who in turn was subject to the sovereign pontiff whom he had appointed.

A hundred years later, Buddhism underwent important changes, and the forms of worship were introduced which present such a striking analogy to the Catholic liturgy. The Lama reform arose in the country of Amdo, to the south of Koukou-Noor, where we resided six months in our travels through Thibet in 1845. This part of the country is inhabited by the Si Fans and is wild and melancholy in appearance. On all sides the eye beholds nothing but hills of red or yellow ochre, almost devoid of vegetation, and traversed by deep ravines in every direction. Nevertheless, amid this sterile and desolate land, you sometimes encounter valleys abounding in pasturage, where the nomadic tribes feed their flocks. The following curious legend was related to us in that district concerning the Lama reforms which arose there.

Towards the middle of the fourteenth century of our era, a shepherd of the country of Amdo, named Lambo-Moke, pitched his black tent at the foot of a mountain, near the opening of a large ravine, at the bottom of which flowed on its stony bed an abundant rivulet.

Lambo-Moke shared the cares of a pastoral life with his

wife Chingtsa-Tsio. They were not the owners of numerous flocks; about twenty goats and a few yaks, or long haired oxen, composed all their wealth. For many years they lived childless and solitary in the heart of the wilderness. Lambo-Moke led his cattle to the neighbouring pastures, while Chingtsa-Tsio, alone in the tent, took care of the dairy or wool, a kind of coarse cloth, which the women of Amdo prepare from the long hair of the yaks.

One day Chingtsa-Tsio having gone down the ravine to fetch water, was seized with giddiness, and fell senseless upon a large stone, which was engraved with characters in honour of Buddha. When Chingtsa-Tsio came to herself and arose, she felt a great pain in her side, and became aware that the fall had rendered her pregnant. In the year of the *Fiery Hen* (1357), nine months after this event, she brought into the world a child, whom Lambo-Moke named Tsong-Kaba, after the mountain, at the foot of which his tent had been pitched so many years. This miraculous child had at its birth a white beard and a face of extraordinary majesty. There was nothing puerile in his behaviour: as soon as he saw the light he was able to speak, and expressed himself with clearness and precision. He spoke little, but his observations always bore a deep meaning concerning the nature and destiny of man. At the age of three years, Tsong-Kaba resolved to renounce the world and to embrace the religious mode of life.

Chingtsa-Tsio, full of respect for her son's holy project, shaved his head with her own hands, and cast down the long and beautiful tresses of his hair, outside the entrance to the tent. From this hair there sprung up a tree, whose wood gave forth an exquisite perfume, and each leaf of which bore a character of the sacred language of Thibet engraved on it.*

From that time forth, Tsong-Kaba lived in such complete

---

* For an account of this tree, see our "Travels in Thibet."

seclusion, that he even fled the society of his parents. He withdrew to the summits of the most desolate mountains, or to the bottom of the wildest ravines, and passed days and nights in the contemplation of eternal things. His fasts were frequent and of long duration: he respected the life of the smallest insects, and rigorously denied himself every kind of animal food.

Whilst Tsong-Kaba was thus occupied in purifying his heart by assiduous prayer and austerity of life, there came by chance into the country of Amdo, a lama from the farthest regions of the West, and he requested hospitality in the tent of Lambo-Moke. Tsong-Kaba astounded at the science and holiness of the stranger, threw himself at his feet, and entreated him to be his guide and master. The Lama traditions say that this strange lama from the West was remarkable not only for the inscrutable profundity of his doctrine, but also for the peculiarity of his face, above all for his large nose, and eyes glittering with supernatural fire.

The stranger was equally struck with the marvellous qualities of Tsong-Kaba and did not hesitate to accept him as a disciple. He established himself in Amdo, where he did not survive many years; but after initiating his disciple in the doctrines of all the most renowned saints of the West, he went to sleep upon the summit of a mountain and never woke again.

Tsong-Kaba became more than ever eager for religious instruction, when deprived of the counsels of the holy stranger; and resolved to abandon his tribe and journey into the West, to imbibe the sacred truths at the fountain head. He set off, therefore, alone and on foot, but with a heart strong in superhuman courage, and turned his steps towards the south at first, and, after long and painful wanderings, reached the frontiers of Yun-Nau, the extremity of the Chinese Empire. He then turned to the northeast, following the bank of the great river Yaroa-Dsangbo. Thus he reached the capital of Thibet, and was continuing his route, when a Lha (or spirit), surrounded by dazzling light, appeared to him and forbade him going farther. "Oh! Tsong-Kaba," said the spirit, "all these countries form part of the great empire which has been allotted to thee. Here thou must promulgate the new truths thou has learned; here the last days of thy mortal life must be passed." Obedient to the supernatural voice, Tsong-Kaba entered the city of spirits (Lha-ssa), and chose a poor dwelling in the most retired part of the town; but he was not slow to win disciples. Before long, the new doctrines he taught and the unknown rites he introduced into the Lama ceremonies began to attract attention. Tsong-Kaba then boldly announced himself as a reformer, and declared war against the ancient faith. His party augmented from day to day, and were called Yellow-cap Lamas, in distinction to the Red-cap Lamas, who defended the ancient worship. The Chakdja, living Buddha and chief of the Lama hierarchy, began to inquire into this new sect, which was bringing religion into confusion; and he ordered Tsong-Kaba to appear before him, that he might judge whether his doctrine was as marvellous and profound as his partisans pretended.

The reformer disdained, however, to accept this invitation, for, as representative of a new system of religion which was to replace the old, it was not for him to do homage to it, or perform any act of submission.

As the sect of the Yellow-caps continued to increase, and the multitude did homage to Tsong-Kaba, the Buddha Chakdja, seeing his authority decline, resolved to pay a visit to *the little Lama of Amdo*, as he contemptuously called the reformer. He repaired to his dwelling, surrounded with all the pomp and attributes of his supreme office; but as he entered the lowly cell of Tsong-Kaba, his great red cap knocked against the lintel of the door and fell to the ground an accident which was regarded by the monks and the people as an omen of triumph to the Yellow-caps.

The reformer was seated cross-legged on a cushion, and paid not the slightest attention to the entrance of the Chakdja, but continued gravely to tell the beads of his chaplet. The Chakdja, without disturbing himself either at the fall of his cap or his cool reception, abruptly commenced a discourse. He pronounced a pompous panegyric on the ancient rites, and dwelt upon all their claims to pre-eminence; but Tsong-Kaba without raising his eyes, interrupted his opponent thus:—

"Cruel that thou art! restore to liberty the hapless creature writhing between thy fingers! My heart is penetrated with grief at the sound of its cries of suffering."

In fact the Chakdja, while occupied in describing his own merits, had seized upon an insect which was biting him unpleasantly, and, despite the doctrine of metempsychosis, which inculcates respect for the life of every creature, was endeavouring to crush it between his fingers. Not knowing what to reply to the severe words of Tsong-Kaba, he prostrated himself before the reformer and acknowledged his supremacy.

From that day Tsong-Kaba met with no obstacle to his scheme of reform; but it was adopted throughout Thibet, and established itself by degrees in all the kingdoms of the Tartar empire.

Even a slight examination of Tsong-Kaba's reforms and innovations will suffice to show their resemblance to Catholicism. We have already spoken of the striking analogy between the government of the Grand Lama and that of the States of the Church. During our residence among the Buddhists of Thibet, we remarked, besides the cross, the mitre, the dalmatic, and the chasuble, that the superior lamas carry with them, when travelling, or performing some ceremony out of the temple, the choral service, the exorcisms, the censers supported by five chains, and made to open and shut, the blessings which the lamas bestow on the faithful, laying their hand upon the head of the supplicant, the rosary, the practice of ecclesiastical celibacy, of spiritual retreats, the worship of saints, fasts, processions, holy water, litanies, and many other details of ceremonial, which are in use among the Buddhists, precisely as in our own Church, and are evidently of Christian origin.

At the time when the Buddhist patriarchs established themselves in Thibet, all the countries of Northern Asia numbered Christians among their inhabitants. We have seen that the Catholic missionaries founded many flourishing colonies in China, Tartary, Turkestan, and even among the nomadic tribes of Thibet, who were converted by Oderic de Friuli. In their apostolic wanderings, the monks carried with them the paraphernalia of the Church; and they performed the ceremonies of their religion before the Mongol princes, who received them hospitably, and suffered them to erect chapels even within the precincts of their palaces; and they were thus enabled to witness and admire the pomp of Christian worship. The envoys of the Mongol conquerors, too, visited the capital of the Christian world several times, and assisted at the second œcumenic council of Lyons in 1274. These barbarians must have been greatly struck with the splendour of the Catholic religion, and have carried back to their wilderness an indelible impression of its grandeur. The new dignity of the Buddhist patriarchs being founded at this epoch, it is not surprising that, desirous of augmenting the number of their sect, they should have sought to increase the magnificence of their worship by adopting some of those splendid ceremonies of the Christian service which attract the multitude, and even have introduced into their system something of that ecclesiastical organisation with which the missionaries had made them acquainted.

Is not the legend of Tsong-Kaba, which we have ourselves heard in his native country from many of the lamas, a striking proof of the Christian origin of the Buddhist reform?

Stripping the narrative of all the marvellous details added to it by the imagination of the lamas, it is easy to suppose that Tsong-Kaba was a man remarkable for intellect and virtue, that he was instructed by a stranger who came from the West; that after the death of the master the disciple, turning his steps westward, arrived at the capital of Thibet, where he taught the doctrines which he had imbibed. The stranger *with the large nose* may have been one of the numerous Catholic missionaries who at that time appeared in China, Tartary, and Thibet, and it is not surprising that tradition should have preserved the remembrance of the European face, so different from the familiar Asiatic type. Whilst living in Amdo, the native country of Tsong Kaba, we often heard the lamas making remarks on our strange faces, and declaring without hesitation, that we must come from the same country as Tsong Kaba's instructor.

A premature death may have prevented the Catholic missionary from completing the religious instruction of his disciple, who afterwards wishing himself to become an apostle, and either being but half acquainted with the Christian dogma, or having seceded from his faith, merely introduced a new liturgy. The slight opposition which he met with would seem to indicate that the progress of Christianity in those parts had already affected the stability of the religion of Buddha.

The coincidence of time and place, as well as the testimony of history and tradition, all point to the fact, that the lama hierarchy borrowed largely from Christianity; and the assertions of Voltaire and Volney show either profound ignorance or wilful misrepresentation.

Communication between Europe and Asia was long interrupted by the sanguinary and devastating wars of Tamerlane. When a new attempt was made at establishing relations between them, the time was past for that weary and interminable land travelling which was formerly the only means of intercourse, and the ocean was beginning to be the highway uniting the most distant lands of the two hemispheres. The discovery of the compass was bearing fruit; and mariners, emboldened by the possession of a certain guide, steered their vessels far away from land, and ventured to traverse the vast and pathless plains of ocean.

After a long and adventurous voyage along the coast of Africa, Diaz returned to Lisbon in 1487. As he related the story of his voyage before the court, he said that at the extremity of Africa was a cape so celebrated for its storms, that he had called it the Cape of Torment. "No," cried Juan II., "it shall be called the Cape of Good Hope, as a happy omen of the advantages to be derived from this great discovery."

Ten years afterwards the good hope of the King Juan II. began to be realised; a man of genius and rare courage had doubled the stormy cape which arrested Diaz's progress, and discovered by sea China and the Indies.

At that time, not far from Lisbon, might be seen a rustic chapel, which the Infante Don Enrico had built upon the seashore in honour of the Virgin, to animate the devotion of the sailors, and to ensure them her protection.

One day towards the end of July, 1497, there knelt, at the foot of that statue of the Virgin, a party of men, whose tanned complexions and energetic faces showed them strangers to idleness and ease. They passed the night in prayer; and the next day, after hearing mass, and communicating with fervour, they returned to Lisbon in procession, each one carrying a taper, and chanting hymns and psalms, accompanied by priests, monks, and an immense concourse of people drawn together by the novelty of the spectacle. These men were Vasco da Gama and his companions, preparing to brave the perils of an unknown sea. Diaz had given so terrible an account of the Cape of Storms, that all these sailors were looked upon as so many victims, destined to almost inevitable destruction. Their procession was regarded almost as a funeral array; and the crowd melted into tears at the sight of the youth and manly vigour which was bidding adieu to its native land, to rush into a sadly-certain doom. Thus were the adventurers escorted to the port; and here, throwing themselves on their knees, they received general absolution as for death, and embarked amid the cries and lamentations of the people. The bold adventurers then set sail with a favourable wind, and were soon lost to view on the vast plain of waters.*

Before a year had elapsed, Vasco da Gama had planted the Christian cross and the flag of Portugal on the coast of Malabar; and he was not a little surprised to find churches and Christians already established there. The Nestorian missions, founded in the East during the earliest ages of the Catholic Church, were still flourishing; and at the very time when Vasco da Gama landed on the shore of Malabar to form the first European settlement at Goa, the patriarch Elie was sending four bishops to India and China.

These were Thomas, Jaballah, Denha, and Jacob, all monks of the monastery of St. Eugène in Mesopotamia. They set out in 1502, and, by a singular coincidence, arrived in the Indies precisely at the time when the Portuguese were seeking to establish themselves in the country. They witnessed their first struggles, of which we find details in a letter addressed by them to their patriarch, and which has been preserved in the Oriental library of the learned Maronite Assemani; we quote this document as a curious specimen of the accounts of the Nestorian missionaries:—

"To our patriarch, to whom is given, in heaven and on earth, power to feed the flock of Christ; happy are the people possessing such a prelate! To Mar Elie, Patriarch Catholicos of the East, may the Lord fortify him, and surround him with honour and magnificence, for the glory of the Christian religion, and the exaltation of the Church! Amen!

"Your humble servants and unworthy disciples, the pilgrims, Mar Jaballah, Mar Thomas, Mar Jacob, and Mar

---

* Lafitau, " Histoire des Découvertes et Conquêtes des Portugais dans le nouveau monde."

Denha, men full of infirmities and misery, adore the footstool beneath your pure and holy feet. From the depths of their abject poverty, they implore your efficacious prayers, and supplicatingly entreat 'Your blessing, lord! your blessing! your blessing!'

"We address our salutations to John, the tabernacle of God, the treasurer of His ministry, the prince of saints, the Metropolitan Bishop of Atèle; to the upright monks, pure priests, immaculate deacons; to the faithful, the elect, and all Christian people who reside in Atèle.

"Be it known to your amiable charity, that, assisted by the divine grace, and the virtue of your prayers, we have reached the land of the Indians in safety.

"We therefore humbly thank God, the Lord of all things, who never confounds those that place their trust in him. We were received with general rejoicings. Our holy father, Mar Jean, is still living, and sends you greeting. There are here about thirty thousand Christian families, united to us in faith, and praying the Lord to preserve your life. The faithful have begun building new churches; they are in the enjoyment of abundance, and are peaceful and gentle in disposition. Blessed be the Lord!

"The temple of St. Thomas is undergoing restoration by the Christians, to whom it belongs. They are separated from the rest of the faithful by twenty-five days' journey. They live on the seashore, in a town called Meliapour, the capital of the province. The Indies are vast and fertile, it takes six months to journey from one end to the other; and each province has a special name. That inhabited by the Christians is called Malabar. It contains more than twenty towns, of which the three most important are, Cranganor, Palaor, and Colam; but the rest are little inferior to these. They all contain Christians and churches. There is in the neighbourhood an opulent city named Calicut, inhabited by idolaters.

"We have also to announce to our father, that powerful

vessels have been sent hither by the Christian king of the Franks, our brother.* Their voyage occupied a whole year. After visiting Ethiopia, they landed on the shores of India, purchased pepper and other merchandise, and returned to their own country. Their powerful king (whom God preserve!) having discovered and explored this new route, despatched six immense vessels; and after six months' navigation, these skilful mariners reached Calicut. There are at Calicut many Ismaelites, who, urged by their inveterate hatred to Christians, have sought to slander them to the king. They have said that these Western men were so much pleased with the town and its environs, that they intended to return to their own country to fetch a formidable army, with which to invade and conquer the kingdom.

"The infidel king believed in the words of the Ismaelites, and in a great rage put to death all the Franks in the town, to the number of seventy, and five priests who accompanied them: for the Franks never travel any where without priests. Those on board the vessels raised anchor immediately, and sailed away in great distress, and weeping bitterly, towards our town of Cochin.

"That country belongs also to an infidel prince; but when he saw the strangers plunged in distress, he received them kindly, consoled them, and swore not to abandon them. News of this having reached the ears of the impious king of Calicut, he raised a great army, and commenced hostilities; and the Franks, together with the king who had shown them hospitality, were forced to retire into a fortified camp on the seashore. There they remained some days, when Christ took pity on them, and there arrived several more Frank vessels, which made war upon the king of Calicut. By means of their cannon they cast great stones into his army, which caused great ravage, and he was at length driven away. The Franks

---

* The King of Portugal. It was, as is well known, the Eastern custom to call al Europeans Franks.

Vol. II.—2

then marched to the town of Cochin, and constructed there an immense camp, which they garrisoned with three hundred of their own countrymen. Some were charged with the management of the cannon; others were fusileers.* There were fifty large guns, and a hundred small, besides a great number of firelocks.

"The hostile king (may his memory perish!) sought to repair his defeat, but was entirely vanquished in the first battle, through the glory of Christ. Three thousand of his soldiers were swept away by the cannon, and he was forced to retreat upon Calicut. The Franks pursued him by sea—for the town is built upon the shore; they seized his person, sunk his ships, and destroyed the town by a cannonade.

"After this war was thus concluded, the Franks visited another infidel king on the coast of Malabar, and demanded a portion of his town named Cananor, where they should be permitted to transact trade freely. This king received them joyfully, treated them hospitably, and assigned to them a certain portion of land and a large house. The Christian chief presented him, in return, with magnificent garments embroidered with gold, and pieces of purple stuff; and shortly after, they sailed away with a great cargo of spices to return to their native land.

"There are about twenty Franks left residing in the town of Cananor. When we arrived there and made ourselves known to them, they received us with joy, and gave us clothes and twenty drachms of gold. We stayed with them two months and a half; and on certain days they requested us to celebrate the holy mysteries. They have an oratory, where they pray, and where their priests daily celebrate divine worship. On the Lord's day, after their priests had officiated, we also were admitted to perform our devotions. On leaving them we repaired at once to our community, which is only

---

* "Alii ad tormenta tractanda deputabantur, alii sclopetarii erant."

eight days distant. The Franks number four hundred men; and their presence has struck terror into the Ismaelites and infidels of these parts. Their country is called Portugal, their king is named Emmanuel*, and we pray to the divine Emmanuel to protect him! Complain not, brothers, of the length of this epistle; for we have thought it good to communicate these details to you. May the Lord be with you all. Amen!"

Such was the beginning of the rapid conquests and extraordinary power which Portugal afterwards attained in Asia. It is curious to find the details of it in the letter of a Syrian monk, and to see with what promptitude European intelligence availed itself of the advantages of gunpowder and the compass,—those two great discoveries which the Asiatics possessed so long without being able to make much use of them, and which were so soon turned to fatal account against them.

No sooner had the Portuguese set foot in the Indies, than the spirit of commerce, and the taste for distant expeditions and adventures, inspired them with a desire to go in search of Cathay, that vast mysterious empire of which so many wonders had been related in preceding ages. They had already encountered many Chinese coasting the Malay peninsula in their junks; and the great Albuquerque entered into communication with them when he took possession of Malacca. It was at the instigation of that renowned warrior and profound politician, that the court of Portugal resolved to send an expedition and an embassy to China. A squadron of nine vessels, commanded by Ferdinand d'Andrada, set sail from Lisbon in 1518; and Thomas Pirès, who had resided long in the Indies, was named ambassador. As soon as the Portuguese vessels hove in sight of the numerous islands near Canton, the Mandarin of the Sea, astonished at the strange apparition, armed his war-junks, and went forth to meet the European flotilla.

* Emmanuel the Great reigned in Portugal from 1490 to 1521.

D'Andrada, who was of an amiable and gentle disposition, allowed his vessels to be inspected, won the friendship of the mandarin, and obtained permission to visit Canton and lay before the governor of the province the object of his mission. They ascended the Tiger river, admiring the rich country on both sides, the fertile well-cultivated lands and flourishing villages, whose inhabitants were peacefully occupied with agriculture and commerce. The great city of Canton with its hard-working intelligent population, its great shops overflowing with the thousand products of an advanced state of civilisation, filled the travellers with astonishment and admiration; and they felt that moderation and gentleness were the only means to establish relations with this remarkable people. D'Andrada insinuated himself by degrees into the good graces of the mandarins of Canton, and succeeded in making a commercial treaty with them, subject to the sanction of the Emperor.

Thomas Pirès then set out for Pekin, as ambassador, expecting to find the court well disposed towards him; but, unhappily, his hopes were doomed to destruction by various untoward circumstances. News reached the court from Canton, that Simon d'Andrada, the brother of Ferdinand, had come from Malacca with four vessels, built a fortress on the Isle of Tu-men, pillaged the Chinese junks, and let loose his sailors on the coast to commit every excess of licence and piracy. At the same time came an ambassador to Nankin from the Mussulman king of Bantam, to represent to the Emperor that his sovereign had been unjustly deprived of Malacca by the Portuguese, and to demand that, as a vassal of the empire, he should be placed under Chinese protection. The governor of Nankin had listened to these complaints; and he besought the Emperor not to enter into any alliance with the greedy, audacious Franks, who only sought, under a pretence of commerce, to study the weak points of the countries where they were received, and to establish themselves as merchants, before assuming the airs of masters. It is apparent that the European disposition to conquest was already well-known in Asia.

This advice, to which the recent conduct of the Portuguese in the Indies, their audacious enterprises, and rapid conquests, gave much weight, was not of a nature to forward Pirès' hopes, and the letter of the King of Portugal to the Emperor of China, with which the ambassador was provided, was a fresh subject of discontent. Written according to the usual style adopted by Western sovereigns towards the potentates of the East, it could not be received in that form at the court of the Son of Heaven; and, by a stratagem attributed to the Mohammedans of Malacca, it was literally translated into Chinese,—the most certain way of making it offensive, and more was not needed to cause Pirès to be regarded as a spy usurping the style and title of ambassador.

The Emperor dying at this juncture, it was ordained that Pirès should be conducted back to Canton, and that in the meantime the Portuguese should be ordered to quit the town. They refused to do so; and there arose a struggle in which they were defeated. Pirès and his followers arriving just after this unlucky occurrence, fell victims to it. They were thrown into prison, and threatened with being judged according to the laws of the empire, as responsible for the insolent letter which they had brought from the Frank king, for the audacity with which that king's subjects had attacked the Chinese vessels, and plundered and otherwise ill-used the inhabitants of the Celestial Empire.

Such crimes were sufficient in the eyes of the Chinese to justify the most rigorous treatment of the ambassador. Portuguese historians say that he expired in prison; but that is not the fact. He was released, but only after suffering, in common with twelve of his companions, tortures so cruel that five of them died under the infliction. The rest were banished separately to different parts of the empire.

Pirès, who was one of these latter, married in his place of exile, and converted to Christianity his wife and the children she bore him.* Such was the fate of the first European ambassador bold enough to attempt a negotiation with the Chinese.

Notwithstanding this misfortune, the two Andradas having conducted very profitable commercial transactions with China, the Portuguese were not disposed to lose sight of so wealthy a land. Another expedition was fitted out in 1522, consisting of four vessels under the command of Alphonse de Mello They were not without fear that the Chinese would give them bad reception; and these fears were realised, for, as soon as the arrival of the Frank vessels was made known, the magistrates of Canton gave orders to pursue them, to listen to no treaty, but to destroy all the vessels, and every man in them. A naval engagement took place, in which the Portuguese were not victorious. One of their vessels blew up, the powder magazine having caught fire; another was captured; and Mello was forced to retreat, leaving a great many prisoners in the hands of the Chinese. Many died of starvation in the prisons of Canton, escaping by that death the merciless sentence of the Emperor, which condemned them to be cut to pieces as spies and robbers. "And in this matter," says a Portuguese historian, "the Chinese did wrong them more in the first particular than in the second." Twenty-three underwent this cruel sentence; but even this fresh disaster did not discourage the Portuguese, and urged by the thirst for gain, and the love of adventure, some privateers from Goa ventured on a smuggling traffic along the Chinese coast. The mandarins, gained over by bribes, shut their eyes to it; and permission was at last granted to them to trade with the Isle of Sancian. The Portuguese brought gold from Africa, spices from the Moluccas, elephants' teeth and precious stones from

---

* In 1543, Pinto encountered in China a woman who spoke Portuguese and was acquainted with the Dominican church service. She was found to be a daughter of of Pirès.

Ceylon; and in exchange they took silks of all kinds, porcelain, varnishes, and the tea which is become almost a necessary of life to Europeans.

Whilst the Portuguese sought by every means in their power to establish and extend their commercial relations with China, St. Francis Xavier was propagating Christianity in the isles of Japan. In his discussions with the priests of the idols, he found that they constantly referred to Chinese authorities, and declared that, if there was any truth in the Christian religion, the Chinese, being gifted beyond all other nations with knowledge and wisdom, would certainly be acquainted with its principles. This renown of the Chinese nation inspired the apostle of the Indies and Japan with a great desire to visit them; and he hoped that, when he had vanquished idolatry in China, it would be an easy task to lead the Japanese to follow in the footsteps of the people they admired so much.

The countrymen of Vasco da Gama had not then established themselves at Macao; and it was, as we have said, at Sancian that they traded with the inhabitants of the Celestial Empire. St. Francis Xavier having embarked from Japan for India, touched at Sancian, and there met James Pereira, a celebrated mariner, and wealthy merchant. The apostle made known to him his project of going to China, and of proposing to the government and bishop of Goa to send an official embassy to Pekin, of which he might be a member. Pereira approved this plan, and promised his ship, his fortune, and all his influence, to aid in its success.

Arrived at Goa, St. Francis Xavier communicated his design to Don Alfonso Doronia, the viceroy of India, and Juan Albuquerque, Bishop of Goa. The embassy was resolved upon, James Pereira was appointed chief of it, preparations were immediately made for departure, not forgetting the providing a stock of rich presents to offer to the Emperor, and brilliant hopes were entertained of the important results, both commercial and political, to be expected from the undertaking; but the sainted and zealous missionary thought only of the glory of God, and the salvation of souls. Pereira being at that time in the Straits of Sunda, it was agreed that he should join St. Francis Xavier at Malacca; but a certain Alvarès, the governor of the citadel of Malacca, a personal enemy of Pereira, was jealous of his elevation to the dignity of ambassador, and resolved to effect the failure of the enterprise. As soon as Pereira arrived, he pretended falsely that the town was in danger of being besieged by the Malays, and that having but a scanty force to oppose them, it was necessary that Pereira should remain in the port with his ship and crew; and to insure obedience to this order, he demanded that the rudder of the vessel should be deposited in the palace.

In vain St. Francis Xavier used all his influence to persuade the governor to alter this determination. He even produced and exhibited to him his credentials as Apostolic Nuncio, which he had hitherto kept in reserve out of modesty, and which threatened with excommunication all who should oppose him in his mission. The governor of Malacca was insensible alike to prayers and menaces. St. Francis Xavier seeing that men, instead of aiding him, only raised obstacles in his path, threw himself upon the mercy of Providence. He changed his plan, resolved to get to Sancian the best way he could, to strike up a friendship with some Chinaman, and to land somewhere (he cared little where) upon the coast of China. If he had the good fortune to be arrested and thrown into prison, at least he could preach Jesus Christ to the prisoners, and thus deposit a germ of the true faith in the bosom of that infidel nation.

The governor of Malacca having succeeded in his design of wrecking the hopes of Pereira, retained him prisoner, but consented that his ship should convey the apostle to Sancian. St. Francis Xavier embarked, traversed the Strait of Singapore, and came in sight of the coast of China. The desert and uncultivated isle of Sancian was only thirty leagues off the continent. In the trading season the Portuguese used to gather together on the shore, where they pitched tents and erected temporary huts out of branches, to protect themselves from the fierce rays of the sun; for the Chinese would not permit them to build houses within the limits of the Celestial Empire. These temporary dwellings were abandoned and destroyed as soon as the return of the favourable winds enabled them to re-embark for the Indies.

The Portuguese of Sancian hearing that their sainted and indefatigable missionary intended to penetrate into China, endeavoured to dissuade him from what they regarded as a rash and dangerous act. They represented to him the insurmountable obstacles which he could not fail to encounter in a country which strangers were forbidden to enter, under pain of the severest penalties. But no consideration of personal peril could shake the courage of the man of God. Privation, suffering, imprisonment, torture, death itself, were of little moment in the eyes of that sublime monk, who thought only of the salvation of his fellow-men.

A Chinese merchant of Canton had promised St. Francis Xavier to convey him to China in a junk manned only by his own sons and persons in whom he could place confidence. He was to keep him for a few days in his house at Canton, after which the apostle intended to be guided by the inspiration of his zeal and the grace of God. The Portuguese were alarmed at this scheme. Feeling certain that the enterprise would miscarry at the outset, they expected to see themselves exposed to the anger of the Chinese authorities, who would not fail to make it a pretext for robbing them of their merchandise, and forbidding them all future commercial intercourse with China; they therefore entreated the missionary to abandon his project, or at least to defer the execution of it till the return of the monsoon should enable them to re-embark for the Indies, and escape from the anger of the mandarins.

The time arrived for the Portuguese ship to set sail; and St. Francis Xavier contemplated with delight his approaching entrance into the Land of Promise, where he hoped to win souls to Christ, at the price of his suffering, and perhaps of his blood. But though he was no longer delayed by the exaggerated prudence of his compatriots, there arose a new obstacle. The Chinese merchant did not make his appearance, though the appointed time was already passed. St. Francis Xavier, who had not yet studied the Chinese character, had committed the imprudence of paying him beforehand, with a quantity of pepper and spices which the Portuguese had bestowed on him as alms; and the wily Chinese decamped with his cargo, no doubt considerably astonished at this simple mode of doing business.

Whilst St. Francis Xavier was awaiting with patience and resignation the return of the faithless merchant, the Lord, content with the labours and sufferings of his servant, resolved to reward him by taking him unto himself. St. Francis Xavier had been for some time suffering from a violent attack of fever, in spite of which he continued to visit the sick and attend to the other duties of his apostolic ministry.

One day, a Portuguese, who had remained on the island, found him lying on the ground, completely overcome by his malady. He carried him into a hut and lavished the tenderest care upon him; but the disease increased, and on the 2d December, 1552, the holy apostle of the Indies and Japan rendered up his soul to its Creator, actually in sight of the vast empire into which he had hoped to carry the light of the Gospel.

Three years after the death of the sainted Francis Xavier, Gaspard de la Croix, of Evora, one of the twelve Dominicans who first left Portugal for the Indies, succeeded in entering China.

Cardoso tells us, in his martyrolgy, that he had read a

narrative written in Portuguese by this missionary of his adventures in China, and the hopes for conversion which that land held out, if properly cultivated.* It appears that his efforts were not entirely fruitless, for the Chinese, touched and persuaded both by the actions and the arguments of Gaspard de la Croix, pulled down with their own hands a temple consecrated to their idols. Many requested baptism, and some received it; but the mandarins, alarmed at the influence which the stranger was obtaining, arrested him with the intention of putting him to death.

Not daring, however, to proceed to this extremity with a man whose holiness was evident, they contented themselves with banishing him from the empire; and, thus cruelly torn from the new family in Jesus Christ which he had founded, Gaspard took refuge in the little kingdom of Ormuz, where he effected fresh conversions; but worn out at length with incessant labours, he returned to his native land, where he devoted himself to the plague-stricken populace of Lisbon, and died—the last victim of this curse, of which he predicted the end. Thus, in spite of the efforts of St. Francis Xavier, it was reserved for a Dominican monk† to have the honour of first entering China as a missionary, and of inaugurating that celebrated series of missions which have excited so much interest both in a religious and historical point of view.

Although the Portuguese had succeeded in reaching by sea the Cathay of Marco Polo, many years elapsed before they were able to establish any regular commercial and political intercourse with the jealous and suspicious people of the land.

The unfavourable disposition of the Chinese was kept up and fomented by the Mohammedans resident at Canton, who constantly depicted the Franks as an adventurous, audacious

---

* Touron, " Histoire des Hommes Illustres de l'Ordre de Saint Dominique," vol. vi. p. 729. Fontana, " Monumentum Dominicana, ann. 1555 "

† Le Quien, "Oriens Christianus," vol. iii. p. 1854.

race, whose irresistible power was tending to subjugate all nations.

Nevertheless, the love of commerce and thirst for gain was operating by degrees on the minds of the Chinese; their aversion became less virulent, and after permitting these dangerous strangers to trade at Sancian, they at last authorized them to come to Canton, on condition that they should only appear during a certain season, at the end of which the Canton market was closed, and the Europeans re-embarked with all their goods and chattels, and returned to the Indies.

This method of trade lasted many years, until a fortunate incident enabled the Portuguese to found a less temporary and precarious establishment.

A powerful pirate had taken possession of an important island not far from Canton, named Ngao-Men, whence he held in blockade the principal ports of China. In their distress the mandarins appealed to the Portuguese, who had some vessels at Sancian; and the latter immediately came to their assistance, gave battle to the pirate, and thoroughly vanquished him.

The Emperor, on hearing of this signal service, in his gracious munificence, granted the strangers permission to reside at the eastern end of the island of Ngao-Men; and little by little arose the town of Macao, destined to become the centre of an immense trade, and the rendezvous of all preachers of the Gospel in that part of Asia.

At that time Catholicism and its missionaries always accompanied, sometimes even preceded, the envoys of politics and commerce in their expeditions into new countries. Monks of various orders were not slow, therefore, to establish themselves in the Portuguese colony of Macao, where a bishopric was soon instituted under the pontificial authority; and the Society of Jesus, already widely spread, founded a house there, and prepared to extend its apostleship yet further.

For many years the range of missionary labours was circumscribed within the limits of the Portuguese colony, and the propagation of the faith was confined to the numerous Chinese who settled at Macao, to share the fortunes of the adventurous strangers. But the moment at length arrived when Providence had decreed that the Apostles of Christ should again kindle the torch of truth in the heart of that vast empire, lost in the darkness of idolatry, and sinking day by day into the yet blacker darkness of scepticism.

An Italian Jesuit, Father Alessandro Valignani, had been appointed visitor to all the missions in the Indies; and in the fulfilment of this difficult and toilsome duty, he arrived at Macao, and rested there on his way to Japan.

The ardent zeal of this missionary could not endure to see that the project of penetrating into the interior of China appeared to be given up in despair, and that an innumerable population was to be left plunged in error, without any attempt to rescue them.

He reflected on the best means of founding Chinese missions; and seeing that the monks already at Macao scarcely sufficed for the wants of the colony, he wrote to the provincial father of the Indies on the subject, and before setting sail for Japan, drew up instructions for any monks who might undertake that mission.

The provincial hastened to comply with Valignani's request, and despatched to Macao, Father Michael Roger, a native of Naples, recently arrived from Europe. He reached Macao in July, 1579, read the instructions left by Valignani, and immediately followed the wise counsel contained in them, enjoining the study of the Chinese language, and the learning to read and write its singular characters. When he thought himself sufficiently instructed on this point, he cast about for the means of executing his project. The acquaintance of some distinguished Chinese functionary appeared to him indispensable, and with this view he accompanied the Portuguese merchants to Canton at the appointed season for commercial transactions.

The Portuguese were authorised to enter the town on condition that at sunset they returned on board their vessels, which were anchored in the river. They were furthermore placed under the constant surveillance of several great military mandarins, who regulated their commercial dealings and closely watched their conduct. Father Roger soon made acquaintance with these mandarins, who, flattered to see the European studying the Chinese language, treated him with distinction, allowed him to be exempt from the general rule of returning every evening on board ship, and lodged him in the palace destined for the embassy sent annually from Siam to Pekin.

The attentions of the authorities to Father Roger, made an impression on the Chinese, especially those settled at Macao, and many requested to be received into the Christian religion. Roger now bestowed all his attention on the budding mission, and Father Valignani, hearing of this successful beginning while he was at Japan, requested the provincial to appoint another monk to share Father Roger's labours. Father Matthieu Ricci, who had reached India in company with Roger, and was then at Goa, completing his theological studies, was the elect of Providence for this difficult work.

Ricci was born at Macerato, near Ancona, in the same year that St. Francis Xavier yielded up his breath in the humble hut on the Chinese island. Thus, at the very time that the apostle who had conceived the project of Christianising China was expiring in the heart of Asia, there arose at the other extremity of the world the missionary destined to execute the scheme. The apostolic zeal of Xavier seemed to have passed into the soul of Ricci, who had been originally destined to the law, but, preferring a religious life, entered the Society of Jesus in 1571.

During his noviciate, he was under the tuition of Valignani, who eventually accomplished so much in the Indies, that a prince of Portugal called him the Apostle of the East. After the departure of his master on the foreign missions, Ricci felt a desire to follow him; and only remained in Europe long enough to complete the studies necessary for his enterprise, reaching Goa in 1578. He was twenty-seven years of age when he entered the apostolic career.

The Fathers Roger and Ricci, after a long and dangerous voyage, were brought together at Macao, and found themselves appointed to labour together, at the same work. While they were anxiously seeking the means of entering the Chinese Empire, Providence presented the opportunity to them, by a singular circumstance.

The governor of the province of Kouang-Tong,* who had then, as now, the province of Kouang-Si under his jurisdiction, was residing at Tchao-King-Fou, a town of the first class, lying to the east of Canton.† At that time, the viceroy of the two Kouangs was a certain Tsing-Tsai, a native of Fokien, and a man whose cupidity was remarkable even among the Chinese; and he was bent on making a good income out of the Portuguese merchants of Macao, since their incomparable riches had often been described to him. He therefore sent an edict to Macao, requiring the bishop and governor of the town to appear immediately before his tribunal of Tchao-King. The bishop and governor found this injunction dangerous for their personal safety, and very humiliating for their dignity; but as their infant colony was quite at the mercy of the Chinese, it would have been imprudent to disregard this edict, and thus appear to set at defiance the authority of the viceroy. What was to be done? how harmonise these conflicting considerations?

The Portuguese of Macao had already learned something of stratagem from the cunning and deceitful people whom

* Corrupted by Europeans into the name of Canton.
† In Chinese, Kouung-Tcheou-Fou.

they had to deal with, and the bishop and governor bethought themselves of a perfectly Chinese device to get out of the difficulty.

It was agreed that, instead of the real civil and ecclesiastical authorities, two men should be sent to play their parts before the viceroy. By this apparent, but deceptive obedience, the Portuguese dignity would be saved, and the viceroy's pride satisfied.

Father Valignani, the Jesuit Visitor, thought this an opportunity of entering the empire not to be neglected. Father Roger was to represent the Bishop, and a functionary of the town, named Matthew Penelle, was to play the part of governor. In order that the deceit might more easily find favour in the eyes of the viceroy, they were to carry him rich presents, to which all the merchants of Macao contributed; for it was of the greatest importance to them to conciliate his favour, that no obstacles might be thrown in the way of their commercial transactions.

The pseudo-embassy was received at Tchao-King with the greatest pomp, that is to say, with formidable explosions of fireworks, deafening music, and a rich exhibition of satellites, and mandarins of various coloured balls. But this splendid show was intended less to do honour to the Western barbarians, than to overawe them with the magnificence of the Celestial Empire.

The viceroy received them in his palace with that "lofty dignity" so strongly recommended to great officials on solemn occasions. Nevertheless the proud governor of Kouang softened the haughty arrogance of his features a little on perceiving the rich and curious presents offered to his acceptance, and insensibly assumed a benevolent and agreeable expression. He ordered his interpreter to tell the strangers that they might remain at the port of Macao and continue to exercise their trade, provided they faithfully followed the laws of the mandarins, who were the fathers and mothers of strangers as well as of the men of the Central Kingdom. Then, after casting a glance of longing at the rich offerings of the Portuguese, he told them that he could only accept these presents on condition that he paid for them; and asking the value of each article, he scrupulously paid for it on the spot. This marvellous dignity, however, was only to produce a public effect, for ne caused the Portuguese to be privately informed that with the money thus received they were to buy more presents at Macao, and return with them as soon as possible.

Father Roger expressed to the viceroy his strong desire of residing in the empire, informing him that he had studied the language of the country with zeal, and that his greatest happiness would be to pass his life with the Chinese. The viceroy heard him apparently with great satisfaction, and held out hopes that if he were to return another time the request might be granted. The embassy then took leave, and was escorted back to the vessels which had brought it to the sound of tamtams, and amid an immense concourse of people, gathered to look for the first time upon those curious strangers, to whom they soon gave the soubriquet of "Western devils."*

As soon as the presents demanded by the viceroy could be got ready, they were despatched to him by Matthew Penella; but Father Roger was unable to accompany him, on account of the serious illness which attacked him a few days previous to the departure. The zealous missionary was all the more vexed at this, because he had intended to propitiate the governor by the present of a handsome clock, which Ricci had brought from Goa.

On learning the illness of Father Roger, the viceroy appeared grieved; but when he heard of the marvellous machine which, by means of an ingenious system of wheels, went of itself, and marked the hours with perfect precision, he became tormented with a longing to see and possess this prodigy

* Yang-Koul.

and desired his secretary to write directly to Macao to invite father Roger to come to Tchao-King as soon as his health would permit.

The arrival of this despatch was an event for all the little Portuguese colony, and transports of joy burst forth on all sides, particularly in the Jesuit establishment. The letter of the viceroy granted the request which Roger had made at his first visit, and the monks were formally authorised, by letters patent, to erect a house and a church in Tchao-King. Valignani was the only one who did not share the general enthusiasm. He was quite astounded at this unexpected success; "and he would have let slip the occasion," says Trigault, "if the other fathers had not unanimously advised him to seize such an opportunity."*

The viceroy was so impatient to see Father Roger, or rather to possess the clock of which he had heard, that he sent his secretary to Macao with a mandarin junk to receive the missionary, and conduct him with distinction to Tchao-King.

These precious marks of friendship were eagerly accepted, and on the 18th of December, 1582, Roger embarked, accompanied by Francesco Pasco, another Jesuit who was not yet in holy orders, and several young Chinese.

The viceroy's secretary was astonished to see him thus escorted, knowing that he alone had been invited; but Roger told him that, as a priest, he was not accustomed to go about alone, and that it was necessary he should take with him two members of his order, one to accompany him in his visits to the viceroy, the other to keep house in his absence. This reply was accepted, and the junk set sail with its freight of missionaries, carrying with them the good wishes of all the Christians of Macao. The viceroy was enraptured on witnessing the working of the clock, and no doubt he thought, at the bottom of his Chinese conscience, that men who could in

* Trigault, de l'Expedition Chrétienne, &c., p. 126.

vent such marvellous things were not quite such barbarians as they looked. He wished to show them his gratitude by presents, but the missionaries courteously declined his gifts. They assured him that their only ambition was to be allowed to reside in his country; that their profession was to serve God and cultivate the sciences, that they had heard of the intelligence, laws, customs, manners, and knowledge of the Chinese, and had not hesitated to quit their native land, and undertake a weary voyage of three years, that they might come and learn of them; and their studies, they added, would be much better carried on in the interior of the empire than at Macao. The viceroy thought it a great honor for the Chinese that such men should come so far to live among them; and as he piqued himself on cultivating philosophy and mathematics, in which the missionaries were versed, he agreed to their wishes, and assigned to them as their residence a Buddhist temple in the environs of the town. He often sent them provisions from the palace, and granted them frequent private audiences.

The civil and military functionaries, and all the important personages of Tchao-King, moved either by curiosity or by a wish to please the viceroy, paid frequent visits to the pagoda of the Catholic monks; and thus by degrees the vast empire, so long hermetically sealed to foreigners, appeared opening to the zeal and devotion of the preachers of the gospel. Father Roger had already composed a catechism in Chinese, and translated "The Lives of the Saints," in order that Christian ideas might be communicated to the populace. He had obtained the viceroy's consent to Father Ricci also establishing himself at Tchao-King, and everything appeared to smile upon their efforts, when suddenly an unlooked for event again destroyed all their hopes.

CHAPTER II.

The Missionaries are forced to abandon Tchao-King.—Return to Macao.—New and fruitless efforts to re-enter the Empire.—The Viceroy recalls Fathers Roger and Ricci to Tchao-King.—Grant of Land to Build a House and Church.—Buddhist Towers.—Pagodas.—Success and Hopes of the Missionaries.—Erection of a Chapel.—Preludes to Preaching the Gospel.—A Dying Man Baptized.—Interpretation of Christian Charity by Letters.—Success and Persecution.—Ricci applies himself to the Sciences and Letters.—Singular Map of the World in the Chinese Taste.—Completion of the Church.—Attempt at a Spanish Embassy to Pekin.—Two more Missionaries in the Interior.—Journey of Father Roger to Han-Tcheou-Fou.—Chinese Alchemists.—Rascality of the Neophyte Martin.—His Judgment.—Fresh Persecution.—Peace Returns.—Fête of Old Men.—Memorial against the Europeans.—Defence of Father Ricci.—His Popularity.—Solemn Visit of the Imperial Commissioner to the Mission of Tchao-King.

One day, when the missionaries were conversing with delight on their future propagation of the faith in China, they were visited by an officer of the chief tribunal of the town. Overwhelmed with sorrow, he announced to them that the viceroy had just been deposed, and that he desired them to quit the town immediately, lest their residence, being distasteful to his successor, should sink him in yet deeper disgrace.

As may be imagined, this was a thunderbolt to the monks; but, to console them, the viceroy gave them a letter, enjoining the magistrates of Canton to allow them a residence in that city. But of what value would the letter of a displaced governor be in the eyes of the mandarins of Canton? Nevertheless, the missionaries welcomed even this ray of hope with delight, and, embarking on board a mandarin junk, descended the river to Canton, where, as they had feared, no notice was taken of the viceroy's letter, and they were forbidden even to land. Forced to continue their journey, they reached Macao overwhelmed with grief, but resigned to waiting till it should please Providence to open once more the Chinese empire to the light of the Gospel.

It is customary in China to preserve in the archives of the tribunal, all the edicts issued by the great mandarins, and to write beneath them whether they have been executed or not. The new viceroy of Kouang, therefore, found on examining the archives, the edict which his predecessor had issued to the mandarins of Canton, enjoining them to allow the Europear monks to establish themselves in the town. This edict was unindorsed, so that it was impossible to know whether it had been carried out, and the viceroy wrote to the mandarins of Canton, who knew nothing about the edict, but sent to inquire of the Prefect of Hian-Chan (the Mountain of Perfume), a town of the third class, under whose jurisdiction were included the Chinese of Macao.

As the mandarin of Hian-Chan was equally ignorant of the affair, he sent a deputation of officials to the Bishop of Macao. They were conducted to the Jesuit college, where the viceroy's edict, adorned with his great seal, was shown them; and they immediately endeavoured to possess themselves of it, declaring that such a paper could not remain in the hands of barbarians, without degradation to the dignity of the Celestial Empire. The fathers of the college, however, were unanimously of opinion that it would not do to give up this important document, but at the same time expressed their readiness to carry it themselves to the authorities of Canton, and to request the fulfilment of the promise contained in it. The Chinese officials hereupon became extremely irritated, and declared that such a proceeding was contrary to the "rites," and perfectly impossible. The Jesuits persisted, however, and it was at last agreed that the rites should be set aside, and the Chinese officials should conduct the bearers of the edict as far as Hian-Chan, and that there the mandarin of the town should undertake their further conveyance by water to Canton. This delicate mission was entrusted to the prudence and energy of Fathers Ricci and Roger.

After some hours walking through the island of Ngaomen, of which Macao occupies a rock at the eastern extremity, they reached the town of Hian-Chan, built on the opposite shore. The mandarin received them very badly, and ordered them to deliver the edict up to him, that he might send it to Canton: upon the missionaries formally refusing, he flew into a rage, tore the document from their hands, trampled it under foot, and screamed, " Fools that you are! what do you think is the value of an edict from a deposed viceroy? There, take your piece of waste paper, and get back to Macao as fast as you can!"

The poor missionaries took leave of this insolent mandarin, saddened, but not discouraged by their misadventure; and after they had been to rest themselves a little at an inn, they resolved upon attempting a bold stroke.

Accompanied by a young Chinese neophyte, who acted as their interpreter, they repaired to the port at the moment when a passenger junk was setting off for Canton. The captain, seeing these two foreigners come on board with their little luggage, was seized with misgivings, and refused to take them; but the young interpreter interposed with great presence of mind, and exhibited the edict garnished with the official seal.

"Are you mad, my elder brother," he exclaimed, "to turn away men furnished with the viceroy's passport?"

At the sight of this magnificent document the captain changed his tone, and would have suffered them to remain; but the other passengers, less impressed by the sight of the passport, thought only of the danger of compromising themselves by travelling in the company of barbarians, and so imparted their fears to the captain that, before raising his anchor he ordered the monks to land; and that there might be no doubt of their obedience, he seized their luggage, and threw it on the shore. They were, therefore, forced to resign themselves to their second failure.

Those who do not know the Chinese will conclude that there was now nothing to be done but to return to Macao and wait patiently for a better opportunity; but not so thought the missionaries. Having no doubt studied the people with whom they had to deal, they judged that in spite of repeated failures, all hope was not yet lost, and by means of bribery they persuaded a petty mandarin of the locality to send them to Canton. To effect this, he caused them to be arrested, and sent as prisoners to the marine mandarin of Canton, announcing in his despatch that two barbarians having been seized in the town of Hian-Chan, and pretending to be bearers of an edict from the viceroy, he had deemed it right to send them to him for judgment. By this means they reached Canton without further trouble, and were well received by the marine mandarin.

They delivered to him the edict of the ex-viceroy, together with a petition, in which they set forth that, attracted by the brilliant renown of the Celestial Empire, they had braved the perils of boundless seas, in order to have the happiness of living and dying in so celebrated a country; that all they asked was a corner of land where they might build a temple to the Lord of Heaven, and pass their time in prayer and self-improvement. The mandarin thought this a good and praiseworthy desire, but could not take upon himself to grant their request, as that depended upon the viceroy.

The missionaries begged that they might at least be allowed to reside at the Siamese embassy, until the season came for the Portuguese merchants to visit Canton, hoping that before that time they should have obtained the viceroy's permission.

No objection was made to this plan, and the missionaries installed themselves at the embassy; but before the end of the day, and while they were congratulating themselves on their success, they received an order to return at once to Macao, on pretext that the new viceroy was coming to Canton, and that it would be highly improper for him to find two strangers installed in the town, when it was not the trading season. They were once more forced, therefore, to yield to the ebb tide, and re-embarked.

On passing through the town of Hian-Chan, they perceived the real motive of their expulsion from Canton. On the gates, and in the principal places of the town, they saw placarded an edict of the new viceroy, in which, after various observations on the administration of the province, it was said, " A great many abuses are committed in the neighbourhood of Ngao-Men (Macao), and the laws are openly infringed. These crimes are for the most part to be attributed to the interpreters and linguists, who, in abuse of their office, teach evil to the barbarians and lead them into crime. Thus we learn that some interpreters have actually persuaded certain foreign monks to learn the language of the Central Nation, and then to demand a place in the capital of the province, in which to build a house and church. All this is extremely pernicious to the empire, which cannot benefit in any way by the presence of barbarians." The edict further exhorted the interpreters to reform their evil ways, under pain of having their heads cut off.

The repeated failure of their attempts, and above all this last edict, discouraged the Jesuits considerably. But in China, as elsewhere, unforeseen incidents often determine events Providence, who arranges all things at pleasure, does not allow man to boast of the wisdom and prudence of his manœuvres; and success often comes from the quarter where only obstacles were expected.

The missionaries felt convinced that they must not hope to establish themselves in the province of Kouang whilst the new viceroy governed it, and it was precisely the new viceroy who gave them the opportunity.

Many days had not elapsed when there arrived, at Macao, an official from Tchao-King. Preceded by the tam-tam and followed by a numerous *cortége*, he directed his steps to the palace of the mandarin who governed the Chinese of Macao. Thence he repaired to the Jesuit college, where he announced himself as the bearer of a despatch, in which Fathers Roger and Ricci were invited to Tchao-King, with permission to construct there a church and house.

The missionaries could scarcely believe this welcome news. Nevertheless, the despatch was clear and precise; the indispensable preparations were hastily made, and the two apostles of China set off full of joy and hope. They were escorted back by the same official who had brought the welcome message.

The viceroy received them kindly, and questioned them about their country and their motives in coming to China. The monks replied as before, that they were natives of the extreme West, who, having heard of the greatness and fame of the Celestial Empire, had undertaken a weary voyage of three years to behold it. Having visited a great number of countries, and traversed vast seas, they had at last ascertained with their own eyes that the Celestial Empire was even superior to its brilliant renown. They, therefore, desired to end their days in it, and wished to obtain a little land to construct a house and church, where they might pass their time in prayer and study, in solitude and meditation, which they could not do at Macao, on account of the tumult and bustle which the perpetual activity of commerce occasioned.

The viceroy was of a good and generous disposition, and as he was flattered at these strangers having come from the extremity of the world to have the happiness of living in China, he promised to take them under his protection, and desired them to choose, in the town or its environs, the spot which would best suit them.

Whilst busied in organising the mission, the monks lodged with a family named Ny-Ko. During their former residence in Tchao-King, the Jesuits had made the acquaintance of several Chinese of distinction, attracted to them by curiosity and Father Roger had been particularly intimate with a young bachelor named Ku-Ny-Ko, who appeared to be remarkably gifted, both in the qualities of the heart and the intellect. The Father applied himself to instructing him in the truths of Christianity, which made such an impression on the proselyte, that he soon acquired the habit of repeating, with faith and fervour, a few short prayers which he had been taught. The Jesuits had with them a small portable altar, on which they celebrated mass, in a hall which Ku-Ny-Ko had placed at their disposal; and when they were obliged to leave the town, they had confided this altar to the care of the family of Ny-Ko, whom they already considered as the first Christians of China.

As soon as Father Roger returned to Tchao-King, he went to the house of Ku-Ny-Ko, and had the delight of seeing that the seed of truth, so lately sown, had already germinated, and promised a rich crop.

The young man, after saluting the missionaries with the greatest respect and sympathy, led them into a hall adorned with elegance and simplicity, and where he had erected the altar confided to his care. In default of holy images, he had placed above it a tablet, on which were inscribed the Chinese characters, *Tien-Tcheou*, or Lord of Heaven. On each side of the altar were a profusion of beautiful vases of flowers and bronze vessels, in which burnt exquisite perfumes. In this little oratory, Ku-Ny-Ko daily knelt to pray to the God no longer unknown to him, but already worshipped with truth and fervour.

At the sight of this touching testimony to the faith of the catechumen, for such he might well be called, the missionaries could not restrain their tears, and fell on their knees, thanking the Lord that there was at length a worshipper of the true God among that vast nation, sunk in scepticism and idolatry.

We have already said that the viceroy had invited the Jesuits to choose for themselves the spot on which to erect their church. At that time, there was, in the environs of the town, one of those towers so frequently met with throughout the empire, and which, with the pagodas, form the sole monuments of Chinese architecture. In the neighbourhood of towns of the first, second, and third class, there is almost always to be seen a tower more or less lofty, placed in a solitary spot, like a colossal sentinel.

According to Indian tradition, when Buddha died, his body was burnt, and his bones were divided into eight parts, which were enclosed in as many urns; and these were deposited in an eight-storied tower. This was the origin of these towers, so common in all the countries where Buddhism prevails, the number of stories varying, however, as well as their shape, some being round, others square, hexagonal, or octagonal, and built in stone, wood, brick, or china, like that of Nankin, which, from the porcelain ornaments with which it is enriched, is called the Porcelain Tower.

At the present time most of these monuments are defaced and falling into ruins; but in the ancient poetry of China, there are passages which attest the lavish magnificence which the emperors expended in the erection of these towers. One of these passages is as follows:—

"When I raise my eyes to the tower of stone, I seek its roof amid the clouds. The enamel of its bricks vies in lustre with gold and purple, and reflects, in a rainbow, the rays of the sun, which fall on each story."

A censor, wishing energetically to express the uselessness and enormous expense of the famous tower of Tchang-Ngan, calls it *half a town*. A satirical poet, in speaking of one of these edifices which was 500 feet high, after several verses expressive of astonishment and admiration at the plan and execution of so great a work, continues:—

"I fear asthma, and dare not venture to mount up to the highest terrace, where men look like ants. To mount so many staircases is reserved to those young queens who have the strength to carry on their fingers, or their head, the revenues of many provinces."

The Chinese say, that there were towers of white marble, gilded bricks, or even partially of copper. The number of stories were three, five, seven, nine, and sometimes even thirteen.

Their outward form varied much, as did their interior decoration: there were some with galleries or balconies, diminishing in size at each story; some were built on an immense rock in the midst of waters, on which trees and flowers were cultivated, and cascades arranged. The summit was reached by steps roughly cut in the sides of a rock passing under or through it by grottoes and caverns imitated from nature, and bounded by precipices. On reaching the rocky platform, you found yourself in delightful gardens, in the midst of which rose the towers, whose magnificence must have been extraordinary, to judge from the ruins still remaining.

The pagodas, or idol temples, like the towers, exist in incredible profusion throughout the empire. There is no village which does not possess several; they are to be found on the roads, in the fields, in every place in short; and it is said that in Pekin and its environs there are as many as ten thousand. It should be added, that most of these pagodas are nothing more than little chapels or niches, enclosing some frightful idol, or vases of burning perfumes; but there are many, which for grandeur, richness, and beauty, are well worthy of attention. At Pekin the temples of Heaven and Earth, and in the provinces several celebrated pagodas, to which the Chinese make annual pilgrimages, are particularly remarkable.

The ornaments and decorations of these temples are of course entirely in the Chinese taste, a mass of whimsical confusion. The paintings and sculptures have no great artistic value, for drawing is but little cultivated in China; and the painters excel only in certain mechanical details relative to the preparation and application of their colours; they pay no attention to perspective, and their landscapes exhibit a lamentable monotony. There are, however, some Chinese miniatures and water-colour drawings of great perfection, but very inferior in style to the most mediocre European performances.

The sculptures in the pagodas have some good fragments, but are generally wanting in elegance and correctness of form. The Chinese themselves affirm that their painters and sculptors of former times, especially those of the fifth and sixth centuries of our era, were much superior to those of the present day, and this assertion is confirmed by the museums of antiques, which contain many specimens of real merit.

There are no temples of very great antiquity in China: their architecture is not solid enough to defy the attacks of time and man; and they are allowed to fall to ruin, and new ones are built in their place. A Chinese proverb says, "The Songs made roads and bridges, the Tangs made towers, and the Mings pagodas."*

The tower then building outside the walls of Tchao-King was named the Flowery Tower. It was to have nine stories, but was then only completed as far as the second. A magnificent pagoda was to be built near it, the foundations of which were already laid; and the principal altar of which was to be dedicated to Buddha, the other to Confucius. This Flowery Tower stood on the banks of a beautiful river, continually enlivened by a crowd of junks of all sorts, carrying merchandise from Canton into the interior. The country was rich, and thickly scattered over with farms. Thickets of bamboo, large-leaved banyan trees, papaw trees with their enormous yellow fruit clustered in bunches at the top of the trunk, orange, pomegranate, and many others, always loaded with fruit and flowers, adorned the gorgeous landscape.

The missionaries, struck with the beauty of this enchanting spot, requested the viceroy's permission to fix their residence

* Chinese Empire, vol. II. p. 127.

there; and the viceroy replied that their request was granted, and that on the following day he would repair to the Flowery Tower to fix the exact spot which should be allotted to them.

The next day the viceroy came accordingly to the spot, accompanied by an assessor and a commission of public works; but the members of this commission were unfavourable to the project of the monks.

They had already tried to persuade the viceroy that it was improper and dangerous to suffer strangers and barbarians to establish themselves in the kingdom of Flowers. "Assuredly," they said, "these men will by degrees invite their fellow-countrymen from Macao, their numbers will increase, and there will be danger for the town of Tchao-King." These insinuations, however, did not alter the Viceroy's intentions; he merely warned the Jesuits against inviting any of their friends, and exhorted them to observe obediently the paternal laws of the empire. The missionaries promised faithfully to conform in everything to the laws and rites of China. A space of ground was then officially assigned to them not far from the Flowery Tower; but as it appeared to them too small to build both a house and church upon, they signified as much to the viceroy. "That is only intended for your house," replied he; "you see that a large and magnificent temple is being built here; what need have you then of another?" The missionaries understood by these words that the viceroy intended to convert them into priests and servants of the pagoda; and as this was not precisely the object of their persevering efforts, they immediately replied, "We men of the West do not adore Buddha nor any idol; we worship only the one true God, the Creator and Sovereign of all that exists, the Tien-Tchou, the Lord of Heaven."

The viceroy heard them with astonishment, as if not understanding their repugnance to follow the religion of China. He conversed a moment with his assessor, then turning to Father Roger he said, "What matters your religion, and your woship of the Tien-Tchou? the pagoda shall be built, and you may put any god you like in it."* These words express exactly the scepticism of the mandarins, in whose eyes all religions are on a level.

Afraid that this concession might be withdrawn, the Jesuits hastened to set to work, and, in order themselves to superintend the building of their residence, they hired a little house near at hand, where they divided their time between the duties of the apostle and the architect.

Two Western barbarians building themselves a house on the soil of the Celestial Empire was an unheard-of innovation, and shocking to all Chinese ideas. The news spread quickly through the town and its environs; the roads leading to the Flowery Tower became blocked up by the crowds who flocked to assure themselves with their own eyes of the incredible event, and to have a look at the strangers who were said to have the most extraordinary faces in the world. Curiosity soon became seasoned with ill nature. The men of letters murmured; the founders of the Flowery Tower and the pagoda complained that their neighbourhood had become a scene of discord and disorder. Everybody said that the strangers would do at Tchao-King as they had done at Macao, where their numbers were yearly augmented by fresh arrivals from beyond the seas, so that it would soon be almost impossible to dislodge them from the place of which they had taken possession by degrees. All this grumbling did not deter the Jesuits from continuing their labours, but it caused them some anxiety; they therefore sought out the chiefs of the malcontents, and managed so completely to win their esteem and sympathy, that they were no longer annoyed by anybody.

A fresh obstacle of a serious nature, however, was arising in the shape of poverty. They had intended to build a house in the European fashion, with two stories and a respectable

---

* "Nihil admodum refert: fanum extruemus, in illud deinde quas volueritis deorum effigies inferte."—*Trigault*, lib. ii. p. 164.

appearance, but the funds at their disposal were exhausted by the time the first story was erected. They sent information of their circumstances to the college at Macao, but the superior answered that the resources of the establishment would not permit him to assist them. He was, besides, uneasy at their building a two-storied house, which was completely at variance with the customs of the country, and feared that the jealous and suspicious Chinese might regard it as a fortress prepared for a future invasion. The fears of the superior and the want of money made them, therefore, decide on leaving the house as it was; the roof was placed over the first story, and the Jesuits installed themselves in it, hoping that time would permit them further to develope their modest establishment.

The future hopes of the infant mission rested solely on the good will of the viceroy of Kouang: should this high functionary be dismissed from his place, all the hopes of the missionaries might immediately vanish with him. Their endeavour, therefore, was to obtain a surer footing; and they were rejoiced to receive from the viceroy an official decree, in which was set forth the motive of their visit to China with a pompous eulogy on their merits; that their residence at Tchao-King had been assured to them by the authority of the viceroy; and that it was expressly forbidden, under pain of the severest punishment, to trouble or injure them in any way. The Jesuits caused a copy of this decree to be framed and hung up over the door of their house, according to the custom of the country; and soon after they received two other documents of no less importance and sealed with the great seal. On contained the act of donation of the land on which the house was built; the other empowered the missionaries to go whenever they pleased to Canton, to Macao, or to any place throughout the empire.

Armed with these powers, the apostles of China could now contemplate the future prospects of their mission with lightened hearts, and work with the grace of God at the conversion of that great nation, who had long ceased to believe the doctrines of their Bonzes and Tao-Sse, and were sunk in indifference to all religion.

"In order not to excite the suspicions of the Chinese," says Father Trigault, "by the novelty of our religion, our missionaries at first did not explain it very clearly, but rather employed the time which they could spare from the duties of hospitality and civility to those who came to see them, in learning the language, literature and customs of the country. However, they did all in their power to persuade by a better means than words, that is, by the holiness of their lives, and the example of their virtues, hoping thus to gain the good will of the Chinese, and dispose their minds by degrees to receive what could not yet be taught them in words, without danger of undoing all that had been done, either through their imperfect knowledge of the language or on account of the naturally vicious disposition of that nation. They clothed themselves in garments which are considered among the Chinese as the most modest, and which do not differ very greatly from our own, being long robes with large sleeves The Chinese greatly approved this proceeding."*

By this extract we see how careful the missionaries of Tchao-King were not to shock the feelings of the Chinese or wound their self-esteem, by telling them at once, "Until now you have been sunk in darkness and ignorance; we are bringing you light and truth." On the contrary, they began by cultivating the good graces of the viceroy, the chief mandarins, and the men of letters of the town. They received frequent visits from them, and, during these interviews, of which i must be owned curiosity was the principal motive, they found opportunity of sowing the seeds of faith in their souls, and pouring the words of truth into their ears. There was

* Trigault, p. 141.

in their house, as in all Chinese houses, a room called *the hall of guests*. This they had arranged as an oratory, where they prayed and celebrated the services. The altar was placed at one end of the hall, surmounted by a large picture of the Virgin and infant Jesus, and on the walls around were inscribed, in large Chinese characters, the fundamental truths of religion: "To the Sovereign Ruler of all things," "To the true Source of Being," &c. &c. They also translated the Decalogue, and printed a number of copies for distribution to their visitors.

The picture of the Virgin did not remain long over the altar, however, but was replaced by an image of the Saviour; for a report had been spread that the strangers worshipped a woman; and if such an impression should have been established, it would have been highly prejudicial to the progress of Christianity; such is the abject and despised condition to which women are reduced in China.

As the Fathers became better acquainted with the Chinese language, they began to hold familiar discourses in their chapel on the most elementary truths of our faith. The mandarins, the men of letters, all the most important persons in Tchao-King listened to them with great attention. "But,' says Trigault, "all this brought more applause than fruit."

Then, as now, the mandarins listened to discourses on God, the soul, and salvation, from mere curiosity, or, as they say themselves, "to amuse their hearts a little." They often were even courteous enough to declare the doctrines they heard perfect and unanswerable, but on going away they resumed their habitual indifference, and became just as Chinese as ever. They gravely bestowed their sanction and approbation on the truth and beauty of the new theories, without ever appearing to imagine they could learn anything from barbarians; and instead of becoming disciples, they assumed the airs of arrogant and self-sufficient critics and judges, for their Chinese vanity prevented their observing any other attitude. It is written that "God rejects the proud, but gives His grace to the humble."

One day, as the missionaries were traversing the ramparts of the town, they perceived a poor man lying on the ground scarcely covered with a few rags, and a prey to the greatest suffering. They approached him with emotion, and, addressing him with the tenderest sympathy, asked how it was he lay thus abandoned in the public way. The unhappy man roused by the voice of benevolence and sympathy, made an effort to speak, and informed them in a scarcely audible voice that he had long been a victim to a cruel disease; that his relations were sunk in the direst poverty, and unable to provide for him any longer, had carried him out and laid him there, hoping that some compassionate man might take pity on him, and relieve his misery.

At sight of this affliction, the monks, deeply touched, raised him in their arms, and carried him to their house, as though they had found a precious treasure. They lavished the most affectionate care on him, and built him a little hut beside their own residence, where they bestowed on him all the attentions his condition required.

In the course of a few days, he gained a little strength, and was able to converse with the missionaries, who, though desirous to cure his body, were still more anxious to save his soul. The sick man was soon instructed in the principles of Christianity, and one day Father Roger inquired if he would like to embrace their faith. "Yes, I will be a Christian," said he. "I have not studied books; I am an ignorant creature; but your religion must be true and heavenly, since it teaches love and charity towards our fellow-men."

He received baptism, therefore, with faith and gratitude, and, being soon after seized with a relapse of his malady, he died the death of the just: and this poor deserted sick man was the first Christian that God took to himself, from out that vast and populous nation! They were shepherds who first sought out the manger at Bethlehem, to worsnip the Infant God, and ever since, wherever Christianity has penetrated, the Saviour of mankind has first manifested himself to the poor and humble.

Whilst the poor sick man, touched by the charity of the missionaries, was receiving baptism in simplicity of heart, and passing gently from this Vale of Tears to a better life, it is curious to see how the wits and sages sought to explain the admirable devotion and goodness which the monks had shown him, and ended by making the following ingenious discovery "The Western strangers," said they, "have secrets unknown to us. They knew, on looking at the face of this sick man that he had a precious stone hidden in his head. They, therefore, took care of him while living, that his body might be theirs after death, and that they might be able to extract the jewel of price from his head."

This explanation appeared perfectly natural to the Chinese philosophers, for, as often happens to the proud men of science in every country, although they will not receive with simple faith the simplest things, they will swallow enormous absurdities with the most ludicrous credulity.

Fathers Roger and Ricci were not slow to perceive that they had undertaken to convert a people full of conceit, particularly with regard to their literature. They, therefore, exhibited their little European library to their visitors, who admired the beauty and richness of the binding, and concluded that the books must contain precious thoughts, since so much care was taken to preserve them. Some even went so far as to hazard an opinion, that a people among whom literature was held in such esteem, might not be entirely barbarous.

The missionaries, however, not content with proving that they knew how to read and write in their own language, desired also to show themselves capable of deciphering Chinese books, and even of composing them. They applied themselves closely to this study, with the aid of a well-informed man, whom they had taken into their service; and both being gifted with more than ordinary intelligence, they made rapid progress, and acquired skill enough in writing the Chinese character to compose in it a treatise on the Christian doctrine, considered with regard simply to reason and common sense. Having organized a little printing apparatus in their house, they themselves superintended the printing of it; and a great number of copies were taken, and distributed profusely throughout the empire. The Chinese, always eager for books, and especially those containing matters of novelty, read it eagerly, and the foreign doctors acquired a wide reputation. The viceroy was so satisfied with their performance, that he sent them letters of congratulation, which in China consist of a sort of testimonial, richly illuminated, and adorned with the utmost ostentation of caligraphy. Great personages are in the habit of sending them to those they wish to honour.

The Jesuits caused this document to be hung up in their oratory, that visitors and proselytes might see how high they stood in the favour of the authorities.

The favour and protection of the viceroy, however, did not exercise a very great influence over the Chinese population, which still remained hostile to the missionaries. They were insulted at every opportunity; placards were stuck up representing them as sly, ambitious men, as spies, as *Western devils*, for already had the Chinese bestowed that insulting nickname on Europeans.

The Flowery Tower had changed its name, and was called the Strangers' Tower, on account of its neighbourhood to the monks' residence; and in this name blame was implied to the magistrates for having favoured men, whose presence was a source of trouble and uneasiness to the country.

It happened that Father Roger found himself obliged to undertake a journey to Macao, and to remain there some time, and the enemies of the mission took advantage of his absence to endeavour to dislodge it, and drive the monks from the country. They imagined that, as Father Ricci was alone with a few servants, it would be easy to carry out their designs; persecutions of all kinds became incessant, and even Ricci's personal safety was severely menaced. The populace, not content with assembling round the house, and uttering insults and menaces against the Western devils, threw showers of stones and other missiles upon the roof, from the neighbouring tower.

One day, a boy was attacking the door of the chapel with stones, when a servant came out suddenly, seized him, carried him into the house, and inflicted a salutary chastisement on him. Some neighbours perceiving this raised a great uproar a crowd collected, rushed into the house, and, taking possession of the boy, carried him in procession through the town, heaping curses and insults on the Europeans.

A writer took up the affair, and magnified it into an important business. He drew up an act of accusation against Father Ricci, in which he accused him of having unrighteously arrested the boy, detained him three days in his house, forced him to drink a magic potion, which overset his intellect, and then despatched him to Macao, to undergo some unholy sorcery. This act was laid before the governor, and a crowd of false witnesses were brought to prove the assertions. A frightful excitement prevailed in the town, when the trial came on. Father Ricci was dragged before the tribunal of the viceroy, who at first believed in all this calumny, for the witnesses were numerous. God willed, however, that the truth should be discovered; the accuser and the false witnesses were sentenced to be flogged with bamboos, and Father Ricci returned in triumph to his house, where he was received by his catechumens with transports of joy. A new edict was published the same day by the viceroy, containing a panegyric on Ricci, and menacing with the severest penalties all who should dare to trouble him, during his residence in Tchao-

King; so that this event, which had seemed likely to prove fatal to the mission, only procured for it fresh friends. Since his arrival in Tchao-King, the fathers had had time to understand the dispositions of the people whom they sought to convert, and they saw that the best way to gain the esteem of the Chinese was to show themselves enlightened men, devoted to the study of science, and thus differing widely from the Bonzes of the country, with whom the people were apt to confound them.

They thought justly that the philosopher would make more impression than the priest upon minds so sceptic and so imbued with literary conceit.

Deeply versed in mathematics and geography, which they had studied at Rome under the celebrated Clavius, they undertook to make a large map, in which, to flatter Chinese vanity, China was to be placed in the centre, and all other countries drawn as surrounding the Celestial Empire.*

Trigault thus relates his mode of proceeding:—

"Father Ricci being well versed in mathematics, which he had learned from Christopher Clavius, the prince of the mathematicians of his century, applied himself to the construction of this map, which suited well with his design of preaching the Gospel, knowing that the same means cannot be employed to attract different nations to the faith of Jesus Christ. In truth, by this decoy, many Chinese were drawn to the bosom of the Church. This map was of large dimensions, the better to contain the Chinese characters, which are larger than ours, as well as many annotations, which he thought suitable to his purpose, and to the humour of the Chinese; for in various places, in treating of the manners and customs of different nations, he found an opportunity of discoursing on the

---

* In order better to conform to Chinese ideas, Ricci reversed the ordinary principle of making the central portion smallest. "Ut sinæ regnum in medio majorem partem occuparet, reliqua regna in finibus mappæ oviformis exigua appareret.'— *Riccioli Almagest*, Nov. 1651.

sacred mysteries of our holy faith, until this time unknown to the Chinese,* in order that the fame of it might be quickly spread abroad by every one. I will not either omit to mention a contrivance of his to gain the good graces of the Chinese. They believe that the sky is round, but the earth square, and that their empire is situated in the midst of it; and they are for this reason very angry, when they find our geographers, in their maps, putting it in a corner of the extreme East. Now they are not capable of understanding any mathematical demonstration, by which it might be proved to them, that the earth and the sea together form a globe, and that by the nature of the spherical figure there can be neither beginning nor end to it. He, therefore, altered a little our plan for maps of the world, and by placing the first meridian of the Fortunate Islands at the margin, right and left, he brought the empire of China into the centre, to their great satisfaction." After this account, Father Trigault adds, with much naïveté, "Truly one could not at that time have found an invention more calculated to dispose this people to receive the mysteries of our religion."

In fact, this map, though somewhat irregular in its structure, might have been very useful in contributing to destroy a prejudice which has always been one of the chief causes of the hatred of the Chinese towards strangers. From the earliest times, they have always fancied, that the fixed purpose of the Europeans in coming to China, was to seize upon their empire. Now a mere glance at the map of the world might tend to diminish this fear, by showing the enormous distance that separates it from the countries of the West; the danger would not then appear so imminent, nor the presence of a few foreigners on the coasts give rise to so vivid an alarm.

The impression produced by his map was a great encouragement to Father Ricci, and he pursued with much ability

---

* We have seen how much Father Trigault was deceived when he supposed that the Fathers Roger and Ricci were the first apostles of China.

this method of obtaining influence by constructing terrestrial and celestial spheres, both in copper and iron; and he also made sundials to mark the hours, and presented them to the first magistrates of the cities, so that he acquired a prodigious reputation, and was soon regarded as the most learned man that had ever existed in astronomy, or, as the Chinese say, in "Celestial Literature" (Tien Wien.)

In the meantime, Father Roger returned from Macao, having perfectly succeeded in his enterprises. The Portuguese ships, too, which had been expected from India and Japan, arrived at last; and as their commercial transactions had been fortunate, they were enabled to bestow munificent donations on the mission of China. The Jesuits, therefore, resumed at Tchao-King their architectural labours, and finished building their house, which, says Father Trigault, though small, was not the less beautiful, and the Chinese regarded with pleasure the progress of this European work, differing so much from their buildings, and in which the proportionate arrangement of the windows had so good an effect. The beauty of the edifice was also much heightened by its situation, which was delightful, for there was a beautiful prospect of mountains and woods, and of all kinds of vessels, scattered along the surface of the river. "Every one thought that there could not have been found in the whole town a pleasanter place; and for this reason, and because of the number of things brought from Europe, many people came to see it. Our house was frequented every day by great mandarins, not only from the town, but by those who come from the country to the viceroy, and this gave authority to our people, and benefited the Chinese, by awakening in them by degrees the desire of becoming acquainted with our religion."*

These first successes of the missionaries occasioned grea joy, and a lively sensation amongst the foreigners resident at

---

* Trigault, p. 155.

Macao. The news of so happy a beginning spread rapidly all over the East, wherever there were Europeans, and especially in the Philippine Islands, where the Spaniards already possessed so fine and wealthy a colony. The Governor of Manilla, desirous of establishing commercial relations with the Chinese, formed a plan of sending, in the name of his Catholic Majesty, a solemn embassy to Pekin; and he induced the Dominican monks of Manilla to endeavor to obtain, through the influence of the Jesuits of Macao, and especially of Tchao-King, the requisite Chinese authorisation for the embassy. The negotiations, zealously conducted, had all the success that could be desired; rich presents were prepared for the Emperor, and the missionaries promised themselves, from their presentation at Pekin, great advantages for the propagation of the faith throughout the empire.

The Portuguese authorities of Macao, however, having obtained information of these projects of the Spaniards, wrote officially to the Jesuits of Tchao-King, to adjure them to frustrate the embassy. They declared that if the Spaniards should succeed in their designs, and establish themselves by the side of them in the market of China, it would be impossible for them to support the competition with a people who, having at their disposal all the gold of Peru, would raise enormously the prices of Chinese goods, and ruin the merchants of Macao.

The missionaries of Tchao-King, though by birth Italians, could not but show themselves careful for the interests of the Portuguese, who had assisted them in so many ways, and whose abundant donations had helped them so much in founding and maintaining the mission of China. The rector of the college of Macao, therefore, sent to his brethren at Tchao-King, to desire them to have nothing more to do with the business of the embassy, but to allow it to drop; and although everything had been previously arranged with the mandarins, measures were taken to obtain from the viceroy an edict, by which he formally prohibited the Spanish embassy. He even declared that he would not allow such people to enter the empire, but would punish them severe.y if they attempted it.

All these cares about the embassy, however, and all their astronomical and agricultural labours, did not hinder the Fathers Ricci and Roger from labouring assiduously in their chief duty, that of the conversion of souls; and they had at length the consolation of seeing their long continued toils crowned with some success. They were able to confer baptism on two catechumens, one of whom was a literary man of the province of Fo-kien, and the other the young Bachelor who had kept the altar during the absence of the missionaries, and received them so well on their return at his house in Tchao-King. The ceremony took place in public, and with great pomp, the rector of the college of Macao being invited to perform it; and the new Christians received the names of Paul and John.*

The Chinese talked a great deal of these new rites brought into the empire by the Western nations, and they had the courtesy and politeness to make no objection to them. The number of catechumens slowly increased, and they definitively renounced their idolatry, and received baptismal regeneration.

In the meantime, Father Valignani, visitor-general of the Jesuit mission in the extreme East, came from Japan to Macao. He heard with great joy how God had blessed the apostolic labours of the Fathers Roger and Ricci at Tchao-King; and seeing that even the indefatigable zeal of these two labourers could not suffice to cultivate the immense field opened to them, he asked for assistance from the provincial of India, who sent to him two Portuguese monks, Edward de Sande and Antony d'Almeida. They arrived at Macao in July 1585, but the difficulty was to get them into the interior, notwithstanding the express promise of the Fathers

* Called by the Chinese Pao-Lou and Jo-Han. The Christening was on the 16th December, 1584.

Roger and Ricci that they would never summon any other foreigner.

The fathers were seeking for some skilful device, whereby to reconcile this promise with the entrance of the new comers, when Providence afforded them an excellent opportunity.

The viceroy of the two Kouangs had received from Pekin an imperial despatch, by which he was commanded to send and purchase at Macao sundry European curiosities and merchandise, which he was then to forward to Pekin. The governor of Tchao-King accordingly sent off to Macao a large junk, under the superintendence of Father Roger, who, when he returned with the junk, brought in it, along with the goods, Father Edward de Sande.

The governor did not see any objection to his having accompanied the merchandise destined for the emperor, but after he had rested for a few days, asked whether he was not thinking of going back again. "No!" said the missionary; it has always been my earnest wish and hope, to live permanently among the Chinese; and his entreaties to this effect were so pressing, that at last he obtained the permission, on the express condition that nobody else should come. There was Father d'Almeida, however, all the while waiting at Macao to be sent for; but it really seemed impossible to introduce him, when another incident occurred, that enabled them to overcome the difficulty.

The governor of Tchao-King, who had been so favourable to the Missionaries, was raised to a superior rank, and was succeeded by a certain *Ling-Si-Tao*, a high functionary of the same city, who was extremely intimate with Father Roger. As, according to custom, he would have to make a journey to Pekin before entering on his office, he proposed to Father Roger to take him with him as far as Han-Tcheou-Fou, in the province of Tche-Kiang, and the father eagerly accepted a proposal which might be the means of enabling him to found a new mission in the interior of the empire. Father d'Almeida too, had been warned to hold himself in readiness, and had gone to Canton, where he was taken up by Ling-Si-Tao.

On the 23d of January, 1586, they arrived at Han-Tcheou Fou. The Father of Ling-Si-Tao gave a hospitable reception to the two missionaries, who arranged one of their rooms as a chapel, where they daily expounded the Christian doctrine, whilst the mandarins of the highest rank invited them to their tables. The Bonzes, even, showed them much respect, and asked them for holy water, on account of a tradition, still existing in the country, of a pious personage, who, in former days, had traversed China, giving people a certain sacred water, with which he healed the sick and worked many miracles. It is evident that the memory of the ancient apostles of China was not yet entirely effaced. The Fathers had the satisfaction of conferring baptism on the father of Ling-Si-Tao, an old man of seventy, whom they had instructed sufficiently in the principles of Christianity.

Father Roger then, not content with having established himself at Han-Tcheou-Fou, took advantage of an opportunity that presented itself to make a journey into the province of Hou-Kouang, where he laid the foundation of a new mission, not far from the famous place of Buddhist pilgrimage at Ou-Tan, which, at various epochs of the year, attracts a numerous concourse of people.

In three provinces of the empire, therefore, Kouang-Si, Tche-Kiang, and Hou-Kouang, the missionaries had planted the Christian religion; their reputation was increasing every day, and there seemed to be very prospect of the most complete success, after so many previous efforts had proved fruitless. The West was thrilling with joy at the news; and returned solemn thanks to God when it received these happy tidings from the mission of China. Pope Sixtus V. granted a jubilee to the Society of Jesus,—and Father Aquaviva, general of the order, wrote to the brethren at Macao letters of congratulation and encouragement; promising to the apostolic labourers of the remote East the prayers and alms of Europe. He sent them at the same time some pictures, various devotional articles, and several clocks, with the ingenious mechanism of which the Chinese were always specially delighted.

At the very moment, however, when all these tokens of interest reached China, the missionaries found themselves obliged to abandon the ground that it had cost them so much to conquer. Their protectors and friends at Tche-Kiang and Hou-Kouang were gradually growing cold; they were becoming afraid of compromising themselves by the favourable reception they had been giving to strangers; and they ended by compelling them to abandon their advanced position, and fall back upon Tchao-King, which was in some measure the cradle of the mission. Even there they met with marked indifference, instead of the sympathy of former days. The governor no longer came to visit them, and when he met them by chance even pretended not to know them. Everything presaged a coming storm,—and it was not long before it burst upon them.

The Chinese, like other nations, or rather more than other nations, have occupied themselves with alchemy, in the hope of making important discoveries. Long, and by a thousand methods, have they sought to discover the art of transmuting metals, of making gold, silver, and especially the famous elixir of life—or of immortality. The Chinese alchemists of that time asserted that mercury could easily be transformed into silver, by the aid of a certain herb which grew they said in foreign lands; and they added, that the Portuguese, or rather the "Western devils," possessed this precious herb, and understood the use of it, and that that explained why the foreign ships bought every year such great quantities of mercury, and also how they could bring back so many piastres in exchange. How else, too, could the missionaries have been able to build such a fine house, keep so many servants, live in such abundance, be so well clothed, and make such presents to the mandarins, when they did not either work, or trade, or cultivate the ground? Evidently they were in possession of this grand secret of making silver out of mercury!

Amongst the Chinese whom the Jesuits of Macao had baptized, there was one who had been named Martin. He was a very indifferent Christian, very much absorbed in the care of his *sapecks*, and very little in the care of his soul. He used to go to Tchao-King under various devotional pretexts, but in reality with the hope of making sundry little profits out of the missionaries, or even occasionally of pilfering from them. Father Roger received him well nevertheless, and even gave him some important employments in the establishment, hoping by that means to bring him back to conduct more in conformity with his Christian profession. They were also at Tchao-King two new converts who were ardent alchemists, and passed their days in the midst of crucibles and alembics, though without ever having made any important discovery. One day the Chinese, Martin, went to them, and taking them to the back of their laboratory, told them in great confidence that Father Roger knew how to make silver, and had promised to tell him the secret, but on condition that he should not communicate it to any one. At this grand revelation the two alchemists seemed to see a new world open before them, and felt how important it was to pay their court to Martin. Now Martin was both poor and vain, so they bought him a fine new dress of silk, and begged him to come and lodge with them, and they fed him sumptuously every day. Here then was Martin, established very much to his satisfaction—well lodged, well clothed, well fed; but Martin was still a bachelor, so they bought him a wife and married him, and by dint of presents and cajoleries, our two alchemists obtained from him a promise to make them acquainted with the famous secret, as soon as he should have learned it himself from Father Roger; but of course all was to be managed with the greatest prudence and caution, since doubtless if the "spiritual father" should suspect any thing, the grand plan would fail.

Three or four months passed in this way, Martin living all the while in the most jovial manner, when one day he came to his generous confidants, and announced to them that the moment of the grand discovery was at hand. The very next day, Father Roger was, without any more delay, to instruct him in the art of changing mercury into silver, which art he would forthwith communicate to them.

The next day the alchemists waited, with great emotion and anxiety, for the appearance of Martin; but Martin never came. The day after that, they waited still, but still no signs of Martin; at last they went to seek him, but could find him no where; and it was at length discovered, that he had run away from Tchao-King, and gone to Canton, carrying with him many valuable articles that he had stolen at the mission; and some rather considerable sums of money, that he had borrowed from various neophytes of the place. That was Martin's receipt for making gold, but it was one that has been known and practised in China from the earliest ages to the present day.

This disappearance of Martin made a great noise in the town, especially amongst the Christians, most of whom had been victimised by this villain; and, as the matter came to the ears of the mandarins, the missionaries were obliged to confess that they had been robbed by one of their converts. An order for the arrest of Martin was issued, but he had hidden himself at Canton; at length, however, he was discovered, seized and brought back in chains to Tchao-King, to undergo his trial; but the fellow, when he got back, found means to distribute defamatory libels, in which he accused the missionaries of the most infamous crimes. The trial, as may be supposed, occasioned a great commotion, and the whole future prospects of the mission would have been compromised, if

God had not mercifully permitted the magistrates to discover the truth.

Notwithstanding the most abominable intrigues on his part, Martin was found guilty, severely whipped, and condemned to perpetual imprisonment, with the infliction of the *cangue*.

The missionaries, indeed, implored for him the mercy of his judges, and their generous conduct excited the astonishment and admiration of the Chinese; but this good feeling did not last long.

It is melancholy to relate, that this time they were chiefly the neophytes of Tchao-King who disturbed the peace of the missionaries, and excited the multitude against them. The death of Martin had deprived them of all hope of ever recovering any of the money they had lost by him, and in their distraction, they laid the blame on the missionaries, and declared that they had introduced themselves clandestinely into the empire to cause its ruin. They even appealed to the "corporation of the lettered," to bring an official accusation against the Jesuits, and cause their expulsion from the country.

Affairs were in this unhappy state when, during the rainy season, the river that bathes the walls of Tchao-King burst its banks, inundated the whole country round, and caused much mischief. As soon as the waters had returned to their accustomed channel, the Chinese set to work to construct new dykes, stronger than those that had been carried away; but as wood for this purpose was not forthcoming in sufficient quantity, the mandarins issued a decree authorising, for the sake of the public service, the cutting down all trees that did not bear fruit; and the Chinese in such circumstances, and backed by such authority, become the most pitiless ravagers and never fail to profit by these moments of license to do some harm to those they have a spite against. It was not long before the populace came rushing into the gardens of the mission, cutting down and laying waste whatever they could find. The servants, who were mostly negroes, slaves of the Portuguese, endeavoured to put a stop to the devastation, but only increased the disorder. The house itself was broken into; doors and windows dashed in, furniture broken and destroyed, the very roof torn off, and the inmates put to flight, and pursued with howls and showers of stones. After these exploits, the rioters returned triumphantly to the town, to the sound of the tam-tam, quite proud of the victory they had gained over the nations of the West.

On the following day, Father Ricci went to the tribunal, and while he asked for pardon for the authors of these disorders, he solicited the government to forbid by an edict, for the future, the offering any molestation to the missionaries.

Father Edward de Sande, despairing now of the success of the mission, had returned to Macao.

The situation of the Jesuits in China was in the highest degree precarious, and their only hope of safety hung upon the protection of a few mandarins, who might any day be removed, and must be, sooner or later, or, what was no less probable, might grow cool in their friendship; in either of which cases all would be lost, for the missionaries had against them the fundamental laws of the empire, which prohibited their entrance, and much more their residence in the interior. They were, therefore, daily liable to see the fruit of several years' toil and anxiety vanish in a moment. In order to labour for the conversion of the Chinese with any hope of lasting success, it was necessary for the missionaries to have an established position among them, not at the mercy of every chance, or of the malice of the lowest enemies. The Catholic mission must be recognised and approved by the government of the emperor at Pekin;—this was the unanimous opinion of a council of Jesuits, held at Macao, to deliberate on the subject; and it was, therefore, resolved to get, if possible, a legation apostolic sent by the Holy See to

China. It was hoped that by means of this official embassy the mission might afterwards be established on a more solid basis.

Father Roger, who was better acquainted than any of the missionaries with the manners of China, having resided in the country a considerable time, was commissioned to negotiate this important affair at Rome. He embarked, therefore, at Macao, and arrived in safety at Lisbon, whence he departed for Madrid, in the hope of interesting King Philip in the great cause. At Rome, however, the successive decease of two or three popes caused interminable delays, and the zealous missionary, worn out by so many fatigues and toils, at last terminated his laborious career at Salerno, in the kingdom of Naples.

Father Ricci, who now remained alone at Tchao-King, found means, by prudence and affability, to calm the agitation that had arisen, and in a great measure repair the mischief that had been done. His acquirements in physical science and mathematics procured him respect among the Chinese, especially those of the literary class, who continued to visit him, and pay him much friendly attention. He had contrived to put up in the house a clock that struck the hours, and the sounds, regularly heard at a great distance, excited vehement admiration among the people of the country. They were proud of having such a marvellous machine in their neighbourhood, and they began to show marks of respect to this great lettered man from the West, whose genius had enabled him to combine all those wheels with such astonishing success.

Father Ricci endeavoured to take advantage of this friendly disposition in his admirers, to lead them to a knowledge of the Christian faith; and Father d'Almeida, who had been already appointed to the mission of China, and had been waiting for a long time at Macao, thought he might profit by this interval of peace, to join Father Ricci, and aid him in his apostolic labours. He came, therefore, to Tchao-King, but scarcely had he arrived before the horizon became dark, and threatened another storm.

The Chinese are in the habit of rendering great honour to old age; and they have a custom of choosing every year, among the aged men of the district, the most venerable, not only for a long, but also for an exemplary life, who have never either been themselves brought before any tribunal, nor brought any other person there, a great test of merit in the eyes of the Chinese. The magistrates assemble annually these fine white-bearded old men, have a splendid banquet prepared for them, and wait upon them themselves with every mark of filial respect.

Now, the veterans of Canton had talked a great deal on the day of their meeting, of the strangers who had come to Macao and Tchao-King; and they seemed to have been greatly struck by their audacity in having built, at the latter place, a house with several stories and a tower, that had cost considerable sums.

As we have already said, the "Flowery Tower" had had its name changed to "Stranger's Tower," on account of its vicinity to the house of the missionaries; and the report had then been spread that it was built by the strangers.

This tower appeared to these old gentlemen in the light of a fortress, continually menacing the security of the province, and after a long deliberation, they resolved to address a memorial on the subject to the imperial commissioner, visitor of the two Kouangs. This Chinese document has been preserved, and the translation is as follows:—

"The laws of the empire permit humble citizens respectfully to warn their superiors, when the nation is menaced by some danger. We, the old men of the city of Canton, therefore, having considered certain events, have thought that the provincial visitor should be informed of them, in order that he may take measures to provide a proper remedy for the evil.

"In the first place, it is notorious that barbarians are living at Tchao-King, and that they have come from foreign countries to inhabit the Central Kingdom. Novelties are to be dreaded; they are pernicious; a great misfortune is threatening the empire; this has become obvious to all, and we are only repeating what is too evident. A considerable mass of strangers from barbarous countries have arrived at the port of Macao, on the confines of the town of the Mountain of Perfumes (Hian-Chan), and have been pretending to organize an embassy to the Son of Heaven. Under this pretext they wish to open themselves a way into the Flowery Kingdom, to traffic with our people, and mingle in commerce the productions of all countries; and, although they have not been authorized to act in this manner, nor admitted to make their embassy, they have, nevertheless, remained, living pell-mell, in this port of Macao. In past years they were seen to issue from their ships, and traffic with our people, but without attempting to penetrate into the interior; and when the season of fairs was over, they set sail, and returned to their own country. But now behold they build houses with several stories, and come one after another, and swarm like bees and ants. At this sight the heart of every person in the province trembles, and his hairs stand on end, and so much the more, because it is observed that these strangers encroach every day more and more, by means of artifice and trickery. They have had a high tower built at their own expense, in order by that means to obtain an entrance into the town of Tchao-King, whither they have brought with them a crowd of other wicked men, who are seen continually coming and going upon our canals and rivers.

"We fear, and not without cause, that these barbarian may be so many spies, come to find out our secrets, and tell them to their own people. It is especially to be dreaded that they may connect themselves by degrees with those of our nation who are lovers of novelties, and thus become the source of great calamities to the Central empire, and scatter our people over the vast extent of the seas like fish and porpoises. That is, perhaps, the misfortune which our books foretel, when it is written in them, 'You have sown thorns and thistles on good land; you have introduced into your dwellings serpents and dragons.' Macao is like an ulcer that has been allowed to grow upon the feet and hands. There is not much danger, if the remedy be applied in time; but the mischief at Tchao-King is an ulcer that has advanced to the breast and the heart, and reason points out that there should be an operation without delay. It is for this cause that we, the old men of Canton, have thought it necessary to warn the imperial commissioner, in order that he may as soon as possible, drive away these strangers, and send them back to their own people at Macao. As for Macao, that must be attended to in time, when the moment shall have come. By acquiescing in this request, the imperial commissioner will have restored life to a whole province. We unanimously declare, that by this method we shall receive a signal benefit."

This requisition of the aged men of Canton made a great noise in the tribunals, and among the people, and an investigation was ordered, that the truth of these accusations might be ascertained. As soon as Father Ricci became aware of this formidable attack, he prepared for defence, and he was sufficiently versed in Chinese affairs to know how he ought to go about it, so as to avert the threatened storm. He drew up a memorial, in which he endeavoured chiefly to demonstrate that the missionaries had nothing whatever to do with the construction of that famous tower so much objected to. This was not at all difficult, since the whole town of Tchao-King knew perfectly well the truth of that matter. This main point of the accusation being thus entirely overthrown, al the rest crumbled away of itself; for how, he urged, could any attention be paid to what was said by men who could be so grossly deceived, or allege as a fact what was so notoriously false!

After having drawn up his memorial in a manner entirely conformable to the "rites," and with the strictest observance of Chinese customs, he secured the protection of some of the principal mandarins of Tchao-King; and when the trial took place, Father Ricci came victoriously out of the contest. Father d'Almeida received permission to reside, and the wind changed so favourably, that the Superior of the College of Macao thought he might take advantage of it to send one more assistant, namely, Father Francis de Petris; and at last the missionaries were enabled to devote themselves in peace to the duties of their apostleship.

Tchao-King, a town of great importance both in a commercial and political point of view, is situated on the banks of a great river, constantly furrowed by the passage to and fro of crowds of junks. Almost all the mandarins of the South, who are going to, or returning from Pekin, pass this way; and the house and church of the Jesuits, built outside the fortifications of the town, and close to the water side, naturally attract the attention of all who navigate the "Tiger River." Almost all the travellers who passed by Tchao-King, and especially the mandarins and the "lettered," were in the habit of paying a visit to the residence of the religious men of the West; and all were curious to see closely the faces of the strangers, of whom such wonderful things were told. They wanted to look at those clocks which struck the hours of themselves, those maps which described all the countries of the earth, those pictures painted with such astonishing perfection, that the persons in them appeared alive; and that mass of curiosities unknown to the people of the Flowery Kingdom. The mandarins and the lettered men of China were obliged to admit, when they had seen these things, that the barbarians of the West had some glimmer of intelligence; and that even beyond the limits of the Celestial Empire, there were nations who cultivated industry and the arts with some little success. Father Ricci, too, had made himself familiar with the language of China, and interested and amused them so much by his conversation, that they could not but allow that the "Western Devil" had almost sense enough for a Chinese

The frequent visits paid to them tended much to increase the renown of these men of Europe and their possessions. The visitors felt more inclined to listen to the religious instruction which the missionaries always found means to introduce into their conversation; and thus, by the grace of God, the divine seed was sown, which germinated in many a heart, and bore fruit unto salvation. It was at the mission of Tchao-King that many mandarins, who became grand dignitaries of the empire, received their first notions of Christianity, which they subsequently embraced and practised with fervour, as we shall hereafter have occasion to tell. Some families of distinction at Tchao-King even received baptism; and the number of neophytes was at length found so considerable, that the services of the Catholic Church were publicly and regularly performed.

At this epoch the mission of Tchao-King was visited by the ambassadors from the kingdom of Cochin-China, who go every three years to Pekin to carry to the emperor their homage, and the tribute of their sovereign. When they returned to their country, they took with them several books of Christian doctrine, which Father Ricci had composed and had printed in the Chinese character; and as the people of Annam make use of the same character, they were able thus to obtain a little insight into the principles of Christianity, until it should be permitted to the preachers of the gospel to go thither, and make them truly acquainted with the Saviour of men.

The viceroy of the two Kouangs had been dead for some time, and his successor had just arrived at Tchao-King. Malicious tongues had quickly spread the news that he was not at all favourably disposed towards the missionaries, and intended to expel them; it was even said that he had taken a fancy to the piece of ground occupied by the missionaries, and intended to build a palace on it for himself, as of course his superstitious feelings would not allow him to set foot in the dwelling of his predecessor. He would fancy that it would be unlucky to him, and that it would most likely fall upon him as soon as he entered it.

In the meanwhile the imperial commissioner, the visitor extraordinary to the province, was about to return to Pekin to give an account of his mission. The viceroy, who desired to get a favourable report from this grand dignitary, had even more than the usual honours paid to him on the occasion, and declared his purpose of escorting him himself to a considerable distance up the river. On the day of his departure the entire military force of Tchao-King was on foot, and all the mandarins, great and little, with their balls and peacocks' feathers, their necklaces of honour, and their richly embroidered tunics, were summoned to the ceremony. The whole surface of the river was covered with junks and boats decorated with flags and streamers; fireworks were going off in all directions, and the most infernal music was sounding all along the banks of the river, which were thronged by the good citizens of Tchao-King, feasting their little eyes and their great ears on this gorgeous display. At last the great fan-like sails began to unfold themselves, thousands of boatmen set up their nasal song, the heads of the vast multitude swayed up and down like the waves of the sea, and an innumerable throng of junks of all sizes and shapes began to form into procession.

The Catholic mission, as we have said, had taken up its abode on the banks of the river; and as the brilliant *cortége* moved slowly up the stream, the missionaries, with some friends whom they had placed in their windows, stood watching the progress of the interminable squadron with its daz-

4*

tling escort of mandarins. The imperial commissioner and the viceroy were seated on the deck of the most splendid junk, majestically smoking their long pipes, and inhaling, along with their tobacco, the incense of their votaries, who were shouting enough to burst their throats, " *Wan-Fou, Wan-Fou ;*" that is, " Ten thousand Felicities !" Favoured by a gentle breeze, the great gala junk was moving gaily on, when on a sudden a rapid movement was executed on board, she went about, floated a little way back with the stream, and then came to anchor just opposite the missionaries' door. The two great men, the imperial commissioner and the viceroy, immediately landed, and advanced, sheltered by their enormous red parasols, to the Catholic mission house.

The emotion and embarrassment of the poor fathers at the unexpected approach of visitors of such importance may be imagined; but father Ricci hastened to receive them in his very best manner, according to the prescriptions of the Chinese ritual of politeness ; and the illustrious guests examined with great curiosity the different European articles, the clocks, the paintings, the maps, the astronomical and other scientific instruments, the use of which was explained to them. Father Ricci's cabinet, which contained a rich collection of European and Chinese books, particularly attracted their attention; and at length they went and seated themselves in a gallery overlooking the river, and began talking with the missionaries of men and things in the Western countries. These magnificent mandarins declared themselves enchanted with all they saw and heard from the barbarians ; and addressed to them many amiable expressions of good will, that may perhaps have been sincere. They then returned to their junk in the same pomp as when they had quitted it; the dreadful music and the fireworks began again, the imperial commissioner continued his voyage, and the viceroy returned to his palace, while the friends of the missionaries hastened to congratulate them on the signal mark of honour they had received.

The visit of course did not fail to produce a great sensation in the town. The religious strangers, so often harrassed and molested, seemed suddenly to have become persons of importance, and every one who knew them now boasted of the fact. The avenues to their habitation were choked up with palanquins, for all the civil and military functionaries thought themselves in some measure obliged to pay their court to men protected by the viceroy and the imperial commissioner. The neophytes, who since their conversion to Christianity had been always overwhelmed by care and fear, now saw themselves restored to tranquillity; and Father Ricci no longer doubted that the hour was come in which he would be permitted to gather in peace the fruit of seven years of labour and tribulation

CHAPTER III.

The Missionaries expelled from Tchao-King. — Farewell of the Christians.— Refusal of Indemnity. — Establishment at Tchao-Tcheou. — Monastery of the Flower of the South. — Founder of this Monastery. — Father Ricci refuses to lodge in it. — He founds an establishment not far from Tchao-Tcheou. — First and singular Disciple of Father Ricci. — The Missionaries change the Costume of the Bonzes for that of the Lettered Class. — Father Ricci sets off for Pekin. — Accidents on the road. — Arrival at Nankin. — Returns to the Capital of Khiang-Si. — Scientific Labours and celebrity of Father Ricci in that City. — His relations with the Viceroy. — The Mission of Tchao-Tcheou besieged by the Bonzes. — Tranquillity restored. — Father Ricci named Superior of all the Missions of China. — Father Ricci sets off for Pekin with the President of the Supreme Court. — Agitation in the City of Nankin. — Imperial Canal. — The Yellow River. — Arrival at Pekin. — The Missionaries deceived. — Forced to quit Pekin. — Sufferings on their Return. — Beautiful Chinese Town. — Fêtes of the New Year. — Father Ricci's Dream. — Preaching on Mathematics and the Sciences. — Observatory of Nankin. — Chinese Explanations of Eclipses. — Literary Solemnity. — Philosophical Discussion. — Palace haunted by Evil Spirits.

THE hopes which Father Ricci now thought, not without reason, he might indulge in, were, however, not yet destined to be realised. For a long time still had he to sow in tears and sorrow, before it was granted to him to reap in joy, and the sudden gleam of courtly favour that had shone on him from the attentions of the imperial commissioner was but the immediate forerunner of a storm. Only a few days had elapsed before the magistrates of Tchao received an edict from the viceroy commanding them immediately to drive the strangers from their town, and send them back to their country with sixty piastres, by way of indemnity for the loss of their house; three days only being allowed them to make their preparations. In the copy of the edict officially furnished to Father Ricci, we find the following paragraph:—

"Although Ly-Ma-Teou (Matthew Ricci) may not have come into the Celestial Empire with any bad purpose, and, as witnesses have testified, he has committed no offence against the laws, yet it is quite clear that he ought not thus to abandon his own country, seeing that a man may live religiously anywhere.

"Now, it is by no means proper that strangers should reside for a long time in the city governed by the viceroy and therefore there would be no wrong or injustice in sending these strangers back to the place whence they came. As to the expenses they have been at in constructing their house, it is not denied that they have spent a considerable sum of money, but as it seems this money was given to them by way of alms, it cannot be said that it was really their own.

"I order, therefore, that there shall be paid to them in all, sixty piastres, and that they shall be sent back to their own country." This edict, as will be seen, was quite formal, and manifested very little good-will to the missionaries, and though they tried various expedients to get over the difficulty, they were compelled to submit, and retrace their steps as far as Macao. On the day of their departure the Prefect of the city offered Father Ricci the sixty piastres decreed to him as indemnity, but he refused to accept them, and wisely, for he thus retained an incontestable right over the establishment he had founded at Tchao-King. Instead of the money, the sagacious missionary demanded an official attestation that he and his companions had always lived at Tchao-King, in conformity with the laws and the rites, and that their expulsion was not occasioned by any fault. This was readily accorded them, and, moreover, a magnificent eulogium in addition to it.

The poor missionaries must have been greatly distressed at being thus forced to abandon their dear mission; and their sorrowing neophytes accompanied them to the shore, where a scene took place, exactly like what is described in the Acts of the Apostles, on St. Paul's bidding farewell to the Christians of Miletas:—

"And when he had said these things, kneeling down he prayed with them all.

"And there was much weeping among them all: and falling on Paul's neck they kissed him.

"Being grieved most of all for the word which he had said, that they should see his face no more. And they conducted him to the ship."—(Acts, ch. 20, vv. 36–38.)

The Chinese are, in general, not very susceptible of deep or sincere affection, but the neophytes had nevertheless, it seems, heart enough to attach themselves to those who had enlightened them by faith, regenerated them by baptism, and made them children of God. As for the missionary, he always loves the spiritual family which he has reared with so much trouble, and in the midst of suffering; and when persecution comes to rend asunder those tender ties, when the father has to tear himself from his children, to bid them farewell, perhaps for ever, and abandon them to the mercy of their enemies, then, indeed, it is a cruel grief. Perhaps no one who has not himself been a missionary among infidels, can imagine what Father Ricci felt at the moment when he left his mission, and was borne swiftly away on the rapid current of the Tiger river.

The missionaries waited two days at Canton, until it pleased a mandarin of the sea to place a junk at their disposal, and then they made sail for Macao. Before arriving there, however, they perceived a mandarin galley with two banks of oars, and bearing a yellow flag on its mast, making all speed towards them, and to their surprise it proved to be a messenger from the viceroy sent to order them to return immediately to Tchao-King.

The Fathers did not hesitate a moment about complying with the command, for they feared they might otherwise never have an opportunity of returning to the interior of the empire, and they therefore got into the mandarin galley, and soon, to the astonishment of the multitude, reappeared at the port they had quitted. They were immediately commanded to present themselves at the tribunal of the viceroy, who, though he had quite made up his mind not to allow their residence at Tchao-King, meant to insist on their accepting the indemnity, in order to maintain the appearance of justice, and not leave room for any accusation of his having robbed the house of the stranger. He tried all sorts of methods, tricks, cajoleries, threats and rage; but Father Ricci, who perfectly understood his Chinaman, remained firm and inflexible. He let his Excellency storm, and contented himself with steadily refusing the money, and calmly entered his protest against his expulsion. He agreed to make some concessions, indeed, but only on condition that he should be allowed to go and establish himself in some other province of the empire.

On this new basis, negotiations were recommenced, and the affair was soon arranged. Father Ricci received the indemnity and with it an official authorisation to transport his mission to Tchao-Tcheou, an important town situated on the banks of the river Kin, at a short distance from the frontiers of the province of Kiang-Si.

The sub-prefect of Tchao-Tcheou happened just then to be at Tchao-King, and he made acquaintance with the missionaries, and undertook to conduct them himself to the town under his administration. After a voyage of eight days on the river, proceeding towards the north, they arrived at a vast port, where several civil and military officers were awaiting them. The actual town of Tchao-Tcheou was a little further, but it was intended to instal the missionaries in a large and celebrated Buddhist convent, situated at a short distance from the shore, and in a beautiful country.

Father Ricci declared, however, that it was not his intention to fix his residence in a convent of Bonzes, but in the town;

but as he had heard much of this convent of Nan-Hou (Flower of the South), he should like to visit it.

To reach the town of Tchao-Tcheou, the traveller passes through a magnificent country, surrounded by hills of the most varied and graceful forms; through fine plantations of indigo, and fields of rice, and buckwheat, and sugar canes, which are perpetually irrigated by a copious stream, whose pure transparent waters flow with a thousand windings through this delightful plain. The hills around are richly wooded, and their trees always loaded with flowers and fruit, for in this warm climate there is no winter to dread. The orange, the pomegranate, the banana, the *papaya*, and the *liki*, attain an exquisite perfection; and the thick groves of fruit trees are intermingled with camellias, standard roses, and tea shrubs, whose white flowers, resembling those of the Spanish jessamine, exhale a delicious perfume. The splendid monastery of Nan-Hoa rises on the slope of the principal hill, and commands the whole plain, which forms a part of its estate. At present this convent is, in some measure, deserted and fallen to decay; but when Father Ricci visited it, it was very flourishing, and contained more than a thousand Bonzes, or Buddhist monks. It is said to have been founded towards the eighth century of our era, at which period there dwelt here a sort of hermit renowned for the sanctity of his life and the austerities to which he devoted himself.

His days were entirely occupied by prayer, contemplation, and a certain portion of manual labour. His clothing was of the coarsest kind, and he wore round his body, next the skin, an iron chain, which had so corroded the flesh, that it was in a state of putrefaction and full of worms. According to the traditions of the Bonzes of Nan-Hoa, when it happened that one of these worms fell to the ground, the holy man immediately picked it up again and replaced it, saying: "Hast thou not enough to gnaw? why wilt thou go?"

At the death of this anchorite, the veneration of the inhab

itants of the country for him induced them to raise him a magnificent temple, which soon became a celebrated place of pilgrimage for the southern provinces, and when the Catholic missionaries visited it, it contained, as we have said, more than a thousand Bonzes. The reputation of Father Ricci had been for a long time spreading throughout the Chinese empire, and the inhabitants of Nan-Hoa had heard of this illustrious Bonze of the West, whose scientific knowledge was so marvellous; but when they were told he was coming to reside in their monastery, they were by no means pleased; for they imagined his purpose was to reform the convent and compel the monks to lead a more moral and regular life.

It was, therefore, agreed among the chief of them that they would not try to make him pleased with this place of residence, but endeavour gently to inspire him with the desire to go elsewhere; but the superior and the principal dignitaries nevertheless received him with great pomp, according to the rites, and served up to him a splendid banquet.

They afterwards took him to visit several temples, all of which the Fathers d'Almeida and Ricci found very rich and sumptuous. At Nan-Hoa there were many colossal idols of wood or gilt copper; and those of a rather smaller size were so numerous that in a single temple the visitors counted more than five hundred. In a particular sanctuary, all resplendent with gold and silk, and adorned with fifty lamps, was shown the body of the celebrated hermit, the founder of the monastery, dried and handsomely varnished.

Whilst the missionaries were examining with interest these curious Budhist monuments, they were themselves objects of the liveliest curiosity to the Bonzes, and their little eyes twinkled with cunning and mischief as they peered into the European physiognomies, whose strangeness seemed quite to disconcert them. What they found especially surprising was, that the missionaries made no kind of devotional demonstration in their temples, prostrated themselves before no idol, burnt no incense, consulted no oracle; all which seemed very strange and unaccountable.

The superiors in the meanwhile were in a state of considerable anxiety. "Here are men," they said to one another, "come to be the reformers and heads of our monastery;" and it was, doubtless, a very agreeable surprise to them when they heard the strangers declare to the sub-prefect of Tchoa-Tcheou, that they had an invincible repugnance to reside within the convent, and no more desired to stay with the Buddhists than the Buddhists desired to keep them. No two parties could be better agreed; and the sub-prefect, on the wish to part being so decidedly expressed on both sides, permitted Father Ricci and his companion to proceed to Tchao-Tcheou.

Immediately on their arrival in the city, they hastened to pay their respects to the governor, who seemed exceedingly surprised that, being religious men, they did not wish to remain with the Bonzes. Father Ricci then explained how widely they differed from the Buddhists, both in their creed and in their books of prayer; but the governor not being very learned in theological differences, declared this could not be true, for that there were not in the whole world doctrines and characters other than those of China. Thereupon, Father Ricci drew a breviary from his sleeve, and showed the characters in which it was printed; while the superior of the Bonze convent, who had accompanied him out of politeness, came to his assistance in the other particular, and certified that these were foreigners who were not of the religion of China. "When they visited our temple," said he, "they did not perform the smallest act of devotion; they did not so much as prostrate themselves before the body of our great and holy founder."

These astonishing facts being duly attested, the missionaries obtained permission to establish themselves at Tchao-Tcheou, and a fine piece of land was assigned to them, of which they at their own request paid the price, in order that they might feel more secure of the property; and the work of building soon went on briskly. Father Ricci took care this time not to do as he had done at Tchao-King, build a house in the European style, for experience had shown him that a novelty of that kind might bring him into trouble. The house, the church, and the whole establishment was therefore arranged after the most orthodox Chinese fashion.

Tchao-Tcheou had lately lost one of its great notabilities, namely, the famous Kiu, a man of distinguished learning, who had held the highest offices and exercised a decisive influence in all the most important affairs of the country. His son Kiu-Tai-Sse had followed the literary career with the most brilliant success; but a love of dissipation had afterwards induced him to abandon all serious study, and he had devoted himself with passionate ardour to alchemy.

The rich inheritance that his father had left him was soon dispersed in smoke through his crucibles and alembics, and he then adopted a kind of nomadic life, and traversed all the provinces of the empire, pitching his tent wherever he could find any friends of his father, who, for his father's sake, were generally willing to afford him a welcome.

He had sojourned in this way for a time at Tchao-King, and had made acquaintance with the missionaries, to whom he became a very frequent visitor, as he had heard the report that these strangers from the West knew how to transform the commonest metals into gold and silver.

One day Father Ricci was peaceably engaged at his new abode in Tchao-Tcheou, translating Euclid's Elements into Chinese, when Kiu-Tai-Sse made his appearance. He was attired in a rich costume of ceremony, and accompanied by several attendants, solemnly bearing presents covered with flowers and ribbons. Kiu-Tai-Sse prostrated himself before the missionary, struck the ground three times with his forehead, and said, "Master! suffer me to be your disciple!" This is a customary ceremony with the Chinese when they choose a master; so the next day there was a splendid banquet, and Kiu-Tai-Sse was adopted as a disciple accordingly.

His passion for the occult sciences and the secrets of alchemy, had, however, been the real inducements to this step; but, after having for some time frequented the company of the missionaries, he found that though they were certainly in possession of that philosopher's stone of religious truth which is capable of effecting the most wonderful transformations of the intellect and the heart, they were incapable of manufacturing the smallest morsel of gold or silver.

Kiu-Tai-Sse had applied himself in the first instance to the study of mathematics, geometry, and mechanics, under the direction of Father Ricci, and made very rapid progress, and even, it is said, became capable of constructing instruments and writing on scientific subjects with clearness, elegance, and precision. To the study of religion he devoted no less attention than to that of the sciences, and carried into it the clearness and correctness of thought which the study of mathematics often gives.

He had prepared, among other things, a table with three columns, in the first of which were placed the religious and moral instructions of Father Ricci; in the next the objections that occurred to him; and the third he left blank to receive the master's explanations. He was subsequently admitted to the rite of baptism; and the conversion brought great renown to the mission, for Kiu-Tai-Sse, on account of his reputation as a learned man, exercised a considerable influence over public opinion; and the house at Tchao-Tcheou soon became the rendezvous of the literary men and first functionaries of the province.

In the meantime Father d'Almeida died, and Francis de Petris obtained, in 1592, the permission to replace him. But only two years afterwards this missionary also died, just at the moment when he was beginning to occupy himself usefully in the labours of the mission; for, under the skilful direction of Father Ricci, he had made rapid progress in the Chinese language.

And thus, after so many fatigues and tribulations, Father Ricci found himself once more alone, struggling unaided with all the difficulties of his work; but as he earnestly requested a coadjutor, the Father Cataneo, who had recently arrived at Goa, was sent to him. For a long time Father Ricci had entertained the project of making a journey to Pekin, in the hope of obtaining an audience of the emperor; being persuaded that the smallest success at court would be more useful and efficacious for the propagation of the faith in China than all the efforts he had been making in the provinces.

An opportunity of realising this long cherished project presented itself in the month of April, 1595. One of the principal mandarins of the empire, who was passing through Tchao-Tcheou, to go to the capital, had had the curiosity to go and see the Jesuits, and consult them concerning the health of his son. Father Ricci informed him that he could not cure the child during the short stay which the mandarin was about to make in that city, but that he would willingly accompany him to Pekin, and continue his medical attendance. The offer was accepted, and preparations for departure were made on both sides.

Before quitting Tchao-Tcheou for the capital of China, Father Ricci effected a reform which the superiors at Macao considered of much importance. Up to this time, the Jesuits had adopted the costume of the Buddhist monks of the country, shaving their heads and beards, wearing robes with large sleeves, and collars that crossed over the breast, so as to have externally the appearance of Bonzes, the name, indeed, by which they were known among the multitude. But there were great inconveniences in this practice, for the contempt generally felt in China for these Buddhist ecclesiastics was extended to the Catholic missionaries also. Those who became acquainted with them doubtless learned to appreciate them, but the people in general confounded them with the inhabitants of the Bonze convents in one common reprobation. The Jesuits, therefore, determined to renounce the Bonze costume, and adopt that of the literary class; and they accordingly allowed their hair and their beards to grow again.

The mission of Tchao-Tcheou was now entrusted to the care of Father Cataneo; and Father Ricci, accompanied by two young novices from Macao, set off with the great military mandarin for Pekin. They went by water as far as Nan-Kioung, where they were cordially received by some neophytes, who had come to study their doctrines at Tchao-Tcheou. On leaving Nan-Kioung, they began to ascend the steep and rugged flanks of the Mei-Ling, which separates the province of Canton from that of Kiang-Si. We have ourselves had frequent occasion to cross this mountain; it is traversed by numerous paths, amongst which there is little choice, for all present nearly the same difficulties: their multiplicity arises from the great numbers of travellers and porters who are compelled somehow to make their way across it; since it is, in fact, the only road by which the commerce of Canton can pour its merchandise into the interior provinces of the empire. A most painful thing it is to see these unfortunate men bending under the weight of their enormous burdens, and dragging themselves along these tortuous and almost perpendicular roads; and it is said that those whom poverty compels to adopt this mode of life live but a very short time. We did, however, when we crossed the Mei-Ling, in 1852, see some very old men among them; so old, indeed, that they seemed scarcely able to totter under their painful loads. At certain distances bamboo sheds are found, where travellers can rest in the shade, drink a few cups of tea, and smoke a pipe. On the summit of the mountain is a kind of stone gate, or triumphal arch, to mark the spot where the province of Canton ends and that of Kiang-Si begins.

After crossing the Mei-Ling, the party journeyed through

Kiang-Si, by following the course of the river Kan, famous for the number of its reefs and the rapidity of its current; and on the very first day of the voyage the junk that carried the wife and children of the mandarin was wrecked, and afforded Father Ricci an opportunity of showing his courage and self-devotion. Thanks to his activity and intelligence, not a single person was lost; but the very next day a fierce gust of wind threw the vessel on which Father Ricci himself was upon a reef, so that she foundered instantly, and went down with all her crew and passengers. The zealous founder of the Chinese mission was, however, providentially rescued from this imminent danger of death, for while struggling beneath the water, he had managed to catch hold of a thick rope, by means of which he got to the surface again, and scrambled upon the junk, which was lying on its side. One of the young novices was unfortunately drowned, and never rose again from the bottom of the water. His name was John Barrados.

Terrified by all these accidents, the mandarin refused to continue such a perilous voyage; he disembarked, and resolved to go by land to Pekin, accompanied only by the few servants who were absolutely necessary; and being of opinion that the presence of the European ecclesiastic brought him ill luck, he would not have him any longer in his suite, and advised him to go back to Tchao-Tcheou. The entreaties of Father Ricci, however, so far prevailed, that he was allowed to go on as far as Nankin, and he received letters of recommendation to the civil and military officers whom he might meet on the road.

The intrepid apostle of China, therefore, now found himself alone and without any protection in the midst of this strange and vast empire; but, fortunately, he was well acquainted with the language and manners of the countries he had to traverse. He continued his route by water only, never once setting foot on land as far as Nan-Tchang-Fou, the capital of the province of Kiang-Si, and stopped there some days in a celebrated pagoda, where the Bonzes wished to make him prostrate himself before their idols. Upon his formal refusal, they excited against him the mob, who had run to look at the learned stranger, and a riot took place: but Father Ricci did not allow himself to be intimidated; and the authorities at last interfered, and declared they saw no reason why the illustrious stranger should not be allowed to worship the divinity in the manner he thought most fitting. On leaving Nan-Tchang-Fou, Father Ricci re-embarked to proceed to the lake Pou-Yang, which cannot be crossed in less than two days, during which time you get out of sight of land. It is difficult to fancy oneself in the centre of the Chinese empire while sailing over this immense extent of waters, which is formed by the confluence of four great rivers, and is thirty leagues in circumference,—the long waves raised on it by the wind, and the large and numerous vessels navigating its surface in all directions, almost entitling it to be called a sea, rather than a lake. Sometimes, the countless junks that cover it form a very pretty spectacle, with their variously shaped sails,—some moving majestically before the wind, with their large matting sails all displayed to their utmost extent, others struggling painfully against wind and wave, or crossing in opposite directions, or seeming to pursue one another, like so many sea-monsters rushing after their prey; and the evolutions of all these floating machines are so rapid and multifarious, that the picture is changed every moment.*

The lake Pou-Yang was safely crossed by Father Ricci, and then the junk that bore him entered the Yang-tse-Kiang, "*the River-Child of the Sea,*" and at last brought up under the walls of Nankin, a town famous in the annals of the empire, where, at various epochs, the emperors with their brilliant court have resided. Its numerous palaces, its great pagodas, its tower, celebrated throughout the world, its triple

---

* See "Chinese Empire," vol. II.

enclosure of ramparts, give to Nankin an imposing aspect, worthy of its past renown. The Blue River, which rolls its majestic waves past the walls of the city, is thronged with junks, bearing into the interior of the town, by numerous artificial canals, the wealthy Chinese of the provinces, who desire to pass their days in a fine climate and in the midst of luxury and magnificence. When the court forsook Nankin it ceased to be the centre of politics and business, but became a favourite residence for literary men and persons of fortune.

Father Ricci chose for himself a modest lodging in the suburbs of the city, and resolved to wait in calm seclusion till Providence should allow him to see some favourable opportunity for coming forward and proclaiming to this population of learned sceptics the good tidings of the Gospel. He soon learned that one of the principal magistrates of Nankin was one of his old Canton friends, the Mandarin Hia, for whom he had made a globe and some sundials. He went, therefore, to pay him a visit, hoping he might not have forgotten their acquaintance and his former expressions of friendship.

The grand Mandarin Hia received Father Ricci with measured courtesy and in a manner perfectly conformable to the " rites," and then inquired by what chance he found himself at Nankin, and what important affair had brought him there. " I remembered you," answered Father Ricci, " and could not resist the desire to pay you a visit. Here are the official letters from the Grand Military Intendant, who has authorised me to come and see you at Nankin." On hearing these words, and especially on seeing the letters, the mandarin seemed to be thrown into the greatest consternation, and he could not repress his displeasure. " What rashness!" he exclaimed— " What madness! Your heart has misled your reason! At Canton I treated you with benevolence, and now you come to ruin me at Nankin! Nankin is not a town where a stranger can live: your presence will excite a tumult: you will be the occasion of a riot, and they will accuse me of having caused

Vol. II.—5

it! My enemies will point me out to my superiors as a man who keeps up a secret communication with barbarians and endeavours to bring them into the Celestial empire. My future prospects are ruined; I shall be irrevocably lost, and all because of you!"—and by way of conclusion to these friendly speeches, the mandarin turned Father Ricci out of doors, and desired he would leave the town immediately, and go, he did not care where.

The poor missionary retired, terribly disconcerted at this rough reception, and he had scarcely got home before a party of soldiers came and seized the owner of the house and dragged him before the tribunal. Father Ricci's old friend thought proper, it seems, to vent some of his anger upon this unfortunate Chinese; he ordered him to be beaten with bamboos till he was covered with blood, and told him that by keeping up secret communication with strangers he had committed a crime that the law punished with death; and that if he wished to atone for his fault he must drive this barbarian from his house, or his presence would assuredly bring him some worse misfortune.

Father Ricci could not of course resist a storm of this violence, but yielded to it with resignation, and, after a tedious and troublesome voyage, reached Nan-Tchoung-Fou, the capital of Kiang-Si. "He turned the prow," says Father Trigault, "towards the province of Kiang-Si, and began again to row against the course of the stream, and not less against his own wishes."*

Nan-Tchoung-Fou is one of the finest and most flourishing commercial cities in the empire, and is especially celebrated for the number and merit of the literary men it contains. In 1847, two hundred and fifty-one years after Father Ricci, we ourselves entered that city escorted by mandarins, who, by the emperor's order, were conducting us back to Canton, and

---

* Trigault, de l'Exp. Chért. p. 255.

we installed ourselves in the Palace of Literary Compositions. Father Ricci was not so well accommodated. A persecuted wanderer, he knew not where to ask for hospitality, and had no companions but a young Portuguese novice from Macao, and some Chinese converts who had attached themselves to him, partly from friendship, and partly from self-interest. Whilst he was seeking an asylum where he might obtain shelter without compromising any one, he remembered that there was in the town a celebrated physican from whom he had frequently received visits during his residence at Tchao-Tcheou; and he determined without hesitation to go to the doctor, and explain his embarrassing position. This time he met with a different reception from the former one. The Chinese doctor welcomed him with generous hospitality, and offered him an asylum in his house; and, as he enjoyed a high reputation both in literature and medicine, he lived on intimate terms with the highest functionaries of the town, and even with the viceroy of the province. He had the highest esteem and veneration for Father Ricci, and he exerted all his influence to guard him from persecution.

By the kind exertions of this learned and religious man, the missionary was soon favourably known in a high class of Chinese society; his rare acquirements were everywhere spoken of with praise, and his fame was already rapidly increasing, when he published two works that he had sketched a few years before, and finished at Nan-Tchoung-Fou, namely; "A Treatise on Artificial Memory, or Mnemonics," and a Dialogue on Friendship," in imitation of that of Cicero. The Chinese have always regarded the latter as a model of unsurpassable excellence, and the "Treatise on Artificial Memory" excited at that time no less the general admiration. Father Ricci had been long familiar with the memoria technica, and could recite long series of Chinese characters, either backwards or forwards; and the experiments of this kind that he made in the presence of men of letters procured him many friends.

The viceroy of the province had heard a great deal of Matthieu Ricci, whilst he held high office in the magistracy of Canton, and the wonderful things related of the learned stranger lately arrived at Nan-Tchoung-Fou made him think this must certainly be the famous Ly-Ma-Teou (Matthieu Ricci) whom he had long known by reputation. One day when the father was giving lessons on memoria technica to his Chinese medical friend, he received a despatch upon red paper summoning him to the viceroy's palace, and Ricci, who had met with nothing but annoyance in his relations with the Chinese authorities, expected only a new persecution; but he was mistaken. The viceroy having discovered that this was really the same learned ecclesiastic whom he had heard mentioned at Canton, received him in a most friendly manner, stated that he considered it a great honour to possess in his province so distinguished a personage, and begged him to settle there for good.

The zealous missionary asked no better. He presented to the viceroy the works he had composed, and also offered him a triangular glass prism, a kind of plaything not then known to the Chinese, and which they enthusiastically admired. But the viceroy, though he had the greatest desire to possess it, magnanimously, and with some self-complacence in his magnanimity, refused it.

"It is written in our annals," he said to Ricci, "that a religious man of past times possessed a jewel of great value. A virtuous person went to visit this religious man, who offered him the precious jewel; and he accepted it, but immediately restored it to him, saying, 'This jewel will always remain in your possession, for you will never offer it but to a virtuous man, and such a one will doubtless never accept it. Therefore it will always be yours.' This seems to apply to you and me, Master Ly, for we both follow the paths of virtue."

It does not appear that the "path" of modesty was one often trodden by this worthy viceroy, but he was nevertheless really kind and generous; and, although he had refused Father Ricci's little present, he frankly accorded him his friendship and protection. The example also was very happy in its effect, and the Chinese of rank hastened to seek the acquaintance of the Catholic missionary.

As the people and mandarins of Nan-Tchoung-Fou appeared so favourably disposed, Father Ricci now began to think of occupying himself with religious propagandism, and wrote to Macao to ask for a coadjutor and some pecuniary assistance, in order to provide for the expenses of his establishment.

In good time for the festival of Christmas, 1595, Father John Soerius, a Portuguese, joined him with a sum of money, which, though not very considerable, was sufficient to hire a house and fit it up suitably for the celebration of religious service; and Father Ricci, who had acquired great literary fame by his previous works, now published a Chinese catechism. From that moment all the inhabitants of the city and its environs were occupied about the religious strangers and the new doctrine they had come to propagate among the followers of Confucius, Lao-tze and Buddha; and two princes of the imperial family, who resided at Nan-Tchoung-Fou, surrounded by all the pomp and prestige of their rank, attached themselves to the missionaries, and protected them to the utmost of their power.

Whilst the mission of Nan-Tchoung-Fou was going on thus prosperously, that of Tchao-Tcheou, after having laboured peacefully and with good success in the conversion of souls, had to sustain a violent assault from the inhabitants of a neighbouring village.

Some learned men, excited by the Bonzes, observed with

jealousy that the Catholic chapel was higher than their pagoda, and also frequented by a crowd of visitors, attracted either by the desire of instructing themselves in the principles of the Christian religion, or of examining the European curiosities displayed in the great hall.

One night, while the mission was profoundly quiet, the people of the village in question were celebrating one of their noisy and superstitious fêtes, and when their brains were well heated with rice wine, a tumultuous mob of them set off to lay siege to the dwelling of the strangers. They began by sending a shower of stones against the house, accompanied by savage cries and maledictions; but the servants of Father Cataneo rose immediately, armed themselves with bamboos, and a valiant negro from Goa putting himself at their head, they issued forth, and threw themselves upon the rioters, who took refuge behind some vessels lying along the bank of the river. The village, however, sent forth a reinforcement of combatants, and the battle began again, and raged till morning. The assailants, who were not apparently of remarkable bravery, and some of whom had got some stout blows from the negroes' bamboo sticks, then ran about over the town of Tchao-Tcheou uttering tremendous cries, and knocking at every magistrate's door to demand justice against the Western devils, who were trying, they said, to assassinate them.

The great tribunals remained deaf to their complaints, but they found one petty mandarin who listened to them with favour because Father Cataneo had refused a few days before to give him a sundial.

Not wishing to allow so fair an opportunity for vengeance to escape him, he sent his soldiers to the mission and arrested two of the servants, whom he condemned to receive fifty blows of the bamboo.

A brother coadjutor named Sebastian went to the tribunal to plead for them, but as soon as he appeared the rioters who filled the hall cried out that he was the wickedest of the party and the very man who had given them their hurts. Immediately the mandarin ordered that he also should receive fifty blows of the bamboo, and moreover the punishment of the *Cangue*. This cangue, as is generally known, is a heavy mass of wood with a hole through which to pass the head of the condemned person, and which presses upon his shoulders with tremendous weight, so that the man becomes, as it were, the pillar of a huge round table. The unfortunate brother Sebastian was exposed before the door of the tribunal suffering this torture, and with an inscription in red letters over his head:—" Condemned for having insulted and beaten Bachelors ;" and the enemies of the mission, forgetting their wounds in the proud satisfaction of their revenge, returned exulting to their village.

Father Cataneo, dreading the consequences of such riots as this, had recourse to an expedient to prevent their recurrence which succeeded extremely well. As he had remarked that t'ie height of his little church gave offence to the Chinese, he had the elevated portion demolished, and reserved only a simple hall without any ornament, from which he took away all the pictures and curiosities that had been so much admired.

Some days afterwards several high class mandarins, happening to pass through Tchao-Tcheou, expressed a desire to go and visit the residence of the foreigners, and the governor of the town hastened to conduct his guests to the Catholic mission, but they found only ruins, and what was quite undeserving their attention. They expressed to Father Cataneo their astonishment and regret at the sight of this devastation, and he then informed them of what had lately taken place. The governor severely blamed the conduct of the petty mandarin for having provoked such a disorder, and in order to remedy the evil, published the same day an edict, in which, after pronouncing a eulogium upon the missionaries, he threatened with the severest chastisements those who should dare to trouble them in their residence at Tchao-Tcheou. The Jesuits now profited by this favourable disposition of the magistrates to send for two more preachers of the gospel from Macao— namely, Father John de Roche and Nicholas Lambard,—but the superiors of the college thought it best to recall poor brother Sebastian, who had undergone the fifty blows of the bamboo, and the degrading punishment of the cangue.

For several years the project had been entertained of sending a solemn embassy to Pekin, for it was still thought that this would be the most efficacious mode of establishing the mission of China on a solid basis. It may perhaps not be forgotten that Father Roger had taken a journey to Europe on purpose to interest the sovereign pontiff and the courts of Spain and Portugal in this grand enterprise, but the death of this zealous missionary and other obstacles had prevented the realisation of the project; and on learning the great success of the missionaries established at Nan-Tchang-Fou and Tchao-Tcheou, the visitor-general of the missions of China and Japan was of opinion that it would be advisable to give up the plan of the embassy, since it could not now be of the importance before supposed. The missionaries had now been long established in the interior of the empire of China; they had made themselves perfectly well acquainted with the language and customs of the country;—had acquired much experience in the course of the various tribulations they had gone through, and no longer needed the doubtful aid of an official embassy; they desired only to follow the impulse of their zeal, and continue the propagation of the faith among these numerous populations. Such was the opinion of the visitor-general; but he understood that to ensure the progress and success of the work it would be necessary that the first plan should undergo some modifications. The rector of the college of Macao was at the same time superior of the missions of the interior; and this organisation did not present any serious obstacles as long as the missionaries had been compelled to limit their excursions to the city of Canton and its environs; but now that there were Christians in Tchao-Tcheou and at Nan-Tchang-Fou, towns far in the interior, and at a great distance from Macao, the centre of authority, it was thought, ought not to be in the latter town. The influence so very widely extended could hardly fail to become so much weakened as to be of little service. In the course too of the labours of the mission, circumstances continually arose that made it necessary for some one on the spot to come to a decision without delay, and those who were imperfectly acquainted with such circumstances would be very likely to decide wrong.

It was therefore determined that a superior-general of the missions of China should be appointed, and that he should exercise all the functions of the provincial visitor, and be authorized to decide all questions without appeal. This important office was to be filled by Father Ricci, and his enlightened zeal, his great experience, and his familiarity both with European science and Chinese literature, rendered him in all respects worthy of the distinction. The mission at the same time was to retain at Macao an officer who should provide for the wants of the missionaries, and be the medium of their correspondence with Europe.

Father Ricci was now invested with the authority and power of superior, and devoted himself with renewed ardour to the prosecution of the work in which he had so long been engaged. The various attempts he had made in several important towns had not induced him to lose sight of the capital, and Pekin and the court still continued to be the goal of his wishes. He felt persuaded that the torch of faith borne to that height would shed a far greater light over the empire, and Nan-Tchang-Fou seemed now about to furnish him with the means of realising his hopes; he cultivated the friendship of the imperial princes of whom we have spoken, and who were nearly related to the reigning emperor; but though the kindred of the "Son of Heaven" gave him much encouragement, they

5*

told him that their protection in such a cause would do him more harm than good, since in their quality of princes of the blood they were objects of suspicion at court, and the least movement on their parts might be considered an act of usurpation; that the emperor distrusted his near relations, and never confided to them any important office, but kept them at a distance from the capital, and out of the way of business.

From all these considerations it became evident to Father Ricci that he must renounce the honour of being introduced at court by the imperial princes, and look out for more efficient, though less brilliant protectors.

During the time when Father Ricci was directing the mission of Tchao-Tcheou, he had made acquaintance with a great dignitary of the empire, named Kouang, who was then going as commissioner to Kai-Nan, an island off the south coast of China. One day father Ricci read, in the official paper of Pekin, that his old friend, the grand mandarin Kouang, had just been appointed President of the Supreme Court, and must necessarily take a journey to Pekin. The business of this court of public employments (Li-Pou) is to present government officers for the nomination of the emperor, and distribute civil and literary posts throughout the empire. It has four divisions, which regulate promotions and exchanges; it keeps notes concerning the conduct of official persons, fixes the amount of their salaries, and their leaves of absence during periods of mourning, and bestows the patents for posthumous rank accorded to the *ancestors* of officers admitted into the ranks of the nobility. Obviously the Jesuits could have no better protector than the president of this supreme court, thus holding under its jurisdiction all the mandarins of the empire.

Immediately on seeing the nomination of the new president, Father Ricci despatched a courier to Tchao-Tcheou to inform Father Cataneo of this important news, and urge him not to neglect seeing the mandarin when he should pass through that city. The Mandarin Kouang did in fact arrive there **very** shortly after, and when he received a visit from Father Cataneo, inquired after his old friend Si-Ma-Teou (Mathew Ricci) and expressed pleasure on learning that he had founded a mission at Nan-Tchang-Fou. "We shall see each other there," he said, "and I will take him with me to Nankin—perhaps even to Pekin, for I should like to have his assistance in correcting the imperial calendar, and reforming the tribunal of mathematics." Delighted was Father Cataneo of course at this gracious speech, and he immediately betook himself to Nan-Tchang-Fou, to arrange with Father Ricci the plan for making most advantage of the favour of this well disposed mandarin, who was faithful to his promise, and on the 25th of June, 1590, the two missionaries embarked with him upon lake Pou-Yang, and arrived some days afterwards at Nankin.

The city of Nankin was at this moment in a state of the greatest agitation; ships of war filled the port, and soldiers the streets, and the mandarins were rushing about from one tribunal to another, evidently under feelings of great excitement. Father Ricci scarcely recognised, in this state of martial ebullition, the quiet and literary Nankin that he had known,—the chosen retreat of those who had no pursuit but that of tranquillity, luxury, and pleasure; but it was not long before he learned the cause of the transformation. It seemed that the Japanese, after having been for a long while secretly preparing a formidable expedition, had suddenly invaded Corea, and attempted to make the conquest of it. At the news of this sudden irruption the Chinese had taken arms to defend a people tributary to the empire, and repel an invasion that might be formidable to themselves; and the imperial government was collecting all its forces, both by land and sea, to deliver Corea from the Japanese. An edict was placarded in the streets of Canton, by which all civil and military officers, and even the populace, were called on to watch and arrest individuals who, by their physiognomies or their manners, might be suspected of being foreigners. Only a few days before some Japanese spies had been seized in the town.

The publication of this edict was a terrible annoyance to the missionaries, and the president Kouang advised them not to appear in public, but to remain shut up in the junk while he himself went to the palace prepared for him, to await the time of his departure for Pekin. Father Ricci, however, who was very anxious to know how affairs were going on, ventured to pay him several visits, though with every precaution to prevent discovery.

He always went in a palanquin, carefully closed all round, so that he could be seen by no one; but even in the moment when he was stealing from the vessel to the palanquin on the shore he was one day seen by a soldier, who was just on the point of having him dragged to prison, where he would probably have been massacred as a Japanese, when he declared he was going to the president Kouang. That completely altered the case, for nobody would dare to meddle with the friends of the president of the Li-Pou, and from that time the missionaries went and came in perfect freedom.

After many hindrances and difficulties, the journey to Pekin was at last determined on; the Jesuits were at length to enter that capital of the most immense and ancient empire in the world; the object that Father Ricci had proposed to himself in coming to China would soon be attained: he would present himself at court, see the emperor, and obtain permission to preach the gospel to the people, hitherto so obstinate in rejecting the Christian faith, and remaining buried in the apathy of religious indifference.

The president, Kouang, having to be at Pekin on a certain day, in order to be present at a solemn imperial festival, intended to go by land; but the missionaries had to calculate the length of their purses, and as they could not afford to undertake such a journey by palanquin, they hired two cabins on board the junk that was to take the baggage of their pro tector, and embarked on the imperial canal, which, after having united the Blue with the Yellow River, continues its course to Pekin.

Father Ricci was much struck with the magnificence of this canal, which is capable of bearing the largest vessels, and by a system of locks, as simple as it is ingenious, overcomes all difficulties from the inequality of the ground. The canalisation of the empire has always been an object of great solicitude to the Chinese Government, and the annals of China show that every successive dynasty has paid the greatest attention to it, though none of their works are comparable to those executed by the Emperor Yang-Ti, of the dynasty of Tsin, who ascended the throne in the year 605 of the Christian era. In the very first year of his reign he had new canals dug, and enlarged the old, in order that boats might be able to pass from the Hoang-Ho to the Yang-tse-Kiang, and from these great rivers into their smaller tributaries.

A learned man named Siao-Hoai presented to him a plan for rendering all the rivers navigable throughout their course, and making them communicate one with another by canals of a new construction. The project was adopted and executed, and more than 6,000 leagues of canals were repaired and constructed. The enormous quantity of labour required for this vast enterprise was divided between the soldiers and the people of both town and country. Every family had to furnish a man, between the ages of fifteen and fifty, to whom the government gave nothing but his food; but the soldiers, who had the hardest part of the work, received an augmentation of pay.

Some of these canals were lined with freestone throughout their whole length; and during our travels in China we ourselves saw enough of them to bear witness to the beauty of the work. The canal from the northern to the southern court* was forty paces wide, and had both the banks planted

---

* There were at that time four imperial courts.

with elms and willows; that from the eastern to the western was rather less magnificent, but also shaded with double rows of trees. Chinese historians have severely blamed this emperor Yang-Ti, for the way in which he oppressed the people by *corvees*, to satisfy his immoderate love of pomp and luxury, but it cannot be denied that he has deserved well of his country by the advantage commerce has obtained from these canals.

After a voyage of several days the missionaries entered the Yellow River, which differs strikingly from the Yang-tse-Kiang by the impetuosity of its current, and the muddy colour of its waters. The Hoang-Ho takes its rise in the mountains of Thibet, and crosses the Koukou-Noor, to enter China by the province of Chan-Sou. It issues from it by flowing along the sandy plain at the foot of the Alechan mountains, surrounds the country of the Ortous, and after having watered China, first from north to south, and then from east to west, falls into the Yellow Sea. Its waters near their source are pure and beautiful, and only take their yellowish tinge from the sands of the Alechan and Ortous. They are almost always on a level with the countries they pass through, and to the general want of embankments may be attributed the disastrous inundations caused by this river.

The bed of the Hoang-Ho has undergone many remarkable changes. In ancient times its mouth was situated in the gulf of Pe-Tche-Li, in lat. 39°. At present it is in lat. 34°, one hundred and twenty-five leagues from its former embouchure. The Chinese Government is obliged to spend annually enormous sums to restrain this river in its bed, and prevent some of the inundations that would otherwise occur. In 1779 the dyking works executed cost forty-two millions of francs (£1,680,000), and yet, notwithstanding these precautions, the inundations are very frequent; for, in the provinces of Ho-Nan and Kiang-Sou, the bed of the river is, for an extent of two hundred leagues, higher than the general level of the plain through which it flows. This bed too is continually rising from the enormous quantity of soil that the river brings down; and it is likely that at no very distant epoch there will happen a frightful catastrophe that will carry devastation and death over the regions bordering on it.

These great rivers and numerous canals, which maintain such life and activity over the surface of the whole empire, were well calculated to astonish strangers, in the sixteenth century, when Europe could show nothing of the kind, and are still very striking, covered as they are with countless junks of all shapes and sizes, perpetually in motion, and transporting goods and merchandise from one province to another. The imperial canal was dug chiefly for the purpose of bringing to the capital the tribute from the provinces, which is mostly paid in kind. The environs of Pekin are by no means fertile, and the immense population of that great city has to be fed with the produce of other parts of China. The government maintains a numerous fleet of junks for the transport of the imperial revenues, and merchants are allowed to hire them at a very low price; so that, poor as it is in native produce, the city is remarkably well provisioned.

The fruits and vegetables of the South, fish, meat, and almost every necessary and luxury, are to be had in profusion, and all along the road to Pekin there are ice houses in which the most delicate articles of food can be kept fresh.

Since the establishment of the Portuguese at Macao, people in Europe had gradually become convinced that this vast Chinese empire, so recently made known by sea, was really the famous empire of Cathay, visited by the travellers of the middle ages, and of which they gave their contemporaries such curious descriptions. Father Ricci on arriving at Pekin made many inquiries on the subject, and soon no longer doubted that this was the great city named by Marco Polo Cambalu. The celebrated Venetian had resided in Cathay during the occupation of the Mongol Tartars, who called the capital Khanbalik,—that is to say the place of the khan or emperor. After the expulsion of the Tartars, the capital received the name of Pekin, signifying "Court of the North," as Nankin does "Court of the South."

Immediately on the arrival of the missionaries at Pekin, they were conducted to the palace of the president Kouang, who gave them a very gracious reception, and invited them to stay at his house; and the first eunuch of the court soon paid them a visit to negotiate the grand affair of their presentation to the emperor. He examined with much attention and admired greatly the paintings, clocks, and other curious things from Europe, which the Jesuits proposed to offer to the "Son of Heaven," and appeared well satisfied with these presents; but when Father Ricci frankly declared he knew of no secret for transforming metals into gold and silver, he seemed disappointed. The credit of this knowledge had been given to the missionaries from the very beginning of their residence in China, while they were still at Tchao-King; and their fame had spread so as to reach Pekin and the court, where the government was counting upon the assistance of their talents in this way to help them pay the fleets and armies to be sent off to Corea against the Japanese.

When the courtiers found they knew nothing about manufacturing silver and gold, they began to regard them merely as barbarians, and persons of suspicious character, perhaps spies of Japan. The president Kouang was alarmed at these rumours, especially as he was himself about to return to Nankin, and he advised their returning with him, and deferring to a better opportunity the ceremony of presentation to the emperor, and the attempt to obtain permission to remain at Pekin. Father Ricci, however, did not relish this advice, and preferred letting the president go alone; he would not allow himself to be baffled thus by the first difficulty, and driven from the point that it had cost them so much to attain, almost as soon they had reached it.

The protector of the missionaries had not long left Pekin before most of their new friends appeared to grow very cool; the mandarins gradually left off visiting them, and soon after refused to receive them at their houses; and father Ricci, without being alarmed, began to consider whether it might not be prudent to think of a retreat, and of securing the means of falling back on Nankin. The great point was, to avoid compromising themselves in the capital, and to keep open a door for their re-admission. In spite of their supposed familiarity with the art of making gold and silver, the real fact was that their purse was now empty, and they were considerably puzzled to find the means of paying their passage. They had received from their agent at Macao advice of a rather large sum of money having been paid into a great commercial house at Canton, for which a bill, payable at sight in Pekin, had been given, and which the agent had forwarded, but vainly did the missionaries search through Pekin for the correspondent of the great commercial house of Canton. The too confiding agent of Macao had evidently been made the victim of a scandalous fraud, and the only thing to be done was to embark on the cheapest boat that could be found, and set out on their return voyage with scarcely the common necessaries, and the prospect of travelling very slowly. They were a whole month getting to Lin-King, which they could have reached by land in a week, and, to complete their misfortune, when they got there they were compelled to stop. The progress of this miserable junk had been so slow that the severe cold of winter had set in, the imperial canal was frozen over, and navigation was interrupted. They would have to wait patiently for the return of spring. After remaining a few wretched winter days on board the junk, Father Ricci thought he would make an effort to avoid the loss of so much valuable time, and endeavour to make his way by land as well as he could to Nankin, whilst Father Cataneo should wait with the baggage for the melting of the ice, and then rejoin him. What must have been the courage and energy of this zealous missionary, to support all the labours and disappointments that he had had to encounter in China? Bidding farewell to his only companion, he soon found himself on the road to Nankin, and surrounded by difficulties that would be scarcely comprehensible to any one who has not had the honour of journeying like him through this "Celestial Empire," this "Flowery Kingdom," where assuredly one does not always find oneself upon a bed of roses; and the sky is not always of the tint of heavenly blue.

As he went on his way, the thought occurred to Father Ricci, that he would go and see his friend the doctor Kin-Tai-Sse, who had rendered him such good service at Nan-Tchang-Fou, and who happened now to be at Sou-Tcheou. He turned his steps, therefore, in that direction, and after long and weary wandering, sometimes on foot, sometimes in a boat, for as he got nearer to the south he found the canals and rivers no longer frozen, he at last reached Sou-Tcheou.

The doctor was not there, but resided in a small town a little way off; and thither Father Ricci proceeded and found again his worthy friend, who lavished upon him every attention that the most cordial hospitality could suggest. Father Ricci had, however, undergone an amount of fatigue that was too much for his strength, and he had no sooner arrived than he fell ill. Happily for him, Providence, in subjecting him to this new trial, had granted him the blessing of having by his side this skilful and experienced physician, who never relaxed in his care during a whole month in which the Father remained a sufferer from this dangerous malady. As soon as the crisis was past, he rapidly recovered his health and strength, and then he accompanied his kind friend the doctor to Sou-Tcheou to see whether it would be advantageous to found a mission there.

Sou-Tcheou, where we ourselves lived a considerable time, during our residence in China, is perhaps the most opulent and pleasant town in the empire. It is almost entirely built upon piles, and occupies the circumference of an immense lake fed by the waters of the Blue River. The streets, like those of Venice, are magnificent canals, over the surface of which skim myriads of little junks of the most brilliant colours, and glittering with varnish, and at night these Chinese gondolas have perhaps a still gayer effect, with their coloured lanterns suspended to their prow and poop. These navigable highways of the city are intersected by many bridges of wood, brick, or stone, frequently of a single arch, and always of an original and fantastic construction. During the fine summer nights the wealthy inhabitants of Sou-Tcheou make long pleasure excursions in these magnificent junks, and display all the pomp of their brilliant acquatic equipages. There are certain quarters which are the general rendezvous of Chinese fashion, the Champs Elysées of this voluptuous city, and it is a proverbial saying among the people of the Celestial Empire, that " The blessed ones have Paradise in heaven, and men have Sou-Tcheou upon earth."

Doctor Kin-Tai-Sse was earnest in his entreaties to Father Ricci to found a mission at Sou-Tcheou, which he desired all the more because it was his own native place, and his relations and friends mostly lived there. It seemed also to be a quiet and peaceful city, inhabited by literary men and traders, and likely to offer fewer difficulties than Nankin, with its countless legions of civil and military mandarins, always a jealous and hostile race. There were at this time no less than six supreme courts sitting at Nankin, whilst the emperor and his court inhabited the capital of the North; and Kai-Tai-Sse asserted that it would be impossible for the missionaries to obtain the good will of this crowd of functionaries of all grades: and the hostility of a single one would be sufficient sooner or later to get them driven from the place. He advised, however, the waiting a few days in order to weigh well the advantages and disadvantages on either side, before taking a final resolution.

The fêtes of the new year too were at hand, and it is well known that the Chinese are not in the habit of attending to any serious business during times of rejoicing.

Father Ricci passed the first day of the Chinese year with his friend Kin-Tai-Sse, at Tching-Kiang-Fou, a town on the banks of the Blue River, which the English took by storm during the war of 1842. He then determined to go to Nankin, which he found much more peaceable than on his former visit, and not resounding so much with the tumult of war. China was no longer in any fear of an invasion by the Japanese, for they had been vigorously repulsed by the Coreans, and obliged to return to their own islands. Father Ricci, encouraged by the pacific aspect of the town, presented himself at the palace of President Kouang, who received him in a friendly manner, and advised him to settle there. The fact that a great number of mandarins resided in the town, formed, in his opinion, a circumstance in favour of the plan, and an additional security. "Master," said he, "you will find among us only protectors and friends;" and as this great personage was then preparing to give some entertainments in honour of the new year, he invited Father Ricci to pass three days in his palace. This was in the month of February, 1599.

The Chinese, like most other nations, celebrate the new year with festivals and rejoicings; every one puts on his best clothes, and numerous visits of ceremony and etiquette are exchanged; presents pass from one to another, feasts are given, people go to the play, and mountebanks, conjurers, and cheats hold high holiday, while fireworks of every description are displayed in all their glory.

The Chinese have always been exceedingly fond of gunpowder, and knew the use of it long before the Europeans, but their taste for the kind used in war is not so decided as for that good only for fireworks. They were pyrotechnists before they were artillerymen, and the catharine-wheel is a much greater favourite with them than the cannon. No high solemnity, be it birthday, marriage, or even funeral, the reception of a mandarin, the meeting of friends, or a theatrical representation, is ever thought to go off with due *éclat* without the popping and blazing of fireworks. Squibs and rockets are going off at every hour of the day or night, for anything or for nothing, and the whole Chinese empire may be regarded as one vast firework manufactory.* In the poorest hamlets, where the inhabitants have scarcely the necessaries of life, they are nevertheless sure to find money to buy fireworks.

The three days' festival given by the President of the Li-Pou were on a scale of great magnificence, and Father Ricci was regarded as one of its not least curious ornaments. The high officers of the six supreme courts appeared happy to become acquainted with the learned stranger, whose maps they had seen, and whose books on mathematical and moral subjects they had read.

On the very day when Father Ricci returned to the humble habitation he had taken, he had the honour of receiving a visit from President Kouang, in all the luxury and pomp of Chinese etiquette, and on the day after that, the poor monk's cell was visited by the presidents of the five other supreme courts in succession, all arriving to the sound of fifes and tam-tams, and with a numerous suite of mandarins and satellites.

The Chinese are known to be, of all nations on the earth, the most addicted to visiting, and their book of "Rites" has given the most minute directions for performing this often-repeated act of public or private life in the most unexceptionable manner. He who meditates paying a visit, must send a note by a servant, some hours before, to the person he designs to favour, to inquire whether he will be at home, and have leisure to receive the visit, which is of course a mark of respect and deference to the person visited. The note must be on a sheet of red paper, larger or smaller according to the rank and dignity of the persons waited upon, and the amount

* Empire Chinois, vol. i. p. 318.

of respect you wish to show them. The paper is to be folded a specified number of times, and you only write a few words on the second page, such, for instance, as—" your disciple, or your younger brother—so and so—is coming to bow his head to the ground before you, and offer you his respects." This sentence is written in a large hand when you mean to assert some amount of grandeur on your own part; but the more humble and respectful you wish to show yourself, the smaller must your writing become.

The grand dignitaries of the supreme courts did not limit their condescension to the paying visits of etiquette to Father Ricci; they pressed him earnestly to take up his abode at Nankin, and as a pledge of the sincerity of their desire to keep him in their city, they offered him for a residence a superb palace, lately vacated by the retirement of an assessor of the Court of Domains. Father Ricci, however, feared to excite the jealousy of the petty mandarins by accepting the brilliant offer, and he could not help thinking, too, that a residence of that kind would be very little in harmony with the character of a poor and humble monk. He determined, however, to remain at Nankin instead of going on to Sou-Tcheou, and he was confirmed in this resolution by a circumstance so singular, that he could not but hope he was thus doing the will of God.

It will not, perhaps, be forgotten that when, on the former occasion, Father Ricci came to Nankin with the intention of settling there, he found the town in a state of great military agitation, and had to remain on board the junk on the Blue River, for fear of being taken for a spy. One night during that time, he thought, in a dream, that God had led him into some great city in the Chinese empire, where he was allowed to walk freely about the streets, talk with the inhabitants, and occupy himself in peace with the holy work of his ministry; and that while he was in his vision traversing every quarter of this celebrated town, God had revealed to him that it was there he should establish himself, and labour for the propagation of the faith. On awakening, Father Ricci was much struck by the dream, and thought of it for a long time. Now, when he had returned to Nankin, and was allowed to walk about, he was greatly astonished to recognise in the streets the palaces and the monuments, exactly what he had seen in the vision of his sleep, and he doubted no longer that God had meant to manifest His will to him.

From that moment all difficulties seemed to vanish, and by the advice of his friend Kin-Tai-Sse, he hired a small and suitable house wherein to establish himself. This story of the dream people will doubtless form various opinions about; it is reported by Father Trigault, from Ricci's own memoir.[*]

Father Cataneo had come to join Ricci at Nankin, and when they were fairly installed and secure of the protection of the magistrates, they resolved to devote themselves to the preaching of the gospel, by what may seem rather a round-about method. They thought it advisable to try and gain credit and influence in the first instance by their skill in mathematics. "God," says Father Trigault, "has not throughout all ages made use of the same method to draw men to His law; and we need not be surprised if our brethren (the Jesuits) made use of this bait to attract fish to their net. Whoever wishes to banish from the Chinese Church physical science, mathematics, and moral philosophy, knows little of the Chinese mind, which infuses wholesome medicine prepared without any of these condiments." Now there was no one thing by which Father Ricci could so powerfully rouse the attention of Chinese philosophers, as by the newest European science, supported as it was by irrefragible proofs.

Father Ricci had found the Chinese plunged in the grossest errors in astronomy, geography, and physical science in general, and he hoped that, by showing these self-sufficient literary

---

[*] Trigault, de Exped. Christ., vol. iv. p. 304.

men the gross absurdities of which they had been the victims, in their pretended science, he might perhaps lead them to admit that they were equally in need of instruction in religion. This method appeared plausible and easy. The Chinese declared the heavens to be round, but the earth square; and they explained eclipses in various ways. Some said that the moon was so impudently stared at by the sun, that she became embarrassed and frightened, and at last dark; others declared there was a large hole in the middle of the sun, and that when the moon was just opposite this hole, she could receive no rays of light.

The Tao-Sse, or doctors of reason, gave a still simpler account of the phenomenon. There was, they said, in the skies, a gigantic goddess, who had but to stretch out her right hand to hide the sun, and her left to hide the moon; and that was the whole secret of eclipses. As for the elements, they admitted five; which reciprocally engendered each other;—they were fire, water, earth, metal, and wood.

It was certainly not difficult for Father Ricci to offer to the Chinese theories approaching a little nearer to common sense than this farago of nonsense, but unfortunately he had not always very incontestable truths to put in the place of their absurdities, and after having rejected their five elements, he gave them in exchange *four*. The missionaries of our day have been sometimes considerably embarrassed when the Chinese talked to them of Father Ricci's four elements and other physical theories which were found interwoven with his moral and doctrinal works.

But though attended with some inconveniences, the method adopted by the first apostles of the Chinese empire was well calculated to gain them credit and consideration; though also it must be owned to excite the jealousy of the learned and the mandarins. Every Chinese at Nankin who had the smallest tincture of letters now made a point of getting introduced to these great masters from the West, and nothing was talked of but astronomy, geography, and mathematics. Euclid had dethroned Confucius, and the Chinese threw aside their classical books, to occupy themselves in making maps, spheres, and sun-dials. It was quite a rage among them—a monomania.

Nankin possessed an observatory, situated on a mountain at one of the extremities of the town; beyond the ramparts and on the declivity of this mountain were magnificent habitations, where resided the "*Celestial Literati*," for this is the designation of astronomers in China. During the whole night these celestial functionaries keep watch and ward at the top of their tower, overlook the conduct of the stars, and give notice to the emperor of any extraordinary phenomenon that may attract their attention.

When Father Ricci visited the observatory he was not a little surprised to find in it metal globes of colossal size, dials, astrolobes, and several mathematical instruments, which, though essentially defective, nevertheless manifested some true scientific ideas in their makers. The Chinese informed him that these curious machines dated from the time of the Mongol occupation, namely, the thirteenth century, and it is therefore highly probable that foreigners, Europeans or Arabs, were the authors of these remarkable works.

The observatory of Pekin possessed some instruments of a similar kind, and of the same dimensions, and the Fathers felt convinced they had been made at the same time, and by the same persons.

Within a short time Father Ricci had acquired considerable influence among the higher classes of Nankin, and it became quite the fashion to be his partisan and apologist. The literary men in particular did not hesitate to declare themselves in his favour; in a great measure because he had attacked with complete success the doctrines of the Bonzes and doctors of reason; as well as because he always professed much respect and admiration for the teaching of Confucius. The

European doctor was, in their eyes, a member of the corporation of the lettered—a follower of Confucius, a partisan of their own doctrines, an enemy alike of the superstitions of the Buddhists and the reveries of the sectaries of Lao-Tze.

One day they invited Father Ricci to a sort of solemn sacrifice that they were about to celebrate in the temple of Confucius, and he had made no objection to be present, imagining that the honours rendered to the great philosopher of China were of a purely civil character.

Doubtless, however, he was mistaken, for Rome subsequently came to a contrary decision, and condemned these practices.

After the ceremony in the temple there was to be a splendid banquet, at which the principal literary men, and some Bonzes distinguished for their learning, were to be present. One in particular had acquired great fame both as an orator and a poet, and had the title of " Master" par excellence. He had also held some of the highest offices of the magistracy, but he had shaved his head and his beard to become a monk of the sect of Lao-Tze.

This illustrious doctor of reason, who desired to enter the lists with Father Ricci, placed himself opposite to him, and endeavoured to draw him into a philosophical discussion. " In order that we may proceed with some method," said Father Ricci, " it will be necessary to set out from a point that neither of us will dispute. What is your opinion concerning the first principle of Heaven and Earth?"

" I admit," replied the doctor of reason, " the existence of such a first principle, but I do not occupy myself much with him, since he has no special power; whoever we may be, I or you, we are equal to him, we yield to him in nothing,—our intelligence is his intelligence, our power his power." Father Ricci combated this system of pantheism with the applause of his audience, and the discussion only ceased when the company sat down to table. Every one took the place assigned to him by the master of the ceremonies, and towards the middle of the repast, the Chinese *beaux esprits* began to discuss some very favourite questions of their philosophical books: " What should be thought of human nature? Is it good in itself; and if so, whence comes evil? If, on the contrary, human nature is essentially bad, whence comes good? If it is neither good nor bad, how does it happen that it sometimes produces good, and sometimes evil ?"

Such was the thesis, in which almost every one took part, and a great deal was said that was subtle, and a great deal that was quite irrelevant, without Father Ricci ever opening his lips. The head of the literary class then begged him, in the name of the assembly, to explain what he thought of this important matter. Thereupon he began to speak, and after having given a clear and concise summary of what had just been said on the subject, he explained the Christian doctrine concerning the nature of man. "In the beginning," said he, " the nature of man was holy—*Jen-Tze-Tson-Sin-Pen-Chan*. These are the first words of the elementary book which you use for the instruction of children in your schools. This nature, originally holy, was perverted by sin." Then he spoke of human liberty, of the Fall, of the wickedness that had been the result of it; of the Redemption of grace, and of free will. He explained how, in the Catholic point of view, man, being free, could do what was evil, by abandoning himself to his own desires, and could do good by help of the grace of God. The eloquent missionary obtained the unanimous applause of the assembly, and was proclaimed victor in this philosophical contest; and the zealous Fathers rejoiced in his continually increasing reputation, because they saw in it the germ of many happy conversions to the Christian faith.

One rather whimsical circumstance tended to increase the credit that Father Ricci had gained by his scientific acquirements. A few days after this solemn discussion, the president of the court of public works came to pay a visit to the missionaries; and when he had complimented Father Ricci on the triumph he had obtained in the presence of the men of letters, he expressed the earnest desire entertained by the magistrates of Nankin that he should settle permanently in that city. Father Ricci declared that this was his desire also, and that he was only waiting to see whether he should be able to buy a suitable house. The president of public works thereupon informed him that he would willingly place at his disposal, in the name of the state, a palace that had been built some years before for the residence of a magistrate, but which was at present uninhabited on account of being haunted by evil spirits (or Kony). The Bonzes and doctors of reason had gone many times and practised the most approved ceremonies of exorcism; and various persons had attempted to live in it, but had always been obliged to decamp pretty quickly, for there were perpetually strange noises and plaintive moanings, and in the night terrific apparitions.

The whole town knew that this palace was the favorite resort of demons, and the very neighbourhood in which it was situated was overwhelmed with terror and consternation. Father Ricci said he would gladly go and see this residence, and if it suited him would make no difficulty about buying it, being quite persuaded that the evil spirits, if there were any, would take flight as soon as he should have placed in it the image of the true God.

This palace, which had been built but a very short time, was capable of accommodating ten missionaries, and in other respects particularly well adapted for a religious house. The price having been fixed at one half what it had cost to build, Father Ricci did not hesitate a moment about the purchase, and did not concern himself in the least on the subject of the diabolical apparitions; for besides that the house was an excellent bargain; it was a point of the highest importance to the security of the mission, to possess premises sold thus by an authentic act of the president of the public works. This fact alone constituted a legal authorization, and would serve to cut short many future intrigues of the petty mandarins or jealous men of letters. The contract of sale was signed and sealed by the president, and the missionaries, with great joy, installed themselves in their palace, though not without having previously sprinkled it well with holy water. They never heard any unpleasant noises, nor saw the smallest sign of a ghost, and from that time all Nankin was talking, not only of the knowledge of these foreign doctors, but of their power over evil spirits; and it was inferred also that their religion must be a holy one, since their presence was thus sufficient to silence and put to flight a whole army of demons.

This event did not fail to make a great impression on the Chinese, and disposed them strongly in favour of the European ecclesiastics.

CHAPTER IV.

Mode of Instruction adopted by Father Ricci.— Zeal of the Portuguese for the Missions. — Father Ricci sets out for Pekin. — Influence of Eunuchs in the Government. — Journey from Nankin to Pekin. — The Eunuch Ma-Tang. — The Missionaries taken prisoners at a sea-port. — Arrival of Ricci at Pekin. — The Court of Rites. — Rivalry between the Mandarins and Eunuchs. — Palace of the Ambassadors. — Homage to the Son of Heaven. — Various petitions to the Emperor. — Relations between the Missionaries and the Magistrates. — Conversion of a member of the Academy of Han-Lin. — Great success of the Clocks at Court. — Missions of the Provinces. — Fraternal feeling among the Christians of China. — Chinese Superstitions. — Procession in honour of the Idol of the Eyes. — The Missionaries mimicked by the mountebanks. — Success of the Christian preaching. — Profession of Faith of a Christian. — Native Clergy. — Academy of Han-Lin. — Conversion in the Imperial Family. — Insurrection of the Chinese at Macao. — Father Cataueo accused of seeking to get himself proclaimed Emperor. — Formidable armament at Canton. — Martyrdom of a Chinese Seminarist. — Peace is restored.

THE admiration of the Chinese for the knowledge and virtues of the missionaries was not always a barren feeling, leading to no result. Many people began to understand that these men, who had come to them through a thousand dangers from the ends of the earth, must have had some other object than that of parading their mathematical and scientific acquirements.

In the midst of these masses of sceptics and materialists there were to be found some privileged souls, whom God had enabled to comprehend the true mission of the the Apostles of Christianity. A military mandarin had the honour of being the first person at Nankin to open his eyes to the truth. He was christened Paul. Not long afterwards his son also received the grace of conversion, and soon the whole family made a public profession of Christianity, the domestic pagoda was converted into a chapel, the holy images took the place of the Pou-Ssa, and Father Ricci had the happiness of celebrating the august sacrifice of the redemption on the very spot where incense was formerly burnt to idols. These walls now resounded with the praises of God, and in this great and celebrated city of Nankin, the voices of Christians were heard chanting with fervour, "I believe in God the Father Almighty," &c., and "Our Father who art in Heaven," the prayer taught to His disciples by the Saviour Himself. The words first uttered by the lips of the Apostles at Jerusalem were now repeated, sixteen centuries afterwards, at the distance of half the globe. What emotions must have swelled the heart of Father Ricci when he heard them chanted at Nankin by his dear neophytes! How must he have felt himself repaid for the time he had devoted to his laborious mission, for his journeyings, privations, and troubles of all kinds, by being permitted to celebrate the holy mysteries in the midst of new converts, and listen to their songs of faith, hope, and charity!

Father Ricci had adopted for his neophytes a mode of preaching that was at once simple, instructive, and likely to captivate the attention of his auditory. He described to them the manner in which Christianity was practised in the West, and its influence on families and on society. He spoke of the number and the magnificence of the churches, of the pomp of the ceremonies, of the immense concourse of believers on days of grand solemnity, and of how rich and poor, princes, magistrates, and the lowest of the people, were seen mingled together without any distinction at the foot of the Altar.

He described the organisation of the religious heirarchy, of the diocese and the parish; the lives of monks and nuns in their convents; the care taken of the poor and the sick in the hospitals; and he treated all these subjects by turns, so as to interest and instruct the new converts. It was Christianity in action that Father Ricci thus passed before the eyes of his audience, in a series of pictures in which were unfolded the various phases of Christian life.

Whilst he was thus exerting himself with affectionate zeal to evangelise the inhabitants of Nankin, Father Cataneo was making a journey to Macao to carry the good news of his success to the Portuguese colony, which took such lively interest in the missions of China. It was necessary also for him to make some collections, in order to provide for the expenses of the establishment, for he could not count much on the generosity of the neophytes, and it might have been dangerous to ask contributions from them. It may be supposed with what enthusiasm and emotion the account given by Father Cataneo must have been received at Macao! A man who had been at Pekin, who had sailed on the Yellow River, the Blue River, and the imperial canal, who had sojourned at Nankin at the foot of its famous porcelain tower, who had been in communication with the six sovereign courts of the empire, who had traversed China from one end to the other, could not fail to be a very interesting person to his countrymen.

At that time the European colonies, that were forming in all parts of the world, were not influenced solely by the desire of traffic and money-getting. The religious question was a very real and serious one to these men, and they might be seen melting into tears, or falling on their knees to thank God, when stories of the conversion of idolators were related to them. These touching narratives animated their faith, and encouraged their devotion to the cause of the propagation of the gospel amongst infidels. The visit of Father Cataneo to Macao was in this way productive of the happiest results; it revived the piety of the old Christians, and interested their charity in favour of the Chinese neophytes; and the missionary set out on his return journey with an abundant contribution of alms, besides quite a little stock of European articles pictures, glass vases, linen cloths, clocks, maps, hour-glasses, mirrors, &c., "All of which things," says Father Trigault, simply, "are necessary in the beginning, and serve as oil, wherewith to grease the wheels of affairs that they may roll more softly."*

When the traveller got back to Nankin, and Father Ricci saw the valuable collection he had brought, and amongst which were many things admirably adapted to please the Chinese, he began to think once more of taking a journey to Pekin, and offering to the emperor some of these master pieces of European art and industry. The emperor's first censor, whose influence at court was very considerable, happened just then to be at Nankin; Father Ricci had made his acquaintance, and he now went to pay him a visit, and ask his advice on the subject of the plan, which he entirely approved, and even added that it was a necessary step, for a report had been spread that he had in his possession some rarities from Europe, intended for the emperor, and it might be by no means prudent to disappoint these expectations. Any difficulty about letters of introduction might be easily settled, since he as censor was charged with the introduction of strangers, and was quite willing to furnish the doctor of the West with whatever might be necessary to forward his enterprise.

This amiability exceeded all Father Ricci's hopes, and he thought of nothing more than to profit by it immediately. A selection was made from the articles brought from Macao, of such as it would be desirable to offer at court, and Father Didacus was summoned to be the companion of Ricci's journey, while Father Cataneo was to remain in charge of the mission at Nankin.

The censor drew up, according to his promise, an address to the emperor, and sent it on the appointed day to the missionaries, with several letters of recommendation to the prefects of the towns that the travellers would have to pass through on their way to Pekin. One of the first eunuchs of

* Trigault, p. 828.

the court was at this time at Nankin, whither he had come to fetch the tribute of silks sent to the emperor from the southern provinces; and six large junks were anchored in the port awaiting his orders. One of these he courteously placed at the disposal of the missionaries, offering at the same time to bear them company; and at length all preparations having been completed at the beginning of the year 1600, the six imperial junks weighed anchor, spread their sails, and began to move rapidly along the Blue River.

China was at this time in one of those crises, so frequent in her history, in which the government had fallen into the hands of eunuchs. The considerable armaments that had had to be sent to various points in the empire to repel the threatened invasion of the Japanese, had exhausted the public treasury. The taxes had been doubled, and in order to ensure the payment of them, the emperor had sent into each of the provinces eunuchs armed with absolute power, and independent even of the authority of the viceroy. These bands of tyrants were overrunning the country, committing the most abominable extortions to gratify their insatiable cupidity, and making both the people and the magistrates tremble, no one daring to dispute their behests, for their influence at court was so great that a word from them would suffice to ruin any mandarin, or whoever should displease them.

The eunuch who had taken the Catholic mission under his august protection behaved with the utmost possible politeness, and was very fond of conversing with the Jesuit Fathers; the conversation mostly turned on the nations of the West, or on the manners and customs of the Chinese of Pekin; but occasionally there were discussions on the religion, the philosophy, and the sciences of Europe, so that the voyage was not at all tedious, as Chinese travelling so often is. The navigation of the imperial canal, especially, is apt to be intolerably slow, for there are frequently so many junks collected at the locks, that you have to wait several days for your turn to pass.

But what mandarin would have dared to delay one of these all-powerful eunuchs, and one too who was carrying silks and presents to the emperor? The voyage, therefore, was rapid as well as agreeable, and the magistrates all along the route hastened to visit the famous Ly-Ma-Teou, who was bringing to the court the wonders of the West. After having traversed the Yellow River, the flotilla re-entered the imperial canal, and in a few days reached the port of Tsing-Ning, a town of the first class, where resided the viceroy of the province of Chan-Toung. The eunuch, who seemed never to miss an opportunity of doing what might be agreeable to the missionaries, or increase their reputation, had sent forward an estafette to announce to the viceroy the arrival of these distinguished strangers from the West; and no sooner had the junks come to anchor, than a magnificent palanquin, surrounded by a brilliant escort, made its appearance on the shore. The palanquin was sent to Father Ricci, with an invitation for him to go and rest at the palace of the viceroy, and he accordingly went, accompanied by the eunuch. The viceroy desired to see the address to the emperor, and not thinking it quite suitable, wrote another himself, as well as several letters of introduction for the Jesuits to friends of his, who held important offices at Pekin. It will be seen, therefore, that the missionaries were now in no want of patronage, and that, looking at the matter in a merely human point of view, they could hardly fail of success.

Just as the junk was about to weigh anchor, the viceroy came in grand state to return the visit of Father Ricci, and to wish him "ten thousand prosperities," and then the little squadron once more set forth. The eunuch congratulated the missionaries on the attention shown them by the viceroy, and he himself redoubled his courtesies, and amiabilities, and seemed quite to dread the conclusion of so delightful a journey. In a few days more they reached a port, where lay, as in ambuscade, a terrible eunuch named Ma-Tang, whose extor tions and robberies made him the terror of the whole province of Chan-Toung. No sooner had the six junks come to anchor, than the amiable friend of the missionaries betook himself on shore, and shortly after, Father Ricci received an order to land, and disembark the presents intended for the emperor, as they would have to be examined; and then it appeared that their charming friend who had been overwhelming them with caresses ever since they had left Nankin was, in fact, a most consummate rascal. After having boasted to the eunuch Ma-Tang of the wealth of the strangers, and thus excited his rapacity, he took advantage of the moment when Father Ricci had gone on shore, to turn his baggage and his people out of the junk, and then made off, and left the missionaries to the tender mercies of this notorious robber.

Ma-Tang's purpose was to appropriate to himself the presents brought by them, and he proposed to Father Ricci to undertake to forward them to the emperor. Father Ricci, however, declined to agree to this plan, and after a long contest, the eunuch had the missionaries and their baggage forcibly put on board a junk which had orders to take them to Tien-Tsing, a port at a short distance from Pekin, at the mouth of the Pei-Ho. At the same time he forwarded a despatch to the "Son of Heaven," informing him that he had arrested on the imperial canal some strangers who were bringing presents, amongst which were clocks of various sizes, that struck the hour of themselves; and also images exactly like living persons, and other valuable things from beyond the Western Seas; that he, the humble Ma-Tang, had had the strangers conducted to the port of Tien-Tsing; and that they now awaited his Majesty's orders. In this sea-port the unfortunate missionaries had to wait and endure as severe trials as any they had ever met with in China, far from all their friends and protectors, and vainly hoping for some favourable news from the capital. The eunuch Ma-Tang began after a time to hope that his despatch was forgotten, and no longer fearing to compromise himself, endeavoured to frighten the strangers, and made an attempt to send them clandestinely round by sea to Macao, hoping thus to get possession himself of the presents he so much coveted. In order the better to attain his ends, he wrote to Tien-Tsing to spread a report that the strangers had designed to go to Pekin in order to kill the emperor by means of sorceries, and he spoke mysteriously of a frightful image which they wore on their breasts; representing a person nailed by the four limbs upon a cross, which image would cause the death of the emperor the moment he looked upon it. He added in the same letter that as a measure of public safety it would be well to seize these bad men, and send them back to Canton, loaded with chains. These reports were repeated among the people with a thousand additions, and at length took such a formidable shape, that the persons most favourable to the missionaries advised them to fly, and think themselves fortunate if they could save their lives by sacrificing their property. The Fathers, however, full of trust in God, would not allow themselves to be terrified, but resolved to wait at Tien-Tsing till the goodness of Providence should show them some way of deliverance from the painful position in which the malice of men had placed them. They had been six months in this distressing predicament, when one day the emperor, when he was surrounded by his courtiers, suddenly said, " Where is this wonderful clock that a stranger from the West was to bring me, and which strikes the hour of itself?" The courtiers looked at one another, and the emperor repeated his question. " Where is the clock that Ma-Tang told me about?" One of the courtiers, who saw how the matter stood, then approached the imperial majesty, prostrated himself, and striking the ground three times with his forehead, said, " A memorial concerning that stranger has been laid before the throne of the Son of Heaven, but the imperial pencil has not yet written anything upon it. Who would have dared to introduce a stranger into the capital without orders from the Son of Heaven? The stranger is still at Tien-Tsing."

The emperor demanded to see the memorial, and immediately after that, a courier extraordinary was despatched to Tien-Tsing, with orders to bring the strangers to Pekin; and as it was winter, and the ice prevented them from going by water, eight horses and thirty porters were assigned them, to bring them and their baggage by land.

It was in the month of January, 1601, that the Fathers Ricci and Didacus entered Pekin thus, by express order of the emperor. As we have already said, the eunuchs had such great influence with the government, and had so completely filled all the avenues to the court, that they alone had the privilege of approaching the sovereign. Even the greatest dignitaries of the empire, the ministers of state, and the presidents of the sovereign courts, could do nothing without their intervention. This voluptuous potentate of High Asia saw no one, and was constantly surrounded by women and their ignoble attendants.

Father Ricci's presents were sent to court, and excited general admiration. The great pictures, it was said, had caused some alarm, from the faces being so natural and the eyes so full of animation; but the clocks roused to the utmost the curiosity of the emperor and his court. Unluckily they were a little out of order, and did not go quite regularly, but three eunuchs were appointed to learn the art of winding them up; and a special office was created for the discharge of this great duty.

A residence was assigned to the missionaries in the immediate vicinity of the court; for although they were not admitted to the presence of the Son of Heaven, he liked to converse with them and question them concerning the manners and customs of Europeans, and he carried on these singular conversations by the intervention of his eunuchs, who went backwards and forwards continually.

In order to enable the emperor and his court to understand many details more clearly than they do by verbal explanations, often ill reported, concerning the customs of the West, Father Ricci sent a collection of figures, representing the costumes of the sovereigns and people of rank in Europe, as well as views of the most remarkable public edifices. Among others were views of the Escurial in Spain, and St. Mark's in Venice, and one of the eunuchs told the missionaries that the emperor on seeing these lofty edifices had been touched with compassion for the melancholy case of the unfortunate monarchs who occupied them, and who were evidently obliged to climb up ladders to get to their apartments, a practice that he considered by no means pleasant, and decidedly dangerous.

Our mode of building houses several stories high, is generally much objected to by the Chinese. They say the countries of the West must be very poor and very small, to oblige people to live in this way, piled upon one another.

Among the other presents offered to the emperor, was a spinnet, but as there were no instructions for playing on it, the missionaries had to give some lessons to the eunuchs. They even composed a set of airs adapted to the taste of the country, and set them to Chinese words, and the collection became very popular in the Chinese capital, under the name of "Songs of the Spinnet." These indefatigable preachers of the gospel were, as we see, perpetually engaged in all kinds of occupations, and they were constantly giving lessons to these eunuchs, sometimes in geography, sometimes in music, and sometimes in clock making. Like the great apostle of nations, they made themselves "all things to all men," to gain all for Jesus Christ.

Among the six sovereign courts of the empire the one named the Ly-Pou, or Court of Rites, superintends all public ceremonies and solemnities, the minute details of which are so important in the eyes of the Chinese. It is divided into four departments, which occupy themselves with the ceremo nial, ordinary, and extraordinary of the court; with the forms to be observed in the sacrifices offered to the souls of deceased monarchs and illustrious men; with the regulation of public festivals, with the fashion of clothes and head-dresses for government officers, &c. This court also overlooks the public academies and schools, attends to literary examinations, and to the distribution of privileges to the "lettered" of various classes; its jurisdiction extends to matters of foreign diplomacy, and it prescribes the forms to be observed in negotiations with tributary princes and foreign monarchs, and settles all matters relating to embassies.

One special office named *Ly-Fan-Yuen*, or office of colonies, is charged to overlook the " strangers beyond the empire," that is to say, the Mongol princes, the Lamas of Thibet, the Mahometan princes of Turkestan, and the chiefs of the countries bordering on Persia.

The principal magistrates of Pekin, being jealous of the excessive influence of the eunuchs, exercised often to the detriment of their own authority, never fail, when prudence will permit it, to try and repress their usurpation; and the President of the Court of Rites thought he had found a good opportunity to make a demonstration against them, on the subject of Father Ricci, whom they had entirely monopolised. One day, the dwelling of the missionaries was suddenly invaded by a dozen of satellites or soldiers who summoned them to surrender themselves prisoners to the Ly-Fan-Yuen, or office of the colonies. On their refusal to obey this order, ropes were thrown round their necks, and they were dragged by violence to the tribunal, where they were informed that they would have to appear the next day before the president, who, in order to be sure that he would find them when he wanted them, meant to lock them in a room of his house. The eunuchs hearing this news, and seeing that the violence exercised against the missionaries was really directed against themselves, raised a riot, and went to break open the gates of the

Ly-Fan-Yuen, and deliver the captives. But Father Ricci, who had long been desirous of withdrawing himself from the humiliating and dangerous protection of these eunuchs, refused to follow them, and preferred placing his interests in the hands of the magistrates.

On the following day, the Fathers Ricci and Didacus were conducted by the chief of the Ly-Fan-Yuen to the presence of the President of the Court of Rites, who received them with a stern aspect.

"I am President of the Ly-Pou," said he, "and consequently charged with affairs relating to foreigners. You have offended against the fundamental laws of the empire in sending your offerings to the emperor through the eunuchs. Ever since you have been here you have seen nobody but the eunuchs, and you despise my authority. Such conduct is subversive of the Rites, and ought to be severely punished." Father Ricci answered:

"We have the most profound and submissive respect for the Court of Rites, but we have been circumvented in spite of ourselves by the eunuchs. Is it surprising that we have been unable to escape from their control, when the greatest dignitaries in the empire are compelled to submit to it? Ever since we have been here we have been constantly occupied at the palace by order of the emperor, and though we desired to present ourselves to the Court of Rites, the eunuchs prevented us. It seems to us also that we ought not to be considered as strangers, since we have been living several years in various parts of the empire, that we observe your laws and customs, wear your costume, and speak your language." The president was content with the answer, and told the missionaries that no harm should be done to them, that he would address the emperor officially concerning them, and that while awaiting his answer it would be necessary for them to conform to the Rites, and go and lodge at the palace of foreign embassies.

This palace of foreign embassies is an immense establishment, in which are lodged, better or worse, all persons who come from the tributary countries, under pretext of bringing tribute or presents to the emperor. The chiefs of these embassies are treated and lodged tolerably well, but the throng of subordinate persons accompanying them are crammed into miserable rooms without furniture, and allowed only a scanty portion of rice per diem,—not very splendid fare certainly for the *attachés* to an embassy, but probably as good as they would get in their own country.

Whilst the Fathers Ricci and Didacus were at the strangers' palace, there arrived a numerous legation of Mussulmans from Thibet, Ladak, and Cashmere, bringing as tribute a large quantity of lapis-lazuli, musk, rhubarb, and jade, an extremely hard kind of precious stone, of which the Chinese make pipe-heads, bracelets, and other trinkets, as well as little idols. From the information obtained from these people, Father Ricci became more and more convinced that he was now in the empire of Cathay, and the Kambalu of Marco Polo. He even wrote to his brethren in Europe to correct their maps, on which for many years they had been in the habit of marking China and Cathay as two different countries, and placing Cathay to the north of the Great Wall of China, in Mongolian Tartary.

The missionaries were detained three days at the ambassadors' palace, and then informed that they would be permitted to pay homage to the emperor, according to the rites established for the reception of foreign ambassadors. This ceremony usually takes place in an immense hall, capable, according to the Chinese, of containing 30,000 persons. A numerous body of military, in garments striped with various colours, and armed with pikes, great swords, and weapons of the most unaccountable and threatening aspect, is drawn up round it, and elephants from the kingdom of Siam, with their drivers splendidly equipped, mount guard at the four principal gates. At the end of the hall appears a magnificent throne, on which the majesty of China is displayed in all his glory, surrounded by imperial princes, ministers of state, the presidents of the six supreme courts, and other high functionaries, both civil and military. Their robes, of the richest silk, embroidered with gold and silver, have a most brilliant appearance, and while the hall is shaken by the exulting strains of music, loud enough, but of somewhat equivocal melody, those who are to pay homage to the emperor advance, and, solemnly kneeling down, strike the ground three times with their foreheads; then at a given signal they rise, and then prostrate themselves anew; and after that the agreeable ceremony has to be repeated for the third time. Altogether there are three prostrations and nine knockings of the head against the pavement of the imperial temple, whilst the Son of Heaven regards his worshippers with indescribable majesty.

Every prostration, every knocking of the head, is executed slowly and with solemn gravity and precision, at the signal given by the grand master of the ceremonies, who would be severely punished should the smallest error occur in a matter of so much importance; and before he ventures to introduce any strangers, he takes care to instruct them minutely in what they have to do, and perfect them by numerous rehearsals, lest the barbarians might make some not sufficiently respectful movement in the presence of him who reigns over the whole earth. When the Jesuits had well studied and practised their parts, they were conducted into the great hall of reception, and admitted to the signal honour of the three prostrations and the nine knockings of the head, in presence of a numerous and brilliant court. But there was on this occasion one thing wanting to make the ceremony complete, and that was,—the emperor himself! The monarch then reigning in China was, as we have said, entirely engrossed by the eunuchs, passed his days in effeminate luxury in the interior of his palace, and was never seen even by his own ministers. As, however, there were certain epochs of the year, and certain circumstances, in which, according to the ritual, homage was to be paid to the imperial majesty in person, the eunuchs had consulted together and arranged among themselves that it would do just as well, and come to the same thing, if the ceremonies were performed before the empty throne; the presence of the casket might imply that of the jewel.

When they had rendered due homage to the throne (though not to its occupant), the missionaries were, according to etiquette, to present themselves to the first minister, and as is customary on such occasions, they sent beforehand to announce their visit, stating that as they belonged in their own country to the class of the lettered, they would appear in the costume appropriated to that class.

The minister received them very politely, but inquired what had been their object in quitting their own country, to come into the Central empire. "We have been sent," they replied, "by our superiors, to preach the law of the only true God, the Creator of heaven and earth. That is what we have been doing ever since we arrived in the Celestial empire. We desired to make some humble offerings to the emperor, but we ask for no reward, and no public employments. We implore only one favour, that is, that we may be permitted to remain at Pekin, and preach freely our holy religion. The first minister requested that they would make known this new doctrine to him, and Father Ricci presented him with all that he had had printed concerning the Christian religion. The minister, nevertheless, addressed a petition to the emperor, in which, after having pronounced a panegyric on the strangers, he begged that they should be liberally paid for their presents, and then honourably conducted back to Canton, to be thence returned to their own country by the first opportunity.

The emperor made no answer to this request, and politicians thence inferred that it was not to the taste of the court. After a month had elapsed, the minister sent another petition in nearly the same terms, and it had the same fate as its predecessor. It then became evident that the emperor did not approve the measure proposed to him, though, in order not to infringe the laws of the empire, he would give the Fathers no official permission to remain at Pekin, unless he should receive a formal request to that effect. There were some persons, however, who were sincerely desirous of their remaining in the capital, namely the eunuchs appointed to wind up the clocks. What would become of them, if, after the departure of the missionaries, anything in these wonderful machines should go wrong?

The emperor was enchanted with these marvellous contrivances, and the eunuchs related that when the empress mother, who had heard much of them, requested her son to send her one to look at, the Son of Heaven seemed quite struck with consternation, fearing that when his mother had had the delight of hearing it strike, she would wish to keep it. As he could not well refuse his mother's request, and yet could not bear the thoughts of giving her one of his clocks, the cunning celestial majesty bethought him of playing the old lady a trick, and accordingly sent her the clocks, but took the precaution first to have the striking movements stopped. The empress mother, therefore, when she got the plaything was a little disappointed in it, and soon got tired of it, and sent it back to her son.

As the two petitions addressed by the minister to the emperor had remained without reply, Father Ricci, by the advice of several of his friends, determined to draw up one himself, and some days after its presentation, the first eunuch of the court came to make him an official announcement from the emperor, that he was authorised to remain at Pekin, and that his majesty would be sorry that he should return to his own country, or even quit the capital, and, moreover, that the emperor would make him a regular allowance from the public treasury, sufficient to enable him to live with his household in an honourable manner.

The joy of the missionaries at this good news may be imagined. After so many weary journeyings, fatigues, and tribulations, the mission of Pekin was now at last established on a solid basis, and the courage and perseverance of Father Ricci and his companions were crowned with the most brilliant success. Supported by the authority of the emperor, they might henceforth labour in peace for the conversion of this immense Chinese empire.

The fame of the signal favour granted to these strangers from the West soon spread abroad; and since in China, as in most other countries, prosperity has a wonderful effect in increasing the number of people's friends, friends now came from all quarters, ministers and high dignitaries, and mandarins great and small, to offer their congratulations to the poor missionaries, and declare how much the empire was honoured by their brilliant presence. There was nothing going on for a few days but fetes and banquets, and ovations of all kinds. Father Ricci, however, did his utmost to get released from these ceremonial visitings, as they absorbed so much valuable time that should have been devoted to the preaching of the gospel. He established in the house regular conferences, to which the most famous literary men of Pekin came to hear him unfold the truths of Christianity. The high position he had attained did not make him forget that he was equally " a debtor to all;" and though he received his more distinguished visitors with courtesy and good will, it was remarked that he was no less accessible to those of a low class in society, and liked to hold long conversations with them.

The oral instruction in which he was daily engaged, did not either make him forget what great influence books might have on a people so fond of reading, and amongst whom literature has always been so highly honoured. Aided by some famous *literati*, with whom he had become intimate, he composed several works which are still the admiration of China; and he devoted particular attention to the Catechism that he had drawn up, and of which he desired to publish a new edition. A member of the famous Academy of Han-Lin, who often worked with him, pressed him not to delay the publication of this important work, but Father Ricci wished to revise it carefully with reference to precision and elegance of style.

One day the Academician said to him, "Master, there was in my country a man affected with a terrible malady, so that his life was despaired of. A skilful physician, who was passing that way, saw the sick man, and said to his relations and friends, who were all in tears, 'The death of this unfortunate man is certainly approaching, but I have in my possession an infallible remedy, and I promise to cure him.' 'Oh, quick doctor,' they cried, 'give us this remedy!' 'No,' replied the doctor, 'I must go home and write out in fine language, and with ornamental characters, the prescription for this remedy.' 'What does it matter about the language or the characters?' cried the sick man's friends, 'it is the medicine itself that we want, and that without delay.' "This sick man," continued the Academician, "is the central nation, whose health has been destroyed by the drugs of the Bonzes and Doctors of Reason. You, Master, possess a medicine that will cure us. Give it us then at once, and do not trouble yourself about the language in which your doctrine is expressed." Father Ricci was pleased with the apologue, and hastened to publish his Catechism, the first line of which offers the solution of a great question: "Why hast thou embraced religion?" "To honour God, and to save my own soul." A truth more simple and sublime than was dreamed of by Confucius and the sages of antiquity.

The Emperor of China, the powerful monarch who held sway over three hundred millions of men, without counting the tributary nations, was still quite absorbed in admiration for his wonderful clocks, his *tse-ming-tchoung;* and, shut up within his palace, was constantly occupied in watching the movement of the hands over the dial-plates, or listening with delight to the striking of the hours, the happiest potentate probably upon earth. But *Jen-you-Sse Ou-you-Houai*, that is Men die, and things pass away! One day it happened that the clocks stopped, and the eunuchs who watched over their movements were at their wits' end. His celestial majesty was overwhelmed with grief, and sent for Father Ricci, in hopes that he might discover some method of setting the clocks going again, and so restoring the Son of Heaven to felicity. The great doctor from the West, after alleviating the terrible anxiety of the court, cleaned the works of the clocks, set their hands in motion, and afforded to the emperor, the ladies, the eunuchs, and all the inhabitants of the palace, the ineffable satisfaction of once more hearing them strike; and from that time, to avoid the recurrence of a similar calamity, it was decreed that the missionaries should have free entrance at court, and help to watch over the welfare of the clocks. The news made a great noise in Pekin, and raised to a still higher pitch the renown of the Jesuits.

While the mission of Pekin was thus prosperous, those of Nankin, Nan-Tchang-Fou, and Tchao-Tcheou, after languishing for some years under the indifference or ill-will of the people, seemed suddenly to have received a new impulse, and the joyful news that had arrived from the capital contributed not a little to aid their progress. When the mandarins heard that the Western strangers were preaching their religion freely at Pekin, and had become in some measure the favourites of the emperor and his ministers, their benevolent feelings towards the missionaries became quite lively. At Tchao-Tcheou the magistrates were assiduous in their attentions to Father Lombard, and those who had been formerly hostile to Father Ricci were, if possible, more friendly than any others. Many families even became converted, and received baptism.

This first glow of enthusiasm, however, cooled after a time, for the populations of these towns, entirely addicted as they were to traffic and material interests, were not very anxious concerning the salvation of their souls, and the things that belonged to eternity. Father Lombard thought it probable that the country people might be better disposed to receive the word of God, and therefore resolved to make an attempt to evangelise the environs of Tchao-Tcheou; and he really found these simple rustic men nearer to the kingdom of Heaven than the mandarins, rich merchants, and men of letters of the cities. When he was about to preach in a village, he used to send off, some days before, a zealous neophyte to announce the arrival of a missionary, and prepare the ground for the evangelical seed. The Father then presented himself, and after exhorting the assembled people, gave them a summary explanation of the Decalogue, and the principal articles of the Christian faith. Those who were seriously struck by what they heard, were then asked to write down their names, and an altar was prepared, above which was placed an image of our Saviour, wax lights were kindled, and some prayers chaunted, after which the new catechumens received a catechism from the missionary, and promised to renounce their idols and superstitions. Up to the moment of their baptism, they applied with zeal to the study of doctrine and to the observance of the commandments of God and the precepts of the Church. It was a sort of trial of strength for them, an apprenticeship to the Christian life which they proposed to embrace. A day was then appointed for their baptism, and as much pomp and solemnity as possible given to the ceremony.

The neophytes were invited from all the country round, and at the conclusion of the festival the newly baptized were escorted home to the accompaniment of music, and with a procession like that which attends a mandarin. These little manifestations pleased the Chinese, who always like a fête and a ceremony; and Catholicism, which is destined to be the religion of the human race, is not of a narrow exclusive spirit, but willingly accommodates itself to whatever is harmless and allowable in the peculiar customs of various nations.

Vol. II.—7

Religion does not destroy national, any more than individual character; it only improves and sanctifies it.

The success obtained by Father Lombard among the peasants, reacted upon the towns and quite electrified the citizens. The list of catechumens and neophytes at the mission of Tchao-Tcheou rapidly increased, and soon there was witnessed a spectacle hitherto unheard of in China,—namely, that of festivals celebrated sometimes in the town, sometimes in the country, at which rich and poor, learned and ignorant, peasants and mandarins, partook of a repast together and passed the day in sweet and cordial fraternity, because they had been just kneeling together in prayer to Him who is the Father alike of all. Equality can really exist only among men who can say from the bottom of their hearts, "Our Father who art in Heaven."

The fraternity of feeling thus developed among the Christian neophytes, formed a striking contrast with the cold egotism that withers the souls of most of the Chinese; and the intimate fusion of various ranks of society was, perhaps, one of the most beneficial effects of the missionaries' preaching. In one of the villages there was a considerable family, all the members of which had embraced Christianity, notwithstanding a very strong opposition on the part of their neighbours, who tried in various ways to frighten them into abandoning their faith, reproached them with having adopted a foreign religion, and never ceased threatening them with the anger of the Chinese gods. It happened one day that the house of these new Christians caught fire—and the neighbours, instead of going to their assistance, stood looking at the fire and seeming to derive much satisfaction from its progress, regarding it evidently as a punishment of what they called apostacy. In a short time nothing was left of the house but a heap of ruins.

When, however, the Christians of the environs heard of the disaster, they voluntarily levied a contribution on themselves to rebuild the house of their unfortunate brethren; they brought the necessary building materials, and laboured with their own hands at the structure, and in a very short time a far more beautiful house than the former one arose, as if by enchantment, from the ruins. It was adorned by the voluntary offerings of the neophytes, and provided with furniture and household utensils; and the pagans could not but see with admiration how the pure flame of Christian charity had repaired the mischief that the material fire had occasioned.

The inhabitants of Tchao-Tcheou and the surrounding villages were gradually becoming acquainted with the Christian religion, and observing the beautiful examples of self-devotion of which it was the source. Some few chosen souls were every day added to the servants of God, but the masses still remained insensible. There was no general enthusiasm: excited; indeed, the Chinese seem incapable of enthusiasm they are kept from it both by indifference and by superstition, two things apparently irreconcilable, but which are often seen united. These men, sceptical as they are to the last degree are yet addicted to a number of absurd and extravagant practices, in which they do not the least believe all the while. What has been done in times past they do still, for no better reason than that they will not change any custom of their ancestors.

The Chinese of the mission of Tchao-Tcheou would have willingly admitted the God of the Christians, and retain their idols, especially those kept in their houses in small niches, with a lamp and perfumes burning before them; not, however, that they were very fond of their idols, but they had a vague fear of being without them, and thought something vexatious would happen in consequence. The household god must not be expelled. What would their ancestors think if they did so?

These superstitions, at the same time that they hinder many of the Chinese from embracing Christianity, are to the new converts a perpetual source of annoyance and persecution. They are constantly teased for contributions to processions, to the erection of pagodas, or for the getting up a play, or for procuring rain or fine weather. As it is not allowable for Christians to countenance such practices, quarrels and vexations of various kinds arise out of them, that appear very formidable to these pusillanimous and lymphatic natures, though they would be easily overcome by persons of firmer character.

One day Father Lombard happened to be in the environs of Tchao-Tcheou, in a considerable village, where he had established a small residence for the benefit of the neophytes. The country people were just carrying about, with much noise and pomp, an idol to which they wished to build a pagoda. According to the Chinese mythology, it was the special business of this divinity to attend to the preservation of the eyes—and he was represented with a great supplementary eye in the middle of his forehead. The purpose of the procession was to collect from every family in the district an offering as a contribution to the expenses of his pagoda.

As it passed before the residence of Father Lombard, the procession entered with drums beating, and filled the interior court, and the Father, issuing forth in haste, was much surprised to see on his premises this Chinese Cyclop, borne in triumph by eight Bonzes. He immediately went up to the chief person in the cortége, and asked what they came there for, while all present appeared greatly shocked that he made no manifestation of respect at the sight of their Oculist God. In all the other houses they had entered, people had prostrated themselves before him and burnt tapers and incense.

"We come," said the president of the ceremony, "to levy a contribution for the building a temple to Hao-Kouang."

"I am affected by your religious zeal," said the Father Lombard, "but I am grieved to see that you do not know the only God who merits the homage and adoration of men. I adore this one true God; idols are nothing to me, and I cannot contribute to their worship."

At these words the multitude began to murmur, and soon to demand with loud cries the specified offering. A literary man, who was acquainted with Father Lombard, attempted to withdraw him from this embarrassment, and coming up to him said, "Master, you are a stranger in this country; you receive hospitality in it, why do you refuse the people's request?"

"You know," replied the missionary, "that whenever a contribution has been asked of me for an object that was useful and not against my conscience,—to assist the poor, to repair the roads, to build a bridge, and so on,—I have not been found wanting in liberality; but to make an offering to your idol would be to offer an affront to my God."

The man of letters, who knew well that Father Lombard's refusal did not proceed from avarice, said, " We understand your scruples, but there is a way of getting over them. In making your offering do not think of the idol, but *intend it for the people.*"

Father Lombard would not, however, admit of this subtle distinction of the Chinese casuist, and the procession departed vociferating abuse and curses against the Western devils.

To annoyances of this kind the Christians of China are perpetually exposed, and when the mandarins are not friendly to them, not to petty annoyance only, but to spoliation, imprisonment, and the cangue.

A very disagreeable kind of persecution, and one which paralysed for some time the progress of the mission, was raised in a curious and unexpected manner. There was a fair at Tchao-Tcheou, and in China, as elsewhere, fairs attract a considerable concourse of people, not only of buyers and sellers, but crowds of others, who have no other object than diversion. The Chinese fairs are very noisy and animated, from the great number of mountebanks, jugglers, and players met with at every step. At this fair of Tchao-Tcheou there was a troop of itinerant actors, whose performances excited shouts of inextinguishable laughter among the people. They were just come from Macao, and the pieces they were playing were intended to ridicule the Portuguese, or rather the Europeans or Western devils in general. The stage was surrounded by immense pictures painted by the Chinese, and representing in caricature the manners and customs of the strangers of Macao; and the explanations given of the pictures were so full of fun and the kind of wit adapted to the audience, that the speaker was every moment interrupted by shouts of merriment. The Chinese were never tired of amusing themselves with the tight clothes, the red faces, the immense round eyes and interminable noses bestowed on the figures; and after the exhibition of the pictures was over, the actors gave some low scenes, in which, disguised as Portuguese, they played various absurd and infamous pranks, and parodied the Christian religious ceremonies for the amusement of the populace. These hideous burlesques gained such prodigious favour with the public, as to form a serious obstacle to the success of the missionaries; but the bad impression gradually faded away, for the Chinese of Tcha-Tcheou had the means of judging for themselves, from the Europeans among them, whether they were always wicked or ridiculous men.

These strangers, against whom the buffoons were attempting to excite the contempt and ridicule of the populace, had, by dint of zeal and perseverance, triumphed over the powerful opposition they had encountered in the Chinese empire. Europe and Christianity were now becoming in some measure known to a nation which hitherto had scarcely recognised any other on the earth than themselves. The missions of Tchao-Tcheou, of Nan-Tchang-Fou, of Nankin and Pekin, were like four great light-houses, whence the radiance of the gospel shone already over the provinces of the North and South.

The missionaries were actively proceeding with the composition of catechisms, apologies for their religion, and books of science and geography that had a wide circulation. They were read with equal curiosity by the literary and by the lowest class; and the Chinese, full of pride and self-sufficient ideas of their own superiority in civilisation, were astonished to find that there existed beyond the Western Seas great nations, amongst whom arts, letters, and sciences were held in honour, and whose religious doctrines concerning the Divinity and the immortality of the human soul far surpassed those of their ancient philosophers. Most of them, it is true, contented themselves with ascertaining this curious fact, and then went back to their idols, under the pretence, that though Christianity was doubtless a very fine and excellent religion, it was not fit for the Chinese; and that after all it came from strangers, and their ancestors knew nothing of it.

There were, nevertheless, some privileged souls who, by the grace of God, were enabled to surmount these absurd national prejudices, and after studying in earnest the doctrine of salvation, to attach themselves to it with devout sincerity, and renounce their former superstitions. The number of believers was increasing at all the missions, and these new Christians were often animated by a simple and touching fervour that reminded the observer of the believers of the Primitive Church, who were of one heart and one soul.

The first worshippers of the Saviour of men were shepherds, and in like manner, in China, they were simple and rustic men who first embraced Christianity, though the neophytes were afterwards recruited in all classes of society. Mandarins of the highest rank, and famous men of letters, were mingled with the humble poor and ignorant who knelt at the foot of the cross, and laid down before it their riches, their dignities, and their science.

Numerous chapels were built in the towns and villages, and, after a silence of several centuries, the land resounded once more with the praises of the true God. The ceremonies of the Catholic worship were everywhere performed with splendour, more particularly that of the baptism of adults. The custom was established that before receiving the first sacrament, the catechumen should make some public confession of the sins of his former life; formulas were composed for illiterate persons incapable of expressing their sentiments suitably; but others composed them for themselves, and sometimes they contained a very interesting profession of faith. Father Trigault has preserved that of Ly-Paul, a celebrated literary man of Pekin; and as we shall have occasion to speak of this zealous and fervent Christian, who became a kind of apostle among the Chinese, we will give it here:—

"I, Ly-Paul, a sinful man, desire to embrace with my whole heart and in entire sincerity the very holy law of Jesus Christ; and for that reason, I raise, as far as I can, my soul towards the Lord of Heaven, and conjure him not to disdain to hear my prayer.

"I, a sinful man, confess that having been born in the imperial city of Pekin, I never, during the past years of my life, heard of the law of the true God, nor met any of the preachers of this holy doctrine. Thus, in all that I did, at every hour of the day or night, I was as a man blind and senseless wandering in the dark. But not long since, I became acquainted, for my happiness, with some men of vast renown and high perfection, who were born in the Western countries, and whose names are Matthew Ricci and Didacus Pantoja; from them I received the very holy law of Jesus Christ, and they have permitted me to contemplate and adore his holy image. Then they caused me to know my celestial Father, and the law which he has given for the salvation of the world. Why should I make any difficulty about embracing with all my soul this divine law, observing it and following it?

"But I consider that from the period of my youth, up to the age of forty-three years, having been plunged in ignorance and darkness, I fell into an infinity of errors and sins. I pray, therefore, the Father of mercy to deign to regard me with compassion and clemency, to pardon my acts of injustice, my frauds, my impurities, my slanders, my rash and presumptuous words, my perverse desires, and all the sins, great or small, that I may have committed, either intentionally or otherwise; and I propose for the future, when I shall have received the holy purification, to amend and fly from my sins. I will adore the Lord of Heaven in spirit and in truth, and I will apply myself to obey his ten precepts.

" I renounce, then, my depraved course of life, I abjure the errors of the age, and I condemn all that is not conformable to the Divine law; and as to-day is the commencement of my apprenticeship to a new life,—as the doctrine which I am now to profess contains sublime and subtle things which I do not sufficiently comprehend,—I conjure thee, Father of goodness, Almighty Creator, and merciful Preserver of Heaven and Earth, to grant me to understand all of those things which the mind of man can attain to. Grant me the grace to reduce to practice all that has been taught me, in order that, living or dying, I may be exempt from fraud and error, and may enjoy in heaven thy divine presence. Suffer me, when I have received thy law, to proclaim it everywhere, as do thy servants throughout the world, and to persuade men to embrace it. This wish I have formed in my heart, and I pray thee to hear it.

" Pronounced in the Kingdom of the great dynasty of Ming, the thirtieth year of the reign of Wang-Lié, on the sixth day of the eighth moon."

As the number of Christians had so much increased since Father Ricci had succeeded in founding a mission in the capital of the empire, the evangelical labourers were found insufficient in number. The Visitor of the Indies sent therefore a considerable reinforcement of apostles, and great pains were bestowed at the College of Macao on the formation of a native clergy. Several young Chinese, destined for the ecclesiastical profession, were brought up in tranquil retirement, and those who had received holy orders accompanied the missionaries into the interior of the country in order to discipline themselves to the apostolic life. The Jesuits have been much reproached with having in the greater part of their missions neglected the formation of a native clergy, in order, it was said, to render their presence perpetually necessary, and to govern these rising churches at their own pleasure, and without any control. Such a motive would certainly be too unworthy a one to ascribe to men who devoted their lives to the salvation of souls, and the accusation is also clearly repelled by the information left to us concerning the first years of their apostleship in China. No sooner had Father Ricci established the mission so as to have some guarantee of its stability, than he hastened to organise at Macao a seminary for the Chinese; and if a native clergy could not immediately be qualified, so as to dispense with the assistance of European missionaries, it arose from special causes of which we shall speak elsewhere, and in no way from any want of willingness in the religious orders.

The remarkable works in science and religion, that Father Ricci published at Pekin, had greatly influenced public opinion in favour of the missionaries, especially in the classes of mandarins and men of letters. Many brilliant conversions had been made among the first magistrates of the capital, and even in the Imperial College of Han-Lin.

This famous Academy, which is composed, as is well known, of literary men of the first rank, furnishes the examiners for the competitions in the provinces, orators for the public festivals, and generally encourages all studies, and favours all kinds of intellectual progress. A committee, formed from its members, draws up all public official documents, and another revises the works in the Chinese, Tartar, and Thibetan languages, which are published at the expense of government. The two presidents of the Academy reside in the emperor's palace, and overlook the studies and labours of the other academicians. The college of historiographers, and the society of annalists, also depend on the Academy of Han-Lin, the former being employed to write the history of remarkable epochs and special reigns, while the annalists, twenty-two in number, write day by day the history of the reigning dynasty, which can never be published till another has succeeded it; and they are summoned by turns, four at a time, to accompany the emperor in all his journeys, and note down his words and actions. It may be well believed, therefore, that this academy is a very influential body, and its members are regarded as oracles and shining lights throughout the empire.

When it became noised abroad that two of them had received baptism, there was a marked increase in the respect and consideration with which Christians were treated. No one would presume to question a doctrine professed by the renowned Doctor Scu, the famous Academician who had been first in all the competitive examinations.

In 1605 the mission of Pekin already counted more than 200 neophytes, and this same year was distinguished by some conversions that gave Father Ricci the highest hopes for the progress of the faith throughout the empire. One of the imperial princes received baptism, and was named Joseph, and his exhortations soon induced several of his relations to follow his example. His elder brother, who had diligently studied the Christian books, demanded to be admitted into the ranks of the catechumens; two of his cousins followed his example, and they were all three solemnly baptized together on the day of the Epiphany, receiving, in commemoration of the three Magi-Kings, who came to adore the Saviour, the names of Melchior, Gaspard, and Balthasar.

The mother of prince Joseph was greatly addicted to the superstitions of the Bonzes, and for more than ten years had been a member of the sect of the "Abstinent." The women who join this association make a vow never to eat either meat, fish, eggs, or anything that has ever had life, but to live entirely on vegetables. They believe that after death, if they have faithfully observed their vows, their souls will migrate, and they will be born again as men; and the hope of obtaining so great an advantage enables them to endure continual mortification, and supports them under all the troubles and vexations inflicted on them in this life by men.

They promise themselves, doubtless, an ample compensation, and it may even be imagined that they sometimes enjoy a little foretaste of the revenge they will take when they find their husbands transformed into women. At various periods of the year the members of this society make processions to certain pagodas which are in high repute; and the poor women may be seen tottering along, by the help of a stick, on their little goats' feet, performing painful pilgrimages, in the hope of some day retaliating their wrongs on the men.*

The aged princess of the dynasty of Ming performed, with much assiduity and devotion, the most slavish observances of the Society of Abstinents. But when her sons became Christians they had the happiness of opening her eyes to her mistake, and showing her that the numerous mortifications she underwent were incapable of procuring for her the felicity of which she dreamed. She therefore at length broke her long fast, and desired to receive instruction in Christianity. Father Pantoja was charged with the office, but as Chinese women, especially those of the highest class, cannot appear before strangers, she received the teachings of the missionary through a door covered by a curtain. When the day arrived that had been appointed for her baptism, it appeared that instead of one female convert, there were a great number, as all the friends and attendants of the princess had listened with her to

* Chinese Empire.

Father Puntoja's explanations of the Catechism, and were willing also to become Christians.

While Christianity, in the interior of China, was thus penetrating even into the bosom of the imperial family, a dark cloud was gathering on the horizon at Macao, that threatened to ruin both the Portuguese colony, and the Catholic missions.

The Dutch, jealous of the daring and successful expeditions of the Portuguese into the Indies, and envious especially of the riches they had amassed there, had armed numerous vessels, and sent them to practise piracy in the Eastern Seas. These audacious villains carried desolation through the Moluccas, and into the islands of the Straits of Sunda; and not content with the rich booty thus obtained, they equipped a flotilla, and attempted to seize on the island of Formosa. Having, however, been vigorously repulsed by the Chinese, they next cast their eyes on the little colony at Macao; but the Portuguese, having gained information of their projects, endeavoured to fortify themselves, and built in a short time a strong wall, on the steep cliffs next the sea, in order to be prepared for the Dutch pirates should they present themselves.

The Chinese, always ill-disposed towards foreigners, profited by this opportunity to rise against them. They pretended that the Portuguese wished to seize on the Chinese empire, that they had already erected several citadels, for so they thought proper to designate the churches lately built, and now they were erecting fortifications next the sea. They even went so far as to say that Father Cataneo had been fixed on to be made Emperor of China, perhaps for no other reason than that this missionary, having lately returned to Macao, still retained his Chinese costume. His captains and partisans, it was said, were already in the interior, and occupying strategic points of great importance, namely, the four missions already mentioned. These absurd reports had been maliciously spread among the people, and at last led to an insurrection, in which the Chinese populace laid siege to a Portuguese church, which they persisted in taking for a fortress, pillaged and set fire to it. A Portuguese having snatched from a Chinese a picture of the Virgin, that he was going to tear in pieces, made with it a kind of standard, and traversed the town to excite his compatriots to vengeance. The Portuguese negroes, at the sight of this holy banner, formed themselves into a battalion, and, their courage and energy being heightened by religious zeal, they threw themselves upon the pagans and put them to flight; and then, thinking themselves entitled to reprisals, went and sacked the palace of the mandarins, and having found the principal mover of the sedition, imprisoned him in the college, after having severely chastised him with the bamboo; after this, the magistrates of the neighbouring town of Hian-Chan (Mountain of Perfumes) came to an agreement with the Portuguese authorities, and order was restored.

The fire still smouldered nevertheless, and a literary Chinese found means to rekindle the conflagration. He published a pamphlet upon the approaching invasion of foreigners, a mere romance full of malice and bitterness, in which Father Cataneo was represented as a pretender to the throne of the empire. He had, it was said, visited all the principal cities from Macao to Pekin; the roads both by land and water were perfectly well known to him, he was acquainted with the manners and customs of the country, and with the Chinese language; he had already many partisans, and he was only waiting the arrival of a great fleet from the West to take some more decided step. The Japanese and the Malays of Sunda were to be his allies; these formidable forces would soon make their appearance, and then it would be all over with the poor Chinese of Macao; they and their countrymen would be reduced to slavery, and the Flowery Kingdom would fall into the hands of barbarians.

This book, widely circulated and greedily devoured by the multitude, excited a panic terror among the population of Macao. Every Chinese packed up his goods as quickly as possible, and whole families, men, women, and children, fled and took refuge at Canton. The sea was covered with junks carrying away Chinese property, and the shore heaped with goods and furniture; it might have been thought that the redoubtable fleet was actually in sight, and that the people had barely time to escape. In a few days the Portuguese and their negro slaves were the sole inhabitants of Macao.

When the bands of fugitives reached Canton, they commu nicated to the whole town the terror by which they were inspired; magistrates, mandarins, and people, all the inhabitants of the city, from the viceroy to the porters, were convinced they were about to become the prey of the Western devils. The militia was called out, the war junks armed, the guard strengthened, and a watch kept night and day from the ramparts; and in order the better to prepare for the defence of the city, it was ordered that all houses built outside the walls, between them and the river, should be demolished. More than a thousand houses, it is said, were destroyed in this way, and by way of additional security, the gates on that side of the town were walled up with blocks of granite and mortar, and an edict published in which it was expressly forbidden for a citizen to receive into his house any inhabitant of Macao, since "one of them," it was added, named *Kotinion* (Cataneo), was planning to seize upon the empire. The viceroy, not content with these energetic precautions, sent off a courier to Pekin, to warn the emperor of the danger that threatened him.

It will readily be supposed that this astonishing affair occasioned much suffering to the missionaries of the capital; it nearly indeed occasioned the annihilation of all the missions of China.

The Portuguese of Macao were placed in a very critical situation. Not only had their traffic with the Chinese ceased, but they were actually threatened with death by famine, for Macao itself was a barren rock, and the inhabitants of the colony had no other food than the provisions brought by the Chinese from Hian-Chan and Canton. The Portuguese authorities therefore took the resolution of sending off a very humble embassy to represent to the viceroy how far they were from entertaining the ambitious views imagined, and the impossibility of a handful of traders seizing on the Celestial Empire. Thereupon some kind of intercourse began again, and a few Chinese were permitted to go to Macao, and examine the state of affairs upon the spot.

No sooner, however, had the news of this approach to a reconciliation circulated in the town of Canton, than a seditious movement took place among the people, and they complained that the *Hai-Teou*, or great maritime chief, had pulled down their houses on false pretences.

They loudly demanded compensation, and even talked of the expediency of throwing the Hai-Teou into chains, and sending him off to Pekin to be tried and condemned. He, to get out of the difficulty, maintained that he had not given way to an idle panic, but that the strangers really did entertain the project of overthrowing the empire and the reigning dynasty.

In the meantime there happened to arrive at Canton a certain brother Martinez, a young Chinese convert, a native of Macao, who had studied in the college with a view to the ecclesiastical profession. After having taken the first orders, he had been sent, as usual, into the interior, to become accustomed to the apostolic life, in the society of the missionaries. The rector of Macao had, however, recalled him, and he arrived at Canton in the midst of the frightful disorder we have been describing. He was at the time in a burning fever, and, instead of going on to Macao, thought to stay a little while with the Christians of Canton, to recover himself and to wait till affairs should have assumed a more pacific aspect.

An apostate neophyte, who was consequently a furious

enemy of the Christians, having heard of the arrival of Martinez, went to denounce him to the grand maritime chief, and declared that he was the lieutenant and spy of Father Cataneo, the pretender to the throne; and that he had been into the interior purposely to prepare the insurrection, and trace out the route to be taken by the foreign armies shortly to be expected. The Hai-Teou being most anxious to exculpate himself for the demolition of the suburbs, was delighted to receive such an accusation, and sent his satellites to seize the unfortunate Martinez in the night. The supposed conspirator, ill as he was, was obliged to rise from his bed, as well as all the other Christians in the house, and they were then dragged with their hands tied behind them, by torch light, and with horrible vociferations, to the tribunal of the Hai-Teou, and immediately on their arrival they were put to the torture; their feet were squeezed between two beams, and at every question the executioners struck the beams closer with two great mallets. Brother Martinez, however, endured his torments heroically, and continued to protest his innocence.

The judge was on the point of acquitting him, when his accuser, the apostate neophyte, presented himself, and confirmed his previous accusation by declaring that Martinez, as soon as he arrived at Canton, had hastened to buy gunpowder, and that a child in the house where he lodged could bear witness to the fact. This new accusation revived the anger of the magistrate, and he sent for the child and interrogated it.

It happens that in the Chinese language the same character *Yo* is used for both gunpowder and a powder used in medicine, and a very slight difference of intonation alone marks the difference. The judge asked the child what it was that Martinez bought directly when he got to Canton; it replied innocently that he had bought *yo*, meaning the medicine, and the accuser cried out, "You hear, he bought gunpowder."

Martinez explained and stated that he had merely bought what was necessary for his malady, and to cure his fever.

The witness, being again questioned, confirmed this statement, but the judge having had the child's fingers cruelly compressed between two pieces of bamboo, and threatening it with worse tortures, it declared at last that Martinez had bought gunpowder. The prisoner was then subjected to a cruel flagellation and condemned to death, but before he should be thus released from suffering, he was to be again interrogated and tortured by the viceroy. But the unfortunate victim had been already so mangled that his body was all one bleeding wound, and while they were dragging him to the tribunal of the viceroy he expired in the street, on the 31st of March, 1606, and at the same hour of the day on which the Saviour of men died on the cross for the salvation of the world.

The fears of a foreign invasion were not yet appeased; and the viceroy commanded the generalissimo of the troops of the province to prepare for laying siege to Macao. The generalissimo, however, was prudent enough before setting out on the march, to send one of his lieutenants to make an official visit to the Portuguese colony, and find out what was really the state of affairs there. This high functionary, being a rational and moderate man, acquitted himself judiciously of his mission.

On arriving at Macao he went to the Jesuits' college and asked to see the much-dreaded *Ko-tinion*, who aspired to the throne of the Celestial Empire; and father Cataneo, who was a man of easy, pleasant manners, invited him to inspect the house, and ascertain for himself that it was not an arsenal filled with munitions of war. "See here," said he, pointing to his books, "these are the arms with which I intend to subdue the empire." The mandarin smiled, and did not seem alarmed; and he was then led to a hall where several seminarists were silently engaged in reading and writing. "Here," said Father Cataneo, "is the army that is to fight under my command, and aid me to mount the imperial throne." The lieutenant declared himself quite satisfied, and after visiting the churches, monasteries, and various establishments of Macao, returned to Canton quite convinced that the approaching formidable invasion was a mere fable. He then rendered an account of his mission to his superior officer and the authorities of Canton, the warlike preparations were laid aside, commercial relations between the Chinese and the Portuguese resumed, and all things returned to their accustomed course.

Father Cataneo himself obtained a passport, and was allowed to return in peace to his mission at Nankin.

CHAPTER V.

Cathay and China. — Father Goès travels by land from India to Pekin. — Cowardice of the Indian Soldiers. — The Robbers of the Desert. — Battle between the Caravan and the Tartar Robbers. — Difficulties of the journey. — Town of Yarkand. — Jade Stone. — Goès visits the Jade Quarries. — The Mussulmen of Yarkand endeavour to Assassinate him. — Encounter of two Caravans in the middle of the Steppe. — News of the Pekin Mission. — Goès' courageous profession of Faith. — Journey through the Steppes. — Desert of Gobi. — Arrival at the frontiers of China. — The Great Wall. — Combination among the Merchants to deceive the Emperor. — Father Goès fails to reach Pekin. — He writes to Father Ricci. — He is sent for. — Death of Father Goès. — His companion arrives at Pekin, and then returns to the Indies. — Death of Father Soerius. — Peculiarity of the Chinese Letters. — Doctor Paul. — Mission of Schang-Hai. — The Influence and Labours of Father Ricci. — Death of Matthew Ricci. — His Funeral. — Grant of a piece of land for his Tomb. — Opposition of the Bonzes. — Virtues of Father Ricci.

NOTWITHSTANDING the numerous obstacles of various kinds offered to the spread of the faith, Christianity was making great progress among all classes of society in China. At this period, when such important discoveries were being made by the Spanish and Portuguese navigators, innumerable preachers of the gospel, full of zeal and piety, were travelling, cross in hand, over all parts of the recently-discovered countries, and planting communities of fervent Christians in the very midst of idolatry and infidelity. The missionaries of different nations communicated to each other the joys and sorrows of their apostleship, and by this invaluable correspondence their courage was upheld in time of trial, their ardour kept alive, and they were enabled to help one another effectually in the great work of conversion.

The accounts of the great success of the Chinese mission had reached India. The missionaries, scattered about on the banks of the Ganges, heard with the utmost interest of the labours of their brethren, who had already erected numerous chapels on the shores of the Yellow River, and even in the capital of the empire. Besides the letters from Macao, telling them of what was being done in China and especially at Pekin, they often met Mahomedan merchants in the Indies who had been travelling in Central Asia, and from whom they received accounts of the riches and grandeur of an immense kingdom, which they called Cathay. They spoke of the manners and customs of the Cathayans, and from their descriptions of certain religious ceremonies that they had witnessed, it became evident that the country contained a great number of Christians. The missionaries wished very much to know exactly where and what this kingdom of Cathay really was that had been so much talked of in the thirteenth century by Marco Polo, and of which the Mahomedan merchants brought such curious accounts. Father Ricci had, it was true, written many letters to show that China and Pekin were in reality the Cathay and the Khanbalu of the travellers in the middle ages, but the identity of the two had never been absolutely proved. In this state of affairs, the monks who were preaching in the Indies came to the resolution of putting an end to the doubt, traversing once more the centre of Asia, and visiting Cathay themselves. They wrote, via Macao, to Father Ricci, and told him that certain missionaries had determined to reach Pekin by land, following the direction of the Indian embassies, which travelled for commercial purposes to Cathay.

The charge of this adventurous expedition was to be entrusted to Father Benedict Goës, a man who, to great courage and energy, united a perfect knowledge of the Indian languages. In order to travel more conveniently, and avoid awakening the suspicions of the natives, he adopted the Armenian costume, and took the name of Abdula Isai, signifying Master Christian; and he was to be accompanied on his route by a Greek priest named Leon, by Demetrius a merchant, and by a certain Isaac, an Armenian, who had resided for a long time in the kingdom of Lahore. Furnished with several letters to Indian princes, he set out on the 6th of February, 1603, with a good escort of converted Mussulmans. The expenses of this important expedition were, at the command of his Catholic majesty, defrayed by the viceroy of India.

The caravan reached Lahore without difficulty, but was here compelled to halt and obtain reinforcements to guard against the robbers of the countries it was about to enter. The King of Lahore, a friend of the Jesuits, placed five hundred Indian soldiers at the disposal of Father Goës, and, armed to the teeth, the party once more set out, determined to exterminate all brigands they might encounter. They had not to wait long for an opportunity of displaying their courage, for as they were peaceably wending their way along a valley, some horsemen suddenly started out from a ravine, shouting loudly and brandishing long sabres. They rushed with great impetuosity upon the soldiers, who instantly dispersed, and set off at full gallop to a neighbouring forest. Nothing was left for Father Goës and his companions but to follow the example of their defenders, so they fled also to the protection of the thicket, and it was some days after the brigands had retired, before the caravan could be again collected; the five hundred soldiers of the King of Lahore having taken to their heels with such vigour that they had got fairly into the middle of the forests. Many indeed never returned at all, and the caravan was obliged to start without them.

This first adventure showed Father Goès that he could place little confidence in his numerous but not very valiant escort. Fortunately however, the banditti of the country were good enough not to reappear, and the caravan arrived in Caboul without any fighting, but suffering greatly from fatigue, and it was obliged to make a long stay through the inclemency of the season. The escort furnished by the King of Lahore left Father Goès without occasioning him much regret, since their conduct on the first alarm had clearly shown their perfect worthlessness; and Leon, the Greek priest, who found a journey of this kind little to his taste, took advantage of the opportunity to return with it. The merchant Demetrius was also compelled, through his commercial engagements, to remain a long time in Caboul, and Father Goès was thus left with only one companion, Isaac the Armenian. This neophyte, however, loved the missionary with a tenderness that was quite filial, his devotion knew no bounds, and he was also a man of determined courage.

After a delay of seven months in Caboul, a caravan of merchants was at last organised, and Father Goès found himself once more upon the road, accompanied by the faithful Isaac. At first the difficulties that the route presented were few, but they increased as the party advanced, and before long they were in the midst of precipitous mountains, great rivers, and rushing torrents, that had to be crossed at the peril of life. The fear of robbers, too, was soon added to the other dangers of the journey, and when the caravan encamped at a little distance from Samarkand*, the governor of the town informed the travellers that as a horde of Tartars had revolted,

* Samarkand, to the east of Bukaria, was the capital of the vast empire of Tamerlane.

and were pillaging and devastating the country, he wished them to retire into the town and place themselves in safety, promising to escort them with his soldiers, and guard them from all attacks. The revolted Tartars being without horses, he feared they might seize upon those of the caravan, and thus become still more formidable to the country. The merchants were desirous, however, of setting out immediately, and getting away from this den of thieves, and the anxiety of the governor to prevent the rebellious Tartars from obtaining possession of the horses was so great, that he did not hesitate to accompany them with a numerous military escort. Scarcely had they got away from the walls of the town, when they saw at a distance some strong bands of Tartars advancing with a menacing air, and at this sight the governor of Samarkand turned with his soldiers, and ran back to the protection of the town. The merchants, however, were prevented, by the large quantity of their baggage, from adopting the Indian military tactics, and they therefore determined to remain and valiantly repulse the enemy. They collected their bales of merchandise, made barricades of them, and entrenched themselves behind them, having previously provided themselves with a considerable quantity of flint stones, to serve as projectiles, when the arrows of their quivers should be exhausted. On seeing this extempore fortification, the Tartars sent forward messengers to assure the travellers, that far from having any hostile intention, they had come to defend them from attack, but the extreme benevolence of such a proceeding prevented the merchants from putting much faith in it.

While the Tartar envoys were returning to their camp, the merchants held a council, and valiantly decided that the best thing they could do was to take advantage of this truce, and make off as fast as they could. This resolution was no sooner taken than executed, and a general scramble, every man for himself, immediately followed. The merchants all made for the nearest woods, and left their merchandise to the robbers, who tranquilly removed all they most cared for. When, however, they came back for the remainder, a chief of the tribe made his appearance, forced them to give back what they had taken, and helped the merchants to reorganise the caravan, and put it in a position to start once more.

The robbers were intimidated by the presence of this valiant chief, and dared not openly repeat their attack on the travellers, but they continued to hang upon their rear, and to harass and pillage the stragglers and rear-guard. One day, when Father Goès had got a little separated from his troop, four brigands, suddenly dashing out of an ambuscade, threw themselves upon him, and were on the point of robbing him, when, adopting an ingenious and novel mode of escape, he tore off his rich Persian head-dress, threw it towards them, and while the robbers rushed after and quarrelled round this magnificent booty, he set spurs to his horse, and succeeded in regaining his companions.

The march of the caravan was a perpetual conflict with robbers, inundations, mountains, and snow. Before reaching the kingdom of Kaschghar, the poor travellers once spent six entire days on a high mountain, where they almost perished of cold and hardship. Many of the men were frozen to death, and some, buried beneath avalanches. While making his way along the steep bank of a torrent, the faithful companion of Father Goès, Isaac, the Armenian, made a false step, and and fell headlong into the abyss. Happily, his companions succeeded in getting him out, but he was so injured by the fall and benumbed by the cold, that for six hours his life was despaired of, though the tender care of Father Goès at last succeeded in restoring animation.

After the mountain had been crossed, the route instead of improving became so frightful, so encumbered with angular rocks, and encrusted with ice and snow, that it was almost impossible to proceed. Six horses, belonging to Father Goès, perished; the travellers, profoundly dejected, could see only an inevitable death before them, and already the horrors of famine and cold had begun to take effect. Father Goës alone was never cast down. Always confiding in the divine mercy, he appeared armed with a superhuman courage, and kept constantly in front of his companions. After unheard of efforts, he at last had the good fortune to reach Yarkand, the capital of Turkestan, and thence he immediately despatched horses and provision to the caravan, which, reanimated and fortified by this unlooked-for help, managed to keep in motion, and to reach the town where the intrepid missionary was waiting for them. They arrived there towards the end of the month of November, 1603, ten months after their departure from the kingdom of Lahore.

Yarkand, the capital of Turkestan, was at this time a large and flourishing town. An immense traffic was carried on there, and notwithstanding the frightful difficulties of the road, merchants thronged to it from all parts of Asia. Those who intended to continue their journey to Cathay were obliged to remain here for some time, and organise a new caravan. The king of the country kept up a sort of monopoly of these expeditions, and sold, for a very high price, the title of chief of the caravan, or rather ambassador. Whoever bought this privilege, had the right of command over the other travellers, as well as of directing the march of the caravan, and in Cathay he enjoyed certain commercial advantages, and was treated with great honour.

It is in this country that *jade* is obtained, a sort of precious stone, much valued throughout China, and which there plays a very important part in the manufacture of trinkets. The Chinese cut this stone with an exquisite degree of taste and wonderful patience, for it is extremely hard; making vases, bracelets, buckles, pipes, and many other articles of luxury and *virtù*, out of it, which are bought at a very high price by the rich Chinese. The most valuable jade is that obtained from rivers, and it is found in the shape of large pebbles, but

Vol. II.—8

an inferior sort is also procured from a mountain, about twenty days' journey from the town. The people who work the quarries in the desert are obliged to take their whole stock of provisions for the year with them, since nothing of that kind can be obtained in these arid solitudes. The jade of the mountain is split up into large sheets, and is conveyed in that state to Cathay.

While the merchants from India were endeavouring to form a new caravan, Father Goës made an excursion to their jade quarries; not only from curiosity, but with a view of obtaining a rather important sum of money that a princess of these districts owed to him. It had happened that, while passing through the kingdom of Lahore, Father Goës had encountered a Mahommedan queen, making a pilgrimage to Mecca; but she had been robbed on the way, together with all the people of her suite, and was reduced to the last extremities, and found it impossible to regain her own dominions. Father Goës, moved with compassion, had generously placed at her service everything that he was able to dispose of, trusting that the good faith of the Mahometan lady would appreciate the piety and charity of the Catholic missionary. A few days after his arrival in Yarkand, Father Goës had set out in search of this princess, the mother of the King of Khatan.*

A month had already passed, and Goës had not re-appeared. A report had got abroad that he had been massacred in Khatan by the fanatic Mussulmans, who, furious at his refusal to pay homage to Mahomet, had torn him to pieces. This news was a source of the most profound grief to poor Isaac, who was quite inconsolable for the loss of his master, and who spent whole days drowned in tears. The Buddhist monks of Yarkand, on the contrary, were delighted, since it is the custom of the country for them to inherit the merchandise and baggage of all travellers who die within the walls of their town,

* In the province of Turkestan.

without having any relations there. The sudden arrival of Goès, however, put a stop alike to the tears of Isaac, and the rejoicings of the pretended heirs. His journey, although long, had been prosperous, and he returned, not only with the sum of money he had lent to the queen, but also with a magnificent present of the jade of the country, that would be quite a little fortune in Cathay.

During his long stay in Yarkand, Father Goès was not unfrequently in danger of losing his life through the fanaticism of the Mussulmans. One day a furious man came suddenly to his house, and placing his scymitar against his breast threatened to plunge it in, if he did not instantly render homage to the prophet Mahomet. The courageous missionary calmly looked at him, gently put aside the scymitar, and said, "Go, I know not who Mahomet is." On another occasion he was obliged to attend a religious discussion, where his profession of faith as a Christian raised such a storm, that the crowd threatened to tear him to pieces. His imperturbable demeanour, however, and a few words uttered with calmness and dignity, served to quiet the tempest.

A large caravan for Cathay was at last definitively organised, at the head of which was a rich merchant of the town who had bought the title of captain from the king. Father Goès prudently said nothing about his wish to join this party; and the captain, who was very desirous of having the company of a man of such known vigour and sagacity, himself went in search of Goès, to try and induce him to undertake the journey. No proposal could have been more agreeable, but he nevertheless appeared to hold back in such a manner that it seemed to the caravan as if he at last, in consenting to go, granted instead of receiving a favour. He exhibited so little anxiety to depart, and made so much of the difficulties of the route, that the captain was obliged to obtain the intervention of the king before he would come to a decision, and at last only agreed to make the journey upon condition of receiving certain letters of protection for the whole extent of the king's dominions.

The friends that Father Goës had made during his long stay at Yarkand endeavoured to dissuade him from undertaking so perilous a journey, and drew a frightful picture of the dangers he would be exposed to. To judge from what they said, he would be liable to death in a thousand forms,—from cold, from hunger, from the sword of the brigand, or the fanaticism of the Mussulmans, who would never have the patience to travel so long a time in company with a Christian. But none of these considerations had any effect upon Goës; he had determined to join his brethren at Pekin, and see with his own eyes whether the Cathay of Marco Polo, and the China of the Portuguese, were really identical or not; and if he lived, to let nothing prevent his accomplishing his purpose. The caravan at last got under weigh, and plunged into the immense wilderness of the steppes of Tartary, where the profoundest silence and solitude had succeeded the tumult of the wars of Tchinguiz-Khan. We need not stop to describe the hardships and vicissitudes of such a journey; we have already endeavoured to give some idea of the trials and miseries to be encountered by travellers in these inhospitable regions. One day while making their way through a wide valley they perceived a multitude of men and horses on the horizon, moving over the side of a hill and coming towards them. An encounter with other men in the steppes of Tartary instead of reassuring the traveller is only a fresh source of alarm to both parties, each fearing that the other is an enemy; so that the two caravans stopped and began to reco-noitre each other's movements. As both seemed to manifest fear, the presumption was, that both troops were composed of honest men, and not of robbers. They mutually advanced, and before long the two caravans, one going to, and the other coming from, Cathay, were mingling eagerly with each other, and pouring out questions that no one would stop to answer.

The valley was spacious and well pastured, and the two parties encamped together, that they might exchange the news of the East and the West more at leisure.

The captain of the merchants coming from Cathay had a long conference with Father Goës. He told him that during his stay at Khanbalu he had lodged at the mansion of an ambassador, in company with a learned monk from the West named Si-Ma-teou (Matthew Ricci.) As it was well known that Father Ricci had, on his arrival at Pekin, remained for some time with strangers from India and Turkestan, there could now be little doubt that China and Cathay, Khanbalu and Pekin, were identical. The captain of the merchants gave Goës many interesting details as to the influence that the missionaries enjoyed at court, and he told him how they had presented the emperor with a clock, a spinnet, and several other things that they had brought with them from the West; also that the princes, the magistrates, and the people held them in great esteem and veneration, and that they made numerous converts. He finally showed Goës a letter, which he preserved with great care in a bag, and which he had picked up from among a heap of sweepings and fragments of paper near Father Ricci's house, as a specimen to show to his friends of the kind of writing in use among the strangers quartered in Cathay. The letter was in Portuguese.

This news gave great joy to Goës and his faithful companion Isaac. They felt their courage redoubled, for everything made them hopeful of seeing their brethren when they should reach Pekin, and of resting after their long fatigues at a Catholic mission. The whole night almost was spent in gossip, but as soon as day reappeared tents were struck, the baggage was packed on the beasts of burden, and the two caravans parted and resumed their route, one to India, and the other to China.

At Tourphan, a celebrated town in Central Asia, the caravan made a halt of several days, to get a fresh supply of pro visions and passports for Mongolia. The sovereign of this country distributed their passports to the merchants surrounded by all his splendour, having collected in his palace the highest functionaries of the town. He was dictating to his chief secretary the names of the travellers, when, on coming to Abdul-Tsaï, the Armenian name which Father Goès had adopted, and which signified Master Christian, he stopped. The assembly was wholly composed of followers of Mahomet, whose countenances became inflamed with anger, and they glared at Goès as at an enemy. The sovereign remained calm, and simply observed to the missionary that the country he was about to travel through was inhabited by Mussulmen, and that it would be more prudent for him to drop his title of Christian. He said, "I am going to write down your name; shall I leave out the word Christian?" Goès, however, cried out firmly, "Write down that I am a Christian; it is a title by which I am honoured, that I have always borne, and no danger, not even the certainty of death, will make me give it up." At these words a venerable old man rose up, uncovered his head, and cried, "Honour to the faithful believer, to the brave man who dares to avow his faith." Then turning to Father Goès, he bowed low before him, while every one present seemed to share his feelings. A sincere belief, when bravely avowed, will always excite admiration, if not sympathy, but an anxiety to avoid a conflict with human opinion will scandalise even disbelievers, and excite contempt for those who are weak enough to adopt such a course.

Leaving Tourphan, the caravan proceeded to Hamil, and then quitted the plateau of Central Asia, taking a southerly course towards the frontiers of China. While crossing the great Tartar plains, it was not uncommon to meet with the bodies of travellers murdered by the robbers who infest these countries. They can only be crossed by large numbers together, and even then it is necessary to use the utmost pre caution to avoid a surprise. While the main body of the caravan marched along the valleys, horsemen were thrown out along the higher ground to keep a vigilant look out, and give the alarm if there appeared the least sign of danger Not unfrequently it became unsafe to travel during the day; the caravan waited till night closed in, and then silently, and under favour of the darkness, left the encampment. One night when this plan had been pursued, Father Goës fell from his horse, and as he was a little separated from his party, no one perceived it. The shock was so violent that he lost his senses, and lay motionless, while the caravan proceeded on its way; and it was not till some time afterwards that the Armenian Isaac noticed that the horse had no rider. Full of anxiety, he retraced his steps, though without knowing where to look, since in these vast solitudes there is no road, and it is easy to miss the right track. At last, however, he heard a voice calling on the name of the Saviour, and eagerly following the direction of the sound, he found the poor missionary, who was feebly dragging himself along, and who had already given up the hope of regaining his companions. Isaac took him on the crupper of his horse, and after much wandering about, they succeeded at break of day in recovering the traces of the caravan, and gaining the encampment.

Before long the caravan entered the deserts of Gobi,—immense sandy plains, where not a blade of grass nor a drop of water is to be met with. We have ourselves crossed this moving sea of sand, which when taken in the hand runs through the fingers like water. The dreary monotony of the desert is only interrupted by the traces of certain small insects, who describe thousands of arabesques upon the white surface of the sand, which is so fine that every turn and winding, even of an ant, upon it can be followed.

After having suffered horribly of thirst for several days, Father Goës arrived at last at Kia-Yu-Kouan, a frontier town of the Chinese empire, and the northern extremity of the province of Kan-Sou, at the termination of the Great Wall. This great work, about which so much is said and so little known, deserves a few words. The idea of raising walls as a protection from enemies is not peculiar to China, and many similar undertakings are mentioned in ancient history. Besides those built by the Medes, Syrians and Egyptians, a great wall was erected on the northern frontier of Britain, by command of the emperor Septimus Severus. No nation, however, ever attempted a wall on so grand a scale as that raised in the year A. D. 214, by Tsin-Che-Hoang-Ti. It is called in China *Wan-Li-Tchang-Tching*, the great wall of ten thousand leagues. An enormous number of workmen were employed upon it, and its erection occupied ten years.

This great wall extends from the western point of the province of Kan-Sou to the Eastern Sea, and its importance has been variously estimated by different writers on China. Some have extolled it prodigiously, while by others it has been only ridiculed. The incongruity of these opinions has arisen through the writers judging only from that small part which fell under their immediate notice. Mr. Barrow, who visited China in 1793, with Lord Macartney, in the capacity of historiographer to the embassy, made the following calculation:—Taking the number of houses in England and Scotland at 1,800,000, and supposing the amount of masonry in each to be on an average 2000 cubic feet, he says that they would not then contain so much material as the Great Wall of China, which, according to him, would supply enough to build a wall that should go twice round the earth. Mr. Barrow, however, has evidently based his calculation upon an examination of the wall at Pekin, where it is in reality beautiful and imposing; but it must not be supposed from this that the barrier raised against the incursions of the Tartars is of equally grand and solid construction in every part. We have ourselves crossed this wall at no less than fifteen different points during our journeys in Central Asia, and we have not unfrequently fol lowed it for days without losing sight of it. Often, instead of the double and embattled wall to be met with in the environs of Pekin, we have encountered one of simple masonry, and sometimes even this has dwindled to a modest erection of mud. We have even come to places where a few flints heaped up were the only signs of this famous wall. With regard to the foundations, which Mr. Barrow speaks of as composed of great blocks of free-stone, cemented by mortar, we must confess that nowhere have we found any traces of them. Indeed, it is easy to suppose that Tsin-Che-Hoang-Ti would have paid more particular attention to the fortification of the capital of the empire, the point to which most of the Tartar attacks were directed. It is only to be expected also that the mandarins who were entrusted with the arrangement of the plans for this fortification, devoted their energies most conscientiously to those portions of the work immediately under the eye of the emperor, and contented themselves with erecting a mere apology for a wall at distant places, where also there was little fear of the Tartars; such, for example, as the frontiers of the Ortous and of Kan-Sou, which are sufficiently protected by the Yellow River, and the great desert of Gobi.*

When he had once reached Kia-yu-kouang, Father Goès had nothing more to dread from the brigands of Turkestan and Tartary. Cold, hunger and thirst, and the accompanying miseries of this long journey, had disappeared; he found himself in the midst of an urbane and courteous population, in an opulent town, where art, industry, and agriculture flourished, and where the savage and adventurous life of the desert was replaced by all the comforts of civilisation. But, in spite of this striking change, the time for repose and tranquility had not yet arrived. Goès had no longer to fear being stopped in his march by mountains and rivers, or being attacked and

* Travels in Thibet, vol. ii. p. 53.

robbed by brigands; but he was still at the mercy of a more polished set of robbers, who were constantly endeavouring to throw a thousand little difficulties in his way, and to lengthen the duration of his journey. Kia-yu-Kouang was a rendezvous for all strangers travelling by land to the Celestial Empire, and was, as Khiaktha in Siberia is at present, divided into two parts, in one of which the Chinese resided, while the other was left to the foreigners. Business was carried on between the two divisions during the day, but as soon as the sun set, each party retired to its respective district. The object of all foreign merchants was to traverse the empire, sell their merchandise at Pekin, and return with Chinese goods. The right of making this journey, however, belonged exclusively to ambassadors; their expenses on the route were defrayed, they were gratuitously quartered in the city, and freed from custom-house exactions, because they were supposed to be bringing tribute to the emperor.

The result of this was, that all merchants who wished to go to Kia-yu-Kouang endeavoured to get up an embassy, and to obtain their numerous privileges and immunities attached to it. The Chinese mandarins wished for nothing better than to help them, provided they were handsomely paid for doing so, and received a large share of the profits of the scheme. They used, in concert with the merchants, to forge credentials, often from sovereigns and kingdoms that never had existed; and when everything was arranged according to the rites, a despatch was sent off to Pekin, informing the emperor that an embassy from a foreign monarch was on its way to offer tribute to the Son of Heaven. The emperor, who always looked upon himself as the suzerain of all the kings upon earth, would feel extremely flattered by these marks of respect, receive the counterfeit ambassadors with honour, treat them with distinction, and on their departure would load them with presents, in return for the pretended tribute which they had brought; so that it was in reality the court of Pekin that paid a tribute to foreign states. These arrangements were at the same time very flattering to the emperor's pride, and very gratifying to the cupidity of the merchants and mandarins.

While at Kia-yu-Kouang, Father Goës often received information concerning his brethren at Pekin, and the flourishing mission under their direction; and though he was burning with the desire of joining them and of resting for a while after the fatigue of his long journey, in their quiet residence, the mandarins were pitiless, and refused to grant him the permission which would enable him to continue his journey, except at an enormous price. He succeeded in obtaining permission, nevertheless, to proceed as far as Sou-Tcheou, an important town in Kan-Sou, but full three months' journey from Pekin.

Meeting with new difficulties even here, he determined to write to Father Ricci, informing him of his whereabouts, and begging him to use his influence in assisting him to reach the capital of the empire. Unfortunately these letters never reached their destination, and Father Goës was kept inactively at Sou-Tcheou for another long and wearisome period. The missionaries of Pekin, on the other hand, were the prey of many anxious fears. They had learned, by letter from the Superior of the Indian mission, that Father Goës had started in the month of February, 1603, and now, in 1606, no news had been received of the expedition.

In the month of November in the same year, a letter from Father Goës at last reached the residence of the missionaries of Pekin. It is easy to imagine the delight with which they heard that the intrepid brother, whom they had long mourned as dead, was in the province of Kan-Sou, and that they would soon be able to hear from his own lips the interesting details of the long and dangerous wanderings. Father Ricci lost no time in sending to him brother Ferdinand, a young Chinese who had just completed his noviciate at Pekin, and had entered the order of Jesuits. He was accompanied by some neophytes who were to form a sort of escort, and conduct the missionary to Pekin; as Father Ricci considered that a Chinese brother would be likely to conduct him more safely than a European.

Brother Ferdinand set out for the province of Kan-Sou, and travelled with great rapidity as far as Si-ngan-Fou, the capital of Chan-Si; but at that point one of the neophytes who accompanied him deserted the party, and no traces of him could be found; and as he was more a Chinese than a Christian, he had carried off the general purse, and without money travelling is no easy matter in China, where hospitality is so little in vogue. Brother Ferdinand had, therefore, to fall back upon his wits, and it was only after much patience, by enduring much annoyance, and by the exertion of no small amount of tact, that he succeeded, towards the end of March, 1607, in reaching Sou-Tcheou nearly four months after he had quitted Pekin.

Father Goës, however, had at length sunk under the sufferings and trials that he had encountered, and brother Ferdinand found him stretched on a pallet, afflicted with a cruel disease, and about to breathe his last. Isaac the Armenian, who had always been devoted to his master, was at his side, in a state of the deepest grief. No sooner, however, had the dying man heard that some one was speaking to him in Portuguese,—that some one had come who could give him news of his brethren at Pekin,—than he seemed to wake up out of a profound lethargy, and his strength revived. The sound of his native tongue penetrated his soul like a sunbeam, and kindled it again to life. When Ferdinand gave him the letter, he read it with deep emotion, and having finished it he shed tears, but tears of joy and consolation. The details that he had found in it, of the success of his apostolic brethren, allayed his sufferings, and enabled him to face death with perfect serenity, and cry out, with the aged Simeon, "Lord, now lettest thou thy servant depart in peace, according to Thy word; for mine eyes have seen Thy salvation." His eyes had seen, really, in the letter from the apostle of China, that the light of the Gospel had been revealed to the remotest nations, and that the day of redemption seemed to shine already for those inhabitants of Cathay whom he had come to seek from the extremities of India. The powerful emotion, however, that had reanimated him for a moment, took away what little strength he had left, and before long he ceased to hear what Ferdinand said, and was no longer able to read Father Ricci's letter, but pressing it to his bosom, he died, with feelings of the strongest affection for the apostle who had laboured with such zeal for the glory of God, and the salvation of souls. He had, with an indomitable perseverance and courage, performed the duty entrusted to him, and had by his journey placed the identity of Cathay and China, of Khanbalu and Pekin, beyond all doubt. In our own times, many learned Orientalists have made this the subject of long dissertations, but none assuredly are of so much value as this evidence of Father Goès.

During the illness of the intrepid missionary, many inhabitants of Sou-Tcheou had displayed the greatest interest in him, and had tended him with a remarkable assiduity, but their charity was neither very pure, nor very disinterested. They robbed him with the greatest effrontery; as soon as they saw his illness becoming serious, all his best pieces of jade disappeared, and, what is still more to be regretted, his diary was taken, which doubtless contained many accounts of the countries he had visited, of the greatest value and interest. The few details that we have been able to give were collected by Father Ricci from the verbal communication with Isaac the Armenian, who continued his journey to Pekin in company with brother Ferdinand. This indefatigable companion of Goès rested for a month with Father Ricci, and then again started on his travels; this time to go right through China, from north to south, as far as Macao. Thence he embarked for India, and on the way was made prisoner by some Dutch corsairs, but was ransomed by the Portuguese of Malacca, who furnished him with the means of returning, after a thousand vicissitudes, to the missionaries, by whom he had been originally chosen to accompany Father Goës. At the present day, great admiration is felt for those who overcome difficulties while travelling in foreign countries, but what are they when compared with the men of former times, whose constancy and energy could be conquered alone by death!

At the same time that Father Goës terminated his laborious career, at the frontiers of the Chinese empire, another missionary also gave up his soul to God, at the mission of Nan-Tchang-Fou, where he had resided for more than ten years. This was Father Soerius, whose apostolic zeal had succeeded in bringing a great number of Chinese to the knowledge of the true God. His body was conveyed to Macao, to be buried in the cemetery of the Jesuits, at the college of that town; but the men who had to take the body there, encountered as many difficulties on the road as if there had been a general persecution. It is a curious fact, that while the missionaries were publicly installed in several parts of the empire, and were known of everywhere, both by mandarins and people, they never enjoyed perfect peace, and although openly protected by the principal magistrates, they had to carry on a perpetual conflict with enemies who suddenly made their appearance when least expected. The poor and destitute class of literary men were invariably hostile to them.

The number of Bachelors, or those who have taken the first literary degree, is very considerable in China; but, either in consequence of a deficiency of money or of brains, those who reach the higher grades and obtain public offices are very few. Those who are in easy circumstances, enjoy at leisure the inestimable blessing of wearing a golden ball in their hats, and of distinguishing themselves from the crowd. They frequent social meetings, public parades, and ceremonies, at which they may always be known by their great display. Sometimes they amuse themselves by their literary powers, writing little stories and pieces of poetry, which they read to their acquaintances, and for which they receive the utmost praise, the condition being always understood that they in their turn will give back the same.

The unemployed and poor literary men form a distinct class in the empire, and lead a very precarious life. All hard work is, in the first place, entirely opposed to their tastes and habits. To be occupied with the ordinary pursuits of industry, commerce, or agriculture, would be beneath their dignity; and those who really wish to earn their living, become the masters of schools, or doctors, or endeavour to obtain some subordinate place in connexion with the courts of law. The others lead an irregular life, feeding upon the public in a thousand ways. Those in the great towns bear a considerable resemblance to decayed gentlemen; their only resource is to bore each other mutually with visits, and discuss the best means of escaping starvation. They frequently decide upon some plan for extracting money from the rich mandarins; and as the latter have often many sins upon their consciences, with reference to their behaviour when they held office, they do not like to have enemies among these poor and unoccupied Bachelors, who are always on the watch to lay some trap for them, or set on foot some intrigue.

Lawsuits, too, when skilfully managed, are made to furnish a considerable addition to the revenues of these gentlemen: they are always ready to foment a quarrel, and embitter the parties against each other; and they will then undertake, for a modest consideration, to make peace again, and throw a little dissertation on some point of law into the bargain. Those whose invention is not active enough to supply all these means of earning a livelihood, endeavour to gain one by their brush, which for the most part they handle with great skill. They get up a complete stock in trade of sentences, written in very beautiful characters upon strips of coloured paper, which the Chinese consume in enormous quantities to decorate their doors and the interiors of their apartments. It is unnecessary to add, that these worthy members of the literary profession, whose merits the world refuses to acknowledge, are the most active agents of secret societies, and the agitators of the people in time of revolution. Proclamations, pamphlets, and placards are the weapons they use, wielding them almost as well as their brethren in the West.*

Such were the implacable enemies of the missionaries. They launched out the most passionate libels against them, and attacked their religion, and often their character as foreigners. They invented skilfully-arranged calumnies against them, and excited the jealousy and suspicion of the multitude, thus raising numerous difficulties and embarrassments, and impeding the progress of conversion. The fearful and pusillanimous catechumens would then withdraw through fear of compromising themselves, and neophytes would often recant their recent profession of faith.

Notwithstanding all these obstacles, the Church of Jesus Christ daily gained ground in China. The seeds of the Gospel, though they did not return a hundredfold, still did not fall on barren ground; and everything favoured the hope, that the time of the great harvest would, through labour and perseverance, at length arrive. The fields that had been first cultivated were becoming extended and more fertile; and occasionally, when an opportunity presented itself, some new piece of ground was brought under tillage. It was on an enterprise of this nature, that Father Cataneo, summoned thither by Dr. Paul, was engaged at Schang-Hai. We have already stated that this illustrious and fervent neophyte had been obliged to quit Pekin, where he was a member of the Academy of Han-Lin, and to pass three years of mourning with his family, in consequence of the death of his father. During this time, the customs of China do not allow any one to hold a public office. A mandarin is obliged to quit his post; a minister of state to

* Empire Chinois, vol. II.

give up the administration of affairs, to live in solitude, and to mourn his loss. He must not pay any visits, and his official relations with the world are entirely interrupted. The present dynasty has, however, reduced the great mourning to twenty-seven months, for all functionaries of the government.

This Dr. Paul was a native of Schang-Hai, a third-rate town, situated on the sea shore, opposite to the isles of Japan; an important point for commerce at all times. In the middle ages, the Arab ships resorted in great numbers to this port; and in our own day, it has been opened to the commerce of the West, and has acquired additional importance through the the erection of a European town by the side of the old Chinese city. Dr. Paul had earnestly requested Father Cataneo to come to his native place, and spread the knowledge of the Gospel there; and the family of Hiu was rapidly converted to Christianity. The princely residence of this important personage was situated in the environs of the town, on the banks of an artificial canal communicating with the Blue River, the mouth of which is at Schang-Hai. A chapel had been constructed in this magnificent house, where divine service was celebrated with much pomp, and attracted all the distinguished Chinese of the town. Dr. Paul enjoyed, both on account of his exalted position, his scientific knowledge and high moral character, a great influence over his fellow-citizens, and his house became the centre of a flourishing Christian community. Two centuries and a half afterwards, in 1850, we had occasion to visit the descendants of this illustrious family, and what a sad change we encountered! We found them plunged in the most obstinate apostacy, and the most abject poverty—but they will again be mentioned in the course of this narrative.

The evangelical labourers scattered over the surface of the Celestial Empire, worked with ardour and devotion at the task that had been entrusted to them; but it may be safely said, that the work of propagating the faith rested especially upon Father Ricci. The relations in which he stood with the court and the great dignitaries of the empire, had a considerable influence on the success obtained by his brethren at Schang-Hai, Nankin, Nan-Tchang-Fou, Tchao-Tcheou, and Pekin. In all their squabbles with the mandarins, the missionaries had but to pronounce the name of Ly-Ma-Teou (Matthew Ricci), and the difficulties came to an end. No one liked to place himself in opposition to men who had so powerful a protector at Pekin. It was not only, however, to the influence and position of Father Ricci, that the missions owed their success, for he was himself one of the most indefatigable and active labourers in the field. Catechising the catechists, exhorting the neophytes, instructing the infidels, formed his habitual occupations; and he also wrote some admirable books, built a large church, the work of erecting which he personally superintended, and carried on an active correspondence with his brethren, and a fatiguing attendance at court.

These multifarious occupations and cares rapidly reduced his strength. On the 3d of May, 1610, Father Ricci was obliged to keep his bed. His brethren thought that he had only a sick head-ache, but he calmly announced to them that his illness was mortal. It soon began to make rapid progress, and on the sixth day he prepared to receive the holy sacrament. Although very much weakened and suffering greatly, as soon as the Eucharist was brought into his room he threw himself from his bed on his knees to prepare for it, while the attendants were all bathed in tears. After he had piously received the Holy Viaticum, he fell into a delirium, and spoke during the whole day of his beloved neophytes, of the conversion of the Chinese, and of the hopes he had entertained of bringing the emperor himself to the religion of Jesus Christ. The following day he blessed his four spiritual brothers, who knelt before his bed, and gave them various pieces of advice about the conduct of the mission. One of them said to him, " Do you know, my father, in what position you are leaving us ?" " Yes," replied he; " I leave you before a door, which may be opened to great merits, but not without much trouble and danger." On the 11th of May, 1610, he quietly resigned his soul to God, at the age of fifty-eight years.

The death of Father Ricci was a great source of grief to all the missions in China. The neophytes of Pekin wept bitterly for him, since they knew they had just lost a father, who had brought them to the Christian faith, and who loved them with all his soul and with all his strength. The whole town seemed to partake their grief; and nothing was heard in the streets, but " The Saint of the West has *saluted the world.*"* " The great Saint has gone to heaven!" The civil and military mandarins, the literary men, the members of the academy of Han-Lin, the principal dignitaries of the supreme courts, all pressed to the funeral of this illustrious missionary, to render homage to his scientific attainments and his virtue. His body was placed in a magnificent coffin, of which a rich neophyte defrayed the expenses, and it was preserved in a room in the residence of the missionaries, according to the Chinese custom, until the time should arrive for it to be buried.

The bodies of missionaries dying in the southern provinces were usually conveyed to Macao, there to be interred at the house of the Jesuits. Pekin was too far, however, from the Portuguese colony; and independently of this, it was desired that the remains of the brave apostle who had founded the mission should be preserved in China. The plan, therefore, was first proposed of buying a piece of land in the environs of the capital, and there raising a tomb to his memory; but afterwards the happy thought occurred to some one of petitioning the emperor to grant a piece of land for a cemetery for the monks of the West whom he had so much appreciated. Father Pantoja, assisted by several learned Chinese Christians, drew up this petition, which has been preserved, and of which the following is a translation:—

* A Chinese mode of expressing death.

"The humble Jacques Pantoja, a subject of the great kingdom of the West, offers a respectful petition on behalf of another subject of a foreign kingdom, recently deceased.

"I humbly pray your Supreme Excellency to grant a place for his burial, in order that your imperial munificence may be extended over all the world, and may embrace the most remote countries. Having heard by report of the renown of the very noble and very Celestial Empire, I devoted three entire years to travelling over the waves of the sea, passing altogether over six thousand leagues, amid perpetual dangers and difficulties; and at last, in the twenty-eighth year of the reign of Wan-Lié, in the twelfth moon, we succeeded in reaching the court, in company with Matthew Ricci, and in offering some little presents from our countries. Since that time we have enjoyed a pension through the imperial favour; and the sentiments of gratitude we feel cannot be contained in our hearts, and we know no way, even by the effusion of our blood, of showing how thankful we are for such a signal benefit.

"In the twenty-ninth year of Wan-Lié, we presented a humble petition, praying for a residence from which to make known to the world the imperial mercy towards strangers. We have now for several years been waiting to hear the manifestation of your will; but at the same time we have always received the pension, though our merit is in reality nothing.

"In the thirty-eighth year of Wan-Lié, and the eighteenth day of the third moon, Matthew Ricci, at an advanced age, died of illness; and I myself remain solitary, worthy perhaps that some one should have pity on my grief, and compassion on my sufferings. The journey back to my native country is long, and sailors are afraid to carry a dead body in their ships.* It is for this reason that it is impossible for me

---

* It is customary in China for the bodies of those who die at a distance from their native country, to be taken back there in order to be buried in the family sepulchre.

to take the coffin with me, and return to my native country. But remembering that we have lived for several years under the protection of your majesty, we may be considered as your subjects; and thus your mercy, like that of Yao,* will not be confined by the limits of the central empire, but extend itself also over all foreign kingdoms. Since during our lives we have been nourished by the imperial munificence, we hope that when we are dead it will also grant us a little earth to cover our bodies. Our hopes are rendered greater also, in consequence of Matthew Ricci having, ever since his arrival in the empire, devoted himself to the study of literature, and to the practice of all the virtues that the books teach. Day and night he burned sacred perfumes before the altar of the Lord of Heaven, and recited earnest prayers for the health and prosperity of your majesty. I, Jacques Pantoja and my companions, are of a foreign kingdom. How then shall we dare to hope more than belongs to such insignificant persons! It is a great sorrow to us not to possess a little piece of ground in which to bury our dead brother; and for this reason do we with abundant tears entreat you to grant us some place where we may lay the body of a stranger. We, who survive him, will always follow faithfully in the footsteps of our brother, and will pray to the Lord of Heaven to grant you and your mother a thousand years of life, in order that we, like very little ants, may live in the peace, consolation, and repose of your great empire. We wait humbly to hear your imperial answer."

It was first necessary for this petition to be endorsed by the Minister of Finance; the emperor then received it, and transmitted it to the president of the Court of Rites, desiring him to report upon it. This report has been preserved; and we subjoin a translation of it, since it is a good example of the forms of Chinese state papers. After having quoted the

---

* The founder of the Chinese monarchy.

petition that we have just given at full length, the president of the Court of Rites continues thus:—

"Your majesty having ordered that this matter should be decided by the court, it has come under my observation. I have written out the laws and customs of the empire, and among them I find one of this tenour:—If any one of the strangers who are in the habit of resorting to this empire, shall die on the road before having arrived at the court, the Intendant of the province in which he dies shall assign him a burial-place, and a stone shall be raised over his grave, on which shall be inscribed the name of the deceased and the objects of his journey. There is another law also, to the following effect:—If the stranger dies after having reached the capital, and if he has not already received, according to custom, the Imperial munificence, the governor of the town shall make him a coffin; but if the emperor has already bestowed his benefits upon him, he shall be buried at his own expense.

"Thus, although Matthew Ricci was not a subject sent by the king of his own country, yet he had come from a very distant nation, having been attracted hither by the renown and splendour of the Celestial Empire. Your majesty has for many years granted him a pension; and now he has died of old age. It is a very great distance to his own country, and, for this reason, his coffin cannot be transported there. Is not this body now exposed upon the surface of the earth a fit object for commiseration? If so, would it not be right to grant something in answer to the petition of Jacques Pantoja, and to put a favourable interpretation upon the laws that I have recited? May not the piece of ground he asks for be given him, in order that your majesty may add new favours to the old ones?

"When this petition came into my hands, I saw and considered that the great renown of the virtues of the Son of Heaven and his government attract people from the most remote countries. Behold how men who, during all past ages have never visited our empire, are now drawn hither by our laws and customs, and flock in from all parts, as shown by the example of Matthew Ricci and his companions ; who, after having travelled for an unmeasureable distance, have at last reached your majesty's court, and have offered you their presents. They have enjoyed your bounty for several years, and Matthew Ricci has been careful to instruct himself, and little by little has learned many things; he has brought out certain renowned books, and has at last saluted the age. Who could help having compassion on the body of a stranger who has come from such a distant land? Jacques Pantoja and his companions now ask for a little ground to bury him; and who could wish to leave the body on the surface of the earth without the rites of sepulture? Jacques Pantoja and his companions pray, that since during his life he experienced your imperial bounty, it may not cease at his death; and I entreat your majesty that it will please you to send an order to the Governor of this town, requiring him to search for an uninhabited and deserted pagoda, and a few acres of ground, to serve as the burial-place of Matthew Ricci and the residence of Jacques Pantoja and his companions, in order that they may practise their religion in what way they like, adoring the Lord of Heaven, and praying for your majesty. It is an act worthy of your majesty's grandeur to extend your benefits to *dry wood* (dead bodies), and to treat strangers with benignity and mercy; thus inducing them more and more to spread the renown of your empire. I think, therefore, that it would be a right thing to grant their petition; though, as I dare not do this on my simple authority, I pray your majesty to command that that may be done which will be most for your service.

"Given this thirty-eighth year of the reign of Wan-Lie (1610), the twenty-third day of the fourth moon."*

* Trigault, pp. 541, 542.

The emperor having received this report, sent it, according to the usual custom, to the prime minister, in order to obtain his advice on the subject. This dignitary wrote upon it, that he agreed with the conclusions that had been arrived at, and then returned it to the emperor; who finally took a brush in his own hand, and traced in vermillion the official sign of approbation, "*che;*" that is to say, "be it done."

Whilst they were in the midst of the grief occasioned by the death of Father Ricci, this piece of good news afforded great consolation to the Christians, who received it with the most lively demonstrations of joy. It was a strange mixture this, of joy and sorrow, happiness and grief. The great propagator of the Gospel in China was no more; but this imperial decree had, in their eyes, placed his work on an imperishable foundation. The authorities were soon engaged in the search after some place that might be bestowed on Father Pantoja, as the emperor had directed; and they decided at last upon a pagoda surrounded with a beautiful enclosure, which had become the property of a eunuch, then lying under sentence of death in one of the public prisons. An objection was raised that this pagoda not only belonged to a eunuch, but was also then inhabited by Bonzes; but the governor of Pekin took his brush and wrote the following words:—"The temple of Discipline and Goodness belongs to no one, since its proprietor has been condemned to death by the emperor; and as to the Bonzes, who inhabit it, let them be driven out, and the establishment be handed over without delay to Jacques Pantoja and his companions."

The missionaries were then officially installed in the "temple of Discipline and Goodness." A few days afterwards some of the Bonzes, taking advantage of the absence of Father Pantoja, made an attack upon the pagoda, and carried off the furniture, pretending that the building alone had been given to the Christians, and not what it contained. After having pillaged the place at their leisure, nobody interfering with them, several of them took their seats in the temple, and began to talk to a neophyte attached to the mission as a domestic servant. "Your master is very powerful," a Bonze said; "he must certainly possess some drug wherewith to enchant the hearts and subjugate the wills of the great mandarins." "Virtue, books, and the law of the Lord of Heaven," said the neophyte, "are the only medicines my master uses to obtain the goodwill of great men." "Since you are his disciple, then," replied the Bonze, "advise him to make them assign him a larger and more beautiful pagoda than this; something that will be worthy of him." "My master is meek, and desires nothing better," was the reply. The Bonze then rose, and addressing a large gilded idol enthroned upon an altar, he made it a bow, and said in a slightly sarcastic tone, "Adieu, adieu for the last time! I shall not be allowed to enter this hall again; adieu!" Some of the Bonzes, however, took leave of their gods with very much less courtesy, pouring out abuse and maledictions upon them. "Since you had the cowardice to allow yourselves to be seized and domineered over by strangers, you are nothing but turtles' eggs, and we curse you."

After some few difficulties, that the magistrates always hastened to smooth over, the missionaries were left to enjoy their new abode in peace. They made a pile of the numerous wooden idols that they found in the pagoda, and the recently converted Chinese amused themselves by seeing them burned, and by cutting jokes at their expense. As soon as the mausoleum inside the enclosure of the mission, which was destined to receive the remains of Father Ricci, had been finished, the funeral ceremonies were performed, the principal magistrates of Pekin being present. The missions of Nankin, Nan-Tchang-Fou, Tchao-Tcheou, and Shang-Hai sent deputations; and as the concourse of Christians was consequently very great, Father Pantoja determined to take advantage of the opportunity to display all the splendours of the Catholic worship. It was indeed not so much a mournful ceremony, as a pompous fête to celebrate the triumph of Christianity in the capital of the Chinese empire.

Some days before the illness that put an end to his apostolic career, Father Ricci had addressed the following words to his companions: "My Fathers, when I reflect upon the means by which I can best further the interest of Christianity among the Chinese, I can find nothing better or more efficacious than my death." The great missionary had without doubt a presentiment of what would be accomplished by patience and courage. He had succeeded in making the seed of the Gospel germinate in the inhospitable soil; he had made the light shine in the midst of the darkness; he had brought the knowledge of the true God to these numerous populations; and it may well be said that his apostleship had been crowned with success, since numerous and fervent neophytes might have been found in many of the provinces. His death, nevertheless, put the seal to all that he had done, and by his burial Christianity was legalised in China. The piece of land that had been granted by the emperor himself, with the approbation of the six supreme courts, and of the ministers and first magistrates, was a splendid proof in the eyes of the people of the favour shown to Christianity. The base had been firmly established, and the evangelical labourers now set themselves heartily to work to construct the edifice, of which the ardent charity of François Xavier and the indefatigable zeal of Matthew Ricci had laid the foundation.

The mission in China was thus established; and the reader who has followed the course of our narrative will have seen how much labour, sorrow, and suffering, the chief of this glorious enterprise had had to endure. Everything depended on him; he had to watch over all the Christian communities, to instruct novices who should perpetuate what he could only begin, to catechise, to preach, to receive confessions, to visit the sick, to cultivate the sciences, to give lessons in mathematics and geography, to answer all doubts and objections which were sent him by the literary men from all parts of China, to obtain the protection of the great men, to provide subsistence for the missionaries and the poor, to be all things to all men, never to think of himself, but to occupy his time only with the work of God; this was what Father Ricci had to do during his long residence in China. He fulfilled all these duties punctually, as we have already observed, and yet found time to write some excellent books in Chinese upon morality and religion. That entitled Tien-Tchou-Che-Y, or " Proofs of the Existence of the Lord of Heaven," is looked upon even in China as a model of neatness and elegance of style. This book is a refutation of the principal errors prevalent in China, a sort of introduction to the Gospel; and the prodigious success which it met with among the Chinese literati, proves that they are capable of following the most subtle and complicated reasoning. The author therein satisfactorily establishes the existence of God, the immortality of the soul, and the free will of man; and, destroying all pagan and irreligious systems known in the country, he prepares the mind of the reader for the conception of a creating and redeeming God.

A courageous and indefatigable zeal, at the same time wise, patient and circumspect, slow in order to be efficacious, and cautious that it might be more daring, were, says Father d'Orleans, essential characteristics of the man destined by God to be the apostle of a fastidious, suspicious nation, inimical by nature to everything new and foreign. A truly brave heart was required to recommence so many times a work so often destroyed, and to know how to turn the smallest resources to advantage; a genius more than common, and a rare and profound sagacity, was indispensable to render itself respected among a people little accustomed to respect any one but themselves, and to teach a new doctrine to men who had till then thought that they could learn nothing from any body.

But at the same time, a humility and modesty like that of Father Ricci was needed to bring this proud race under the yoke of a superior intelligence, which is never voluntarily submitted to, except when it is unperceived. Finally, great virtue and a continual union with God was necessary for the apostle himself to enable him to support by internal power of mind the difficulties of so laborious a life, and one so full of dangers, as that which he had led in China, where it may truly be said that the longest martyrdom known would have spared him much suffering.

CHAPTER VI.

Question of Rites. — The two Schools. — Consequences of these Discussions. — Important Conversions among the Educated Classes. — Doctors Léon and Michel. — Mission of Han-Tcheou-Fou. — Violent Persecution. — Memorial against the Christians. — Apologies from the Christian Doctors. — Edict against Christianity. — Courage of the Neophytes. — Poisoning, Flagellation, and Torture. — Death of two Neophytes. — The Missionaries shut up in Cages. — New Establishment. — The old Missions to Tartary and Thibet. — Father d'Andrada sets out for Thibet in 1624. — Mountains. — Avalanches. — Pagoda of Badid. — Fables of the Lamas. — Halt in the Valley of Mana. — The King of Sirinagar endeavours to arrest d'Andrada. — Terrible Journey of d'Andrada. — Immense Glaciers. — D'Andrada returns. — Reunion of the Caravan. — Arrival in Thibet. — The King of Caparangua. — Decree in favour of the Missionaries. — d'Andrada sets out for the Indies. — Return to Thibet. — Accounts of the Thibetans. — The King desires to turn Christian. — Opposition of the Lamas. — Religious Discussions. — Scarcity of information relating to this Mission. — Conjectures of the Tartar Historians.

Matthew Ricci had pointed out Father Nicholas Lombard as his fit successor in the office of general superior of the Jesuit missions in China. This missionary, born of a patrician family in Sicily, arrived in China in the year 1597. He at first acted as an apostle for several years in the province of

Kian-Si, where for a long time his only companion was one brother, who provided for the subsistence of both, while he himself was preaching both in the towns and the surrounding country. The conversions that he effected were so numerous, that the jealousy of the Bonzes was excited, and they raised violent persecutions against him; and finding himself attacked on all sides by the most injurious accusations and calumnies, he appealed to the magistrates, convicted his enemies of falsehood, and then generously pardoned them. The sagacity, patience, and strength of mind that he had displayed during the exercise of his ministry had struck Father Ricci so powerfully, that he had not hesitated to nominate him his successor.

Father Lombard, though feeling profound respect and admiration for the founder of the mission, did not entirely coincide in the opinions formed by Father Ricci of the religious and philosophical doctrines of China. Father Ricci, after having studied from the very commencement of his apostleship the character and genius of the nation whom he had been called to evangelise, had come to the conclusion that the best means that could be adopted for bringing the Chinese to a knowledge of the truth, would be to subscribe partly to the praises unceasingly lavished upon Confucius by both nation and government, by whom he was regarded as the wise man, *par excellence*, the master of all science, and the legislator of the empire. He thought that in the doctrines advanced by this philosopher as to the nature of God, he found much that bore a considerable resemblance to those of Christianity, and that *Tien*, or Heaven as conceived by the educated classes, was not the material and visible one, but the true God, the Lord of Heaven, the Supreme Being, invisible and spiritual, of infinite perfection, the creator and preserver of all things, the only God in fact, whom Confucius directs his disciples to adore and worship.

With regard also to the honours paid by the Chinese to their ancestors Father Ricci had adopted the same idea, and had looked from the same point of view. He was himself persuaded, and he endeavoured to persuade the other missionaries, that the sacrifices offered to ancestors were purely of a civil nature; that, according to the true meaning of Confucius, they had nothing whatever of a religious or idolatrous signification; and were solely offered in obedience to the feelings of veneration, filial piety and love, by which the Chinese had been, in all ages, inspired towards the authors of their being, and the wise men who had spread the benefits of science and civilisation over the empire. Ricci had thus concluded that these sacrifices and national fetes, if traced to their real sources in the principles of Chinese philosophy, formed no part of a superstitious and pagan worship, but were simply of a civil and political nature, and might be still preserved, at any rate with regard to Confucius, and to their ancestors, by the Christian Chinese.

Such was the opinion of Father Ricci, and of a large number of his brethren. It was a system that offered every facility to the missionaries, and that greatly assisted them in propagating the Christian faith. The ancient and only religion of the Chinese had always been confined to the worship of Tien (Heaven), of the wise men, and of their ancestors. The delusions of Tao-Sse, and the superstitions of the Bonzes, had captivated them at various periods, but had never obtained any well rooted belief, and had never been made a part of their faith. By declaring that the worship of Heaven was similar to that of the true God, and that the homage paid to ancestors and to Confucius was a legitimate expression of filial piety towards the chiefs of families and the benefactors of the race, the missionaries were greatly favoured by the Chinese ideas, instead of coming into collision with them, and never failed to become popular on that account, especially among the educated classes, who willingly abandoned the creed of the Bonzes and of Tao-Sse.

Father Lombard looked at all these Chinese customs from

a very different point of view. The esteem that he had felt for the talents and virtue of Father Ricci had induced him before to suspend his judgment, and his scruples as to the correctness of the system followed by this apostle; but when he found himself placed at the head of the mission, and responsible for all the errors that might arise, he considered it his duty to examine this important question with greater attention. He set himself seriously therefore to the study of the works of Confucius, and of his most celebrated commentators, and consulted such of the literary men as could throw a light upon the subject, and in whom he could place confidence. Many other of the Jesuit missionaries entered into the controversy, and opinions were divided. Father Lombard wrote a book on the subject, in which it was examined to the bottom, and in which he came to the conclusion that the doctrine of Confucius and his disciples was tainted with materialism and atheism; that the Chinese in reality recognised no divinity but Heaven, and the general effect that it had upon the beings of the Universe; that the soul in their opinion was nothing but a subtle aeriform substance; and finally, that their views as to its immortality closely resembled the theory of Metempsychosis obtained from Indian philosophers. Regarded from this point of view, the customs of China appeared to Lombard and the missionaries who took his side, as an idolatry utterly incompatible with the sanctity of Christianity,—criminal acts, the impiety of which must be shown to the Chinese on whom, by the grace of God, the light of the gospel had shone, and which must be absolutely forbidden to all Christians, whatever might be their condition, or whatever part of the empire they might inhabit. The use of the words, *Tien* and *Chang-Ti*, even, by which they designated the divinity, were interdicted. It will be seen from this how widely the rigorous orthodoxy of Father Lombard differed from the excessive tolerance of Father Ricci.

Such was the commencement of the disagreements which

afterwards proved more fatal to the prosperity of the missions, than the most violent persecutions ever raised by the mandarins. They arose in the bosom of the Society of Jesuits, before missionaries of any other order arrived in China, and we shall, further on, see the dispute developing itself, and assuming the lamentable form of a fierce contest. The discussion on Chinese rites, on the worship of ancestors and of Confucius, was not confined within the limits of the Celestial Empire, but spread over Europe, where, as in Asia, the controversy was carried on with the utmost acrimony and passion. Profuse dissertations and numerous pamphlets on the subject were scattered about everywhere; but, instead of bringing out the truth, they served but to envelope it in still thicker obscurity, until at last the Church with her sovereign and absolute authority put an end to this long contest, and restored the peace which this time, it must be confessed, had not been broken by the pagans.

The first years succeeding the death of Father Ricci were wonderfully prosperous to the Chinese missions, and Father Nicholas Lombard commenced his administration under the happiest auspices. The new residence, on the front of which was inscribed "Imperial liberality,"—the pagoda converted into a Catholic church, the splendid funeral of the head of the missionaries, the mausoleum raised in some measure with the ruins of the Buddhist idols, and in the most public manner,—all these things of course made a great noise both at Pekin and in the provinces. People were asking each other who were these religious strangers who had acquired such astonishing and unheard-of celebrity in the capital of the empire; they were eager to read the books published by these men, they applauded the doctrines contained in them, and in all directions a happy movement towards Christianity was perceptible. Conversions were numerous, many even in the highest rank of the magistracy; and one especially notable was that of Doctor Yang, a celebrated mandarin, who had for seven years held the office of governor in the province of Nankin, and was also one of the most distinguished men of the time.

Father Ricci had, as has been already observed, made some valuable conquests among the most illustrious members of the Han-Lin; and the zeal and fervour shown by the Doctors Paul and Léon, in seconding the exertions of the missionaries, has been already mentioned. The latter, having been obliged to retire into the bosom of his family to preside over the funeral rites of his father, and, according to custom, pass the time of mourning in retirement, had carried one of the missionaries with him, in the hope that he might convert his relatives, and found a mission in his native town, Han-Tcheou-Fou, the capital of the province of Tche-Kiang. We have seen from the narrative of the Arab travellers, that in the eighth century a frightful massacre of the Christians took place in that town; and also that in the thirteenth century some monks of the order of St. Francis founded a flourishing mission, which was placed by John of Monte Corvino under the jurisdiction of one of his suffragan bishops; but at the beginning of the seventeenth century no trace of Christianity was left in the place.

Doctor Léon was the apostle destined by Providence to rekindle the flame of the true faith in his native town. From the time of his arrival, Doctor Léon was in frequent communication with the celebrated Yang, one of his nearest relations, and one of the richest inhabitants of the town, though he had renounced his high position in the magistracy to devote himself to the study of letters and philosophy. A zealous disciple of Buddhism, he had had a magnificent pagoda constructed in the interior of his palace, and maintained at his own expense several Bonzes, to whom he was entirely devoted. As religious questions occupied above all else his superior intellect, he entered in his very first interview with his relation Doctor Léon on a discussion concerning Buddhism and Christianity, and the argument was continued with equal earnestness on both sides for several days; till at length the disciple of Buddha, who was seeking for the truth in sincerity and singleness of heart, was struck by the immense difference between the two systems in dispute. On one side he found innumerable superstitions, a multitude of divinities, and the most incoherent doctrines, perpetually varying with various localities and the teachings of various Bonzes; on the other, one only God, one doctrine, one priesthood, and one worship. This admirable unity at length overcame his doubts, and he no longer hesitated to declare himself a Christian. After having been sufficiently instructed in the mysteries of religion, he was baptized under the name of Michel, dismissed the Bonzes that he had had in his service, and converted his pagoda into a Catholic chapel.

With this important conversion the Chinese Christians counted in their ranks the three most celebrated doctors in the corporation of the Lettered; namely, Doctors Paul, Léon, and Michel, who continued during their whole lives to manifest the most ardent zeal for the propagation of the faith, and the most boundless devotion to the missionaries. The high reputation for knowledge and integrity which they enjoyed throughout the empire, and especially among the high and cultivated classes, procured an amount of respect for the religion they had adopted, as well as for its ministers, which had not hitherto been felt. The Bachelors of several towns formed themselves into committees, and drew up petitions with numerous signatures, in which they begged the superiors of the missions of Nankin and Pekin to send them preachers to teach them the true way of salvation.

A new spirit seemed to be awakened from one end of China to the other. New missions were founded, the former ones were enlarged and strengthened: that of Nankin, which already possessed eight missionaries, rivalled even that of Pekin in the number and zeal of its neophytes. Father Semedo, who at that time belonged to the mission of Nankin, witnessed these abundant fruits of salvation, and expressed in these words his hopes and enthusiasm:—"The winter of storms and persecutions is past, and the spring is already producing flowers worthy of the paradise of God: or, rather, it seems that the harvest is ripe and is awaiting only the sickle.*

Father Semedo was, however, soon to see that, on the contrary, the time for great trials and tribulations was only now to begin. The harvest was ripe, indeed, but it was the scythe of persecution that was about to pass over it. The tempest arose in the following manner.

In 1615, the imperial government sent to Pekin a mandarin of the first class, named Kio-Tchin, to take the office of assessor of the Li-Pou, or Supreme Court of Rites, which, among other functions, takes cognisance of costumes, and of the sects of foreigners admitted into the empire. This personage was by no means partial to Christians and missionaries, and had besides some special reasons of his own for owing them an ill will. One of his intimate friends, a learned Bonze, who was a good writer, but overflowing with vanity, had published a book against Christianity, to which he said there could be no reply. Doctor Paul, nevertheless, did reply, and in a style so crushing that the poor Bonze could not survive his defeat, but died of vexation. Kio-Tchin was much grieved at this event, and the more so because he had himself been personally humiliated in a conference on a religious question that he had held with Doctors Paul and Michel: he planned, therefore, a scheme of vengeance against the Christians; and before he had matured his plan, he learned that two of the principal magistrates had presented a petition to the emperor to have all the best European books translated into Chinese by the missionaries, with a view of enriching the national literature. He had, too, hopes of becoming *Colao*, or prime minister, and thought it would serve the purposes of his ambition to put himself forward openly in the character of zeal

* Alvarez Semedo, Histoire Universelle du grand Royaume de la Chine, p. 202.

ous defender of the faith of antiquity, and opponent of foreign innovations. These motives, might, nevertheless, have been sufficient to make the assessor declare open war to Christianity, but, unfortunately for the missions, there was soon added to them another motive which it is always very difficult for a Chinese to resist. The Bonzes of Nankin, terrified at seeing their pagodas more and more forsaken and despised, resolved on making a vigorous effort to save themselves from complete ruin. They levied a contribution on themselves, and made a collection among the devout Buddhists, and from the proceeds offered the assessor a bribe of ten thousand ounces of silver to procure the expulsion of the missionaries. The hatred and wrath of Kio-Tchin against the Christians were at its height, and the temptation of such a sum as this thrown into the same scale completely turned it.

The assessor laid his plan of attack very skilfully. Before accusing the missionaries formally before the emperor, he got the Bachelors of Nankin to draw up a memorial, in which they requested his intervention to drive from the country these dangerous strangers, who had clandestinely introduced themselves into the empire, and were attempting to effect a revolution in it. "Do honest and virtuous men," they said, "thus forsake their families and their property to go running about the world and living in unknown countries? A person who lives near the residence of the missionaries has declared that several times in the year, there is held in that house, under pretext of religion and prayer, a numerous assembly of men and women, who afterwards return to their own houses before daylight; that to every new convert to Christianity they give five ounces of silver, and put them down in a list, under strange unknown names, and that they also accustom them to trace on their foreheads a particular character, doubtless intended as a rallying sign for the time of insurrection; and that finally their houses are filled with arms and munitions of war." The mandarin Kio-Tchin collected carefully all these insinuations, and drew up from them an accusation at once violent and treacherous; which he, in his quality of assessor of the Supreme Court of Rites, addressed to the emperor, in the month of May, 1616. He insisted much on their having fraudulently introduced to the Chinese a religion contrary to that of their forefathers and the sages of antiquity; and he came to the conclusion, that in order to prevent the missionaries and their partisans from increasing to a still more dangerous extent, it would be advisable to put them to death.

The presentation of this memorial, though made very secretly, did not remain unknown to the Christians; as a mandarin, who was a friend of the assessor and of Dr. Michel, communicated the fact to the latter, and he immediately gave information to the missionaries, and advised with them concerning the best means of averting the storm now threatening them and their religion. He also wrote to several influential mandarins, and to the assessor himself, to contradict certain allegations that had been brought against the Christians and their doctrine, though without intimating that he had any knowledge of the memorial presented to the emperor; and in his anxious solicitude for the missionaries, he invited them all to retire in case of danger to his house at Han-Tchcou-Fou, and wait there under his protection till the tempest should have subsided. Doctor Léon, who had been at two days' journey from Nankin when he heard the report, hastened thither, and got an apology for the Christian religion and its ministers printed and circulated in the town; whilst at the same time he addressed the most fervent exhortations to the Christians to keep up their courage in times of persecution.

The news of the danger menacing the missionaries excited the most lively emotion among the neophytes. They ran about communicating to one another their hopes and fears; redoubled their prayers and religious exercises, and by the reception of the sacraments prepared themselves for the probably sanguinary struggle that was about to take place.

One of them, who possessed more than an ordinary amount of courage and energy, had four flags prepared, and inscribed with his Chinese and christian name in large characters, and planted them before his house, in order to encourage his brethren not to shrink from the avowal of their faith, as well as to guard against any feeling of pusillanimity in himself.

Three months passed away, and there was still no answer to the petition of the assessor; but, far from being discouraged, he drew up another, still more violent than the first, and induced one of his brethren in the Court of Rites to draw up a third, to be presented to the emperor at the same time. A member of the College of Mathematics, who had been in friendly relation with the missionaries, having heard of the plot, procured two copies of the petitions, and forwarded them to Dr. Paul; and this zealous Christian, a distinguished statesman, and one of the first writers of his time, spent the night in composing a refutation of the charges, and an apology for Christianity, ready to be presented to the emperor at the proper time. He also sent to the Court of Rites one of his disciples, a keen-witted mandarin, to make the President of that court aware of the intrigues set on foot by his subordinates, and entreat him not to favour the malicious proceedings of his Assessor, Kio-Tchin.

The President assured Dr. Paul of his entire devotion to his wishes, and at the same time fearing to appear less zealous than his Assessor, he hastened to send in a memorial of his own, in which he declared that the complaints of Kio-Tchin were quite just, and conformable to the good of the state; and that for his own part, he should think he was performing a laudable action, and fulfilling the duties of his office, if, without even waiting for the emperor's orders, he should himself undertake to drive these strangers from his dominions. He would except, however, such as resided at Pekin, they being "too powerfully protected." By these last words, the President of the Court of Rites intended, apparently, to throw blame on the high functionaries who had favoured them, and even on the emperor himself.

The petitions of the President of the Court of Rites, and of his Assessor, were forwarded to the court on the same day, namely, on the 15th of August, 1616; and on the 20th of the same month couriers extraordinary were galloping from Pekin in all directions, with orders to arrest the missionaries, and throw them into prison. "Who would not be astonished," says Father Semedo, "at the change in this fickle people, and who could imagine that three of the first mandarins should thus have plotted the ruin of those who were held in esteem throughout the empire; whom so many of the greatest Chinese doctors had honoured with their visits and recommendations; and, moreover, knowing all the while that the accusations preferred against them were pure calumnies?"*

The order sent off from Pekin on the 20th of August reached Nankin on the night of the 30th, and the missionaries threw themselves on their knees before the altar, and offered to God the sacrifice of their lives; they then took away the images and consecrated vessels, and concealed them in the house of a Christian. At break of day, Father Lombard, the superior-general of the mission, set off, in company with Father Jules Leni, in order to proceed immediately to Pekin, and find, if possible, some means of remedying this disaster. The Fathers Alphonse Vagnon and Alvarez Semedo waited in the house until the satellites should come to execute the orders of the emperor. In a short time three mandarins arrived, and signified to the missionaries that they had orders to drive them out of China; and the house was soon entirely occupied by soldiers, who guarded also all the approaches to it. An inventory was then taken of the furniture, and the official seal placed upon it; Father Semedo, being ill in bed, was allowed to remain there, though with a sentinel planted at his door

* Alvarez Semedo, p. 307.

but Father Vagnon was carried in a litter to the tribunal of the Assessor of the Court of Rites, through an immense crowd who made the air ring with their vociferations and insults. The throng was so compact that the satellites were obliged to use their bamboos and rattans pretty freely to get through it.

The Christians of Nankin were not wanting in fervour and devotion in the hour of trial, but as soon as they heard of the imprisonment of Father Vagnon, they ran to the mission house, to make a public protest of their faith, and their sympathy with their spiritual fathers.

The intrepidity of a certain John Yao was especially remarkable: he marched at the head of the procession, holding in one hand a flag inscribed with his name, and his declaration that he was a Christian, and in the other a large placard, on which were written in conspicuous characters the commandments of God and of the church. The satellites, astonished at the novelty of this spectacle, asked him what he was about to do?

"I come," he replied, with calm dignity, "to die, to shed my blood with my spiritual fathers!"

The satellites immediately took him at his word; bound his hands behind him, put a chain upon his neck, and dragged him to the tribunal. When the mandarins asked him who he was, he replied with the same coolness that he was a Christian, and quite ready to render a reason for his faith, if they would listen to him. This courageous bearing, so uncommon in China, in the presence of magistrates, astonished the mandarin, and he ordered the chains to be taken off Yao, and that he should be allowed to sit down.

When the Assessor, Kio-Tchin, learned that one of the missionaries had been left behind in the house, he was exceedingly wrathful, and vented much anger on the subordinates of his tribunal; and the next day, Father Semedo, as well as the Brothers Sebastian Fernandez, and some Christians who lived with them, were sent to join Father Vagnon in prison, where they were kept apart from each other.

Whilst Father Lombard, having reached Pekin, was vainly exerting himself, in conjunction with Father Pantoja and Dr. Paul, to get a petition presented to the emperor, the persecution at Nankin became more and more envenomed. "I will not stay," says Father Semedo, " to relate all the indignities, affronts, and outrages that we suffered, in passing from one tribunal to another. Some struck us with their fists; others kicked us, pushed us about, and slapped our faces, or spit in them, or plaistered them with mud, or tore out our beards, and committed a thousand other such outrages as in this country criminals usually experience, if their purses are not sufficiently well filled to enable them to purchase their freedom from these vexations, and a little humanity from the ministers of justice. We Christians were not rich enough to do this."*

After having been dragged about from one tribunal to another and cruelly maltreated, the confessors of the faith were at length brought before that very Assessor of the Court of Rites, who had been the original cause of this long persecution. He kept them kneeling in chains for six whole hours, in a most painful attitude, while he subjected them to an interminable examination, in the hope of catching at some expression, that might serve as a pretext for having them flagellated and tortured by his executioners, who stood there in readiness, armed with their horrible instruments, and waiting only a sign from him to fall on their unhappy victims. The judge asked them what doctrine they had professed and taught to the people—by what means they had obtained entrance into China—what kind of a life they led—what were their means of existence—what relations existed between them and the missionaries of Macao, and a great number of

* Alvarez Semedo, p. 814.

other questions, to which the accused replied with so much wisdom and truth that even that judge could find nothing in their words to justify his subjecting them to the bastinado or the torture.

The Assessor then addressed Brother Sebastian, who had been flagellated, and asked how he could have the shameless audacity to put forward a criminal, judicially condemned to death, to be adored as a God. The intrepid confessor of the faith collected his strength, which was almost exhausted by the treatment he had undergone, and unfolded with holy ardour the Mystery of Redemption, effected by the death of Christ upon the Cross; but the touching picture he drew of the passion of the Saviour, and of the ferocious persecutors of innocence, appeared to the tyrant too significant. "He could not endure," says Semedo, who was present, "that beautiful but mournful spectacle, and ordered that the prisoner should receive twenty more strokes of the bastinado, to quench the fire that was in him, and then discharged. As his wounds were not yet closed, they burst out again with indescribable torture, and the blood gushed up out of them like water from pipes, till it sprinkled the feet of the judge." With the exception of Father Semedo, who, strangely enough, was spared, on account of the failing state of his health, all these magnanimous Christians were subjected to frightful torments, and afterwards dragged to a hideous prison, where they were left to lie for three months, with chains round their necks and feet, and without any of their friends or relations being allowed to bring them the least solace for their misery. Their food consisted only of a small ration of bad rice boiled in water and a plate of herbs. Father Semedo and Brother Sebastian, on account of their illness, and by extraordinary favour, were allowed *half* a hard salted egg each, instead of the herbs; but if the Christians of the town brought them any thing, the keepers of the prison "were about it," says Semedo, "like wasps round bee-hives, and carried off the greater part, or sometimes the whole, for themselves." Two of the poor prisoners were so much weakened, as to be unable to bear up under this treatment, and died, in a great measure of starvation, in their dungeons. They died, each alone, and only consoled by the consciousness of having bravely performed their duty as Christians.

During this time the enemies of the missionaries at Pekin redoubled their exertions to obtain from the emperor a sentence of banishment against all Europeans; and Father Lombard and Dr. Paul failed in all their attempts to convey their apology for Christianity to the Court. All the avenues to it were so well guarded by the jealousy of the eunuchs, that the emperor, having only the accusation, and not the defence, at last signed the sentence of condemnation in the following terms:—

"Having been informed by the Assessor of the Court of Rites, that certain strangers have sought clandestinely to form establishments in various parts of the empire, and our mandarins having humbly supplicated us that the strangers Vagnon, Pantoja, and their companions should be sent out of the country for having preached an unknown law, and, under pretext of religion, troubled the repose of our people, and endeavoured to excite a revolt among the Hundred Families, and a general rising throughout the empire; we have consequently ordered the Court of Rites sitting at Nankin, to warn the magistrates of the empire, that wherever the said strangers shall be found, they shall be taken, and sent, under a good escort, to the province and city of Canton, that thence they may return to their own country, leaving the Central Kingdom in peace.

"Last year, upon the information given us that these strangers had only entered the empire for our service, and that James Pantoja and his companions were capable of assisting in the correction of the Imperial Calendar, we associated them with the class of mandarins; but notwithstanding this association, we desire that they shall now be dismissed, and sent back to their own country. Let this formal order be obeyed!"

This sentence was every where put in execution, but in no other place with as much rigour as at Nankin. There the missionaries were taken on the 6th of March, 1616, with ropes round their necks before the Assessor of the Court of Rites; and as Father Semedo could not walk, he was carried upon a table. Their persecutor then informed them that they had incurred the penalty of capital punishment, for having preached a religion new to China; but that nevertheless the emperor in his goodness spared their lives, and contented himself with sentencing each of them to ten blows of the bamboo, and to be sent back to their own country. Semedo relates that he was spared the blows on account of his very bad state of health, but they were so severely inflicted on Father Vagnon, that the wounds troubled him for more than a month. As the completion of the same sentence, "our houses, our furniture, and especially our books were destroyed; the executioners crying out that we were unworthy to bear the name of men of letters. Then they put each of us into a small wooden cage, such as is used to transport criminals condemned to death from one place to another; chains were put on our hands and round our necks, our hair was left hanging down, and our clothes in disorder, as an evidence that we were strangers and barbarians; and thus, shut up like wild beasts, they carried us on the thirtieth of April from the prison to a tribunal, to get our cages sealed with the seal of the emperor. I cannot tell you the noise that was made with the iron chains by the serjeants and other officers who were conducting us; but I may tell you that they bore before us three great placards, with the sentence of the emperor written in large letters and forbidding any Chinese to hold the least communication with us; and in this manner we issued from Nankin, and remained thus shut in cages for the space of thirty days. When we arrived at the first town in the province of Canton, we were presented to the governor, who, after having sharply reprimanded us for having dared to preach a new law in China, put us into the hands of the mandarins. They dragged us through all the tribunals, in the midst of an incredible concourse of people, and then cast us out of their town, to take the road to Macao, where we arrived after some days' journey.

"The Christians left in prison after our departure were condemned to seventy strokes each. The two brothers, who were natives of China, after having been cruelly beaten, were sentenced, the one to serve the Masons at the Tartar Wall, the other to drag the imperial vessels with a tow-rope, as oxen and horses do. Of all the Christians it may be said that they displayed the greatest constancy; and, to the no small astonishment of their countrymen, showed in their countenances the joy that they felt in their souls in thus suffering for Jesus Christ."*

The enemies of Christianity, who had raised this violent persecution, and obtained the general proscription of the missionaries, were, nevertheless, not wholly successful, except at Nankin and Pekin; in other places, the Jesuits found help and a refuge among the Christian converts. Even at Pekin, there were two brothers, who, being Chinese by birth, were not included in the sentence of banishment, and continued to inhabit the place assigned by the Emperor as a cemetery for the missionaries, where the remains of Father Ricci had been laid; and though the eunuchs and the Bonzes, the former proprietors of the establishment, made every effort to get possession of it, and overwhelmed the brothers with abuse, Dr. Paul was there to protect them, to assert the inviolability of the emperor's donation, and especially the respect due to a place of sepulture; and this pious appropriation of the house and

* Alvarez Semedo, p. 825-4.

garden caused all the attempts of the Bonzes and eunuchs to fail.

The most recent establishment formed by the Jesuits, was that of the city of Han-Tcheou-Fou, and this became for them in some measure a harbour of refuge in the tempest. We have stated that Dr. Michel had courageously offered them an asylum in his house, in case of persecution; many went there accordingly, and when the sentence of banishment was published, they issued forth in open day accompanied by the principal Christians, in order to seem as if they obeyed the order of the emperor; but they afterwards secretly returned to the house of their generous neophyte, and found there a shelter for themselves as well as a chapel for the celebration of the holy offices.

In the environs of Tchang-Hai, Dr. Paul afforded equal hospitality to the missionaries. It had been thought that by striking at the pastors, the flocks would be more easily dispersed, but, as in the early times of Christianity, the fervour of the apostles and of the faithful triumphed over the malice of their persecutors. They assembled in secresy and silence in private houses, sometimes here, sometimes there, in order not to awaken the suspicions of the enemy, and they employed a thousand ingenious stratagems to elude the vigilance of the mandarins and their satellites; and thus, by prudence and courage, the Christians were still able to be present at the holy sacrifice, and perform in common their religious duties. The scene afforded a touching reminiscence of those which took place in early ages in the Catacombs.

The Almighty, who often brings good out of evil, permitted these times of trial and suffering to become an occasion of increase and progress to the mission of China. The missionaries and Christian converts being obliged to hide themselves in order to escape persecution, were widely dispersed, and often taken to places where they had not hitherto been known, and when the tempest was succeeded by a calm, they were permitted to exercise around them the salutary influence of a good example.

They even founded quite quietly in the neighbourhood of Nankin a college, where several young Chinese prepared themselves by the study of religion and letters, to become one day preachers of the Gospel to their countrymen. After the lapse of about three years, the confessors of the faith, who had been exiled to Macao, endeavoured to return secretly to their missions, and resume their apostolic labours. The first who ventured this was Father Semedo; when his attempt was crowned with success, Father Vagnon made no delay in following his example, and soon not only all the old but several new missionaries were on their way to bear abundant consolation to the long desolate Christian communities.

Such is the appointed destiny of the servants of God upon earth; some few days of serenity, and many of gloom and tempest; a long series of trials alternating with short intervals of peace and joy. Life is a battle, and it is with good reason that the Christian community is called the Church militant.

Whilst the mission of China, after having suffered greatly for a time, was about to re-enter the lists with renewed ardour, there was one heroic gladiator of the faith, struggling with intrepid perseverance against the malice of men and the fury of the elements, in the hope of kindling the light of gospel truths, in the capital of Thibet, the very centre of Buddhism.

The missionaries of the middle ages travelled, as we have seen, over all the countries of High Asia, even into those that were all but inaccessible, to bear thither the light and civilisation of Christianity. They preached in China, Tartary, and Thibet, and numerous churches had arisen among nations so long unknown to Europeans. There was not at that time any one region of the far East, however remote and distant, into which some intrepid monk had not made his way.

These preachers of the Gospel became nomades with the

Tartars of the Desert, and worked their way through the lofty snow-covered mountains of Thibet into the seemingly impregnable fortress of Buddhism. We have seen in the thirteenth century, for example, Oderic de Friuli pursuing alone his apostolic career in those distant regions, scattering the seeds of the doctrine of salvation, and enrolling under the banner of Christ the men of every race and language.

When, however, at the end of the sixteenth, and the beginning of the seventeenth centuries, new apostles appeared in those countries, they found none of the Christians of the middle ages. Those missions which once promised so abundant a harvest, had been devastated by storms, or dried up for want of nourishment, and the field was overgrown by thorns and brambles. At Pekin, when Father Ricci reached it, the flourishing Christian congregation of John of Monte Corvino had entirely disappeared, and left not a trace, nor even a recollection behind it. Father Goès in traversing Tartary made a similar observation. In all his long journeyings he met only Mussulmans and Buddhists; but the religious practices of the latter, borrowed, as we have said, from those of the Catholic worship, deceived the Indian caravans, and induced them to report that they had met numerous Christians going to Cathay. Similarly mistaken information had led the missionaries of India to suppose that there were Christians in Thibet; and one of them, Father d'Andrada, a Portuguese, formed the bold project of penetrating into that country; and accordingly on the 30th of March, 1624, he set off from Agra with Father Marquez, to follow the Great Mogul, who was going to Cashmere. It is known that the Jesuits were at that time very popular in India, and exercised great influence over its sovereign.

When they reached Delhi, they learned that a caravan of devout Buddhists were about to make a pilgrimage to a famous pagoda, distant about six weeks' journey from Agra; and "as for twenty years," says d'Andrada, "our Fathers had been repeating that there were Christian states in those regions, I now resolved, since I could go in company, to find out for myself about those countries; and I could do this the more easily, as one of us would be sufficient to go with the Great Mogul to Cashmere. I set out accordingly for Thibet, with one of our brethren and two attendants."

D'Andrada issued from Delhi at an early hour in the morning, wearing the Indian tunic that formed his customary attire; but he had taken care to put a Thibetan costume underneath, so that as soon as he was beyond the gates of the city he could, by taking off his tunic, appear completely disguised. He did, indeed, meet several Christians and people belonging to the suite of the Great Mogul, who did not recognise him; and he then took an opportunity of leaving the high road, and proceeding by various cross paths, to join the Buddhist pilgrims, then encamped on the frontiers of Hindostan. The caravan began its march, but at Sirinagar (the City of Happiness), the capital of Cashmere, D'Andrada and his companions were arrested as fugitives from the territory of the Grand Mogul; and they were about to be loaded with chains and sent back to their sovereign, in accordance with an international treaty between the two countries, when they explained with such frankness their situation and the purpose of their journey, that they were allowed to pass, and soon reached the foot of the Himalaya.

"We then began," says D'Andrada, "to climb these lofty mountains, which have not their like perhaps on the surface of the globe. It took us two days' march to cross one. In some places the passage between them is so narrow, that we could only just put one foot before the other, and for a long way we had to go first on one side and then on the other, clinging to the rocks with our hands, and at a single false step we should have been dashed to pieces. Some of these rocks are as upright as if they had been formed with a plumb line. The Ganges flows like a gulf at their feet, and the enormous volume of water that it rolls among their cliffs and precipices makes a frightful uproar, which, repeated by the echoes, still further increases the alarm felt by the traveller across these narrow paths. The ascent is difficult enough, but the descent is still more perilous, for one knows not what to cling to. We were several times obliged to turn round and go backwards, as if we had been going down a ladder, and to step with the greatest possible caution; but we had constantly before our eyes the example of pagans who were braving all these difficulties to honour their gods, many even so advanced in years that they could hardly drag themselves along, and we had surely a far better motive for conquering all obstacles than they.*

These courageous pilgrims usually proceeded in single file, one after the other, for the path would seldom allow of two going abreast; and when he who headed the column perceived any danger, he intimated it by chanting in a loud voice the name of the pagoda they were going to visit, and the word was repeated successively by all the travellers. These mountainous regions were mostly without inhabitants, and no living creature was met with in the defiles but troops of wild yaks and musk deer, which exhaled a powerful odour as they fled away. From time to time, however, in some picturesque part of a deep ravine, they came upon a Buddhist temple, the wealth of which quite astonished Father d'Andrada. The Lamas attached to the service of these temples also attracted his attention, though he by no means looked at them as admiringly as he did at the pagodas. "Their aspect alone," he says, "announced that they were ministers of Satan; one, especially, who was very old, and had hair, moustaches, and nails of a hideous length. This monstrous being sat motionless as a statue, receiving the homage of the pilgrims without ever opening his mouth, though they prostrated themselves

* Relation, p. 4.

before him and kissed his feet with the most profound respect.

After having crossed several mountains, some of which displayed all the luxuriance of the most magnificent vegetation, the caravan arrived at a town where the magistrates were struck by the appearance of Father d'Andrada, thinking he had not the manners or the aspect of a merchant, and they subjected him to a severe examination. The missionary declared that he was a Portuguese, and that he was going into Thibet to seek for one of his brothers, who several years ago had been lost beyond the snowy mountains (the Himalayas.) In examining his luggage there were found some black cassocks, which caused great astonishment, as the Thibetans never have garments of that colour; but their suspicions were allayed when the missionary told them that they were mourning robes that he had had prepared, according to the custom of his country, in case he should have the misfortune to find his brother dead.*

By degrees, as the travellers advanced, the country rose higher and higher, and the temperature became more and more formidable. They crossed several arms of the Ganges by means of bridges of rope, along which they had to slide at the imminent risk of drowning in the flood below; and then they came to mountains covered by deep snow, beneath which they could hear the roar of many an impetuous torrent. " It is astonishing," says D'Andrada, " that these rapid powerful streams do not carry away the snow; but it sometimes falls into them from the neighbouring mountains in such masses, that they can only just force an opening in it, through which the water rushes with a terrible noise, and the unfortunate traveller can never assure himself of the solidity of the snow on which he steps, but runs constant risk of being swal.owed up and buried alive in some of these abysses.

* Relation, p. 9.

Six weeks after leaving Sirinigar, the caravan came to the famous pagoda of Badid, to which devout Buddhists flock from all the countries of Asia. There is in the neighbourhood a vast monastery for the numerous monks of the district, and the pagoda of Badid is built at the foot of a mountain, whence issues a boiling spring, which divides itself into three streams, that run into three perfectly cold ponds. The mingling of these waters of different temperatures, forms a tepid bath, into which the pilgrims plunge, in the firm persuasion that this water is able to purify not only their bodies but their souls from every stain; and they undertake these long and dangerous journeys to seek in these salutary baths the remission of their sins.

The monks of the monastery explained to Father d'Andrada the origin of the boiling spring. They told him that formerly the element of fire, touched by repentance for the numerous crimes he had committed in burning so many houses, towns, and forests, and desolating so many countries, had gone to ask pardon of the powerful deity of Badid, who ordered the great criminal to throw himself at his feet, in order to receive absolution for his iniquities. The fire was so happy, however, to find himself at the foot of this beneficent pagoda, that he took up his permanent abode there, and the spring that gushed forth at that spot soon afterwards became boiling. Father d'Andrada ventured to make one remark in reply to this explanation, and asked how it happened that the fire having so clearly seen the error of its ways, and repented of them, should still be found so often committing the same faults? Why, if the fire was thus humble and contrite at the foot of Badid, there should be still so many conflagrations?

The Lamas, however, were not at all at a loss for an answer; they replied with one voice, that the fire that still did so much mischief in the world was nevertheless only the fifteenth part of that element. That the fourteen other parts were certainly subjugated at the feet of Badid; and that if they should ever happen to escape, we should see some rather different effects of fire in the world.

The Lamas also mentioned that this pagoda had the virtue of transforming into gold all metals brought to it, but that at present the deity would not perform the miracle, because he was angry at the avarice of a certain locksmith, who had thrown an immense mass of iron into the water that bubbled at his feet.

"After that," says D'Andrada, "they related to me many other nonsensical impostures, and all that is certain is, that the monks of this monastery receive enormous contributions in gold and precious stones.

The pagoda and monastery of Badid are buried in snow for nine months in the year, and then the neighbouring villages are deserted, and the inhabitants and monks retire to a deep valley, three or four days' journey off, where the cold is not so severe nor the snow so deep.

The people of this country eat their mutton raw, or perhaps slightly scorched on the outside, and the fat and some parts of the feet are regarded as the daintiest morsels; they also tear and devour the entrails, without giving themselves much trouble about cleaning them. Sometimes they cook their meat a very little, but they say that it entirely loses its flavour and goodness when thoroughly done."

The caravan was obliged to stop at a village in one of the valleys, in order to await a favourable moment for crossing the desert, through which lies the way to Thibet, and which can only be crossed during two months in the year. For the other ten it is entirely blocked up and impenetrable. This desert is intersected by a vast range of mountains, which cannot be crossed in less than twenty days; and where there are neither human habitations, nor trees, nor grass; nothing, in fact, but rocks covered with snow. During two months the roads are practicable, not because they are free from snow, but because it is as hard as marble, and even horses do not leave on it the slightest trace of their footsteps. As neither wood nor any kind of fuel can be found on this pitiless soil, travellers are obliged to live on the roasted corn and snow they bring with them, and only people in robust health can possibly endure such a journey, even under its most favourable circumstances.

Whilst the caravan was awaiting the period for this arduous passage, there arrived in the valley some emissaries from the King of Sirinagar, with orders to seize Father d'Andrada and his companions, and to take them back to him bound hand and foot; but no sooner had this intelligence reached the missionary, than he resolved on the, perhaps rash, step of making his escape, and crossing the desert without the caravan, although the proper moment for the passage was not yet come. He passed the night, therefore, in obtaining the necessary instructions, and set off at daybreak with two Christian servants, and a native of the country, who was to serve him as a guide.

The four travellers proceeded on their way, with an iron-pointed staff in their hands, and a wallet filled with roasted barley on their backs. For the first two days they made all possible haste for fear of being pursued, but then a great quantity of snow falling, compelled them to slacken their march, and the next morning they saw three men coming after them, who very soon overtook them. They commanded D'Andrada to turn back, and threatened the severest punishments in case of disobedience; and they informed the guide that his wife and children were already imprisoned, and his goods confiscated by the chief of the tribe. These tidings shook his resolution, and he returned, but Father d'Andrada took no notice of the threats of the emissaries, but continued on his way with his two servants, without any one venturing to stop him.

"Then," he says, "we plunged into the desert and struggled on with difficulty, sometimes up to our waists in snow, sometimes up to our shoulders, and never less than knee deep, and occasionally dragging ourselves at full length along the surface of it, as if we were swimming. Such were the labours of the day, and the night brought us but little rest. We spread our cloaks upon the snow, and covered ourselves as well as we could with others, but very frequently the snow fell so thick upon us that we were obliged to rise and shake it off that we might not be buried. The cold was so severe, that we had lost all feeling in various parts of the body,—principally the hands, feet, and face.

"Once when I tried to hold something, a bone came out of one of my fingers, but I was not aware of it till I saw the blood on my hand; while our feet were so swelled and numbed, that if a hot iron had touched them we should not have felt it. We went on in this way till we reached the summit of those lofty mountains where may be seen the sources of the Ganges, and of another great river that waters the country of Thibet.* We had almost lost our sight, but I myself had suffered less than my two servants from the precautions I had taken, though for five and twenty days I could not read a letter of my breviary."

The reader may possibly think there is some exaggeration in this account; but as we have traversed the same regions ourselves, and undergone the hardships of a similar journey, we know by experience that the narrative of Father d'Andrada is rather below the reality. There are miseries and sufferings to be borne that no description can do justice to, which must be felt to be understood; but those who have always led an easy comfortable life, by the domestic fireside, can have a very imperfect idea of what may be the horrors of cold and hunger and thirst in the midst of a desert like this.

On reaching the summit of the mountain chain, the three travellers discovered before them a vast snow-covered plain

---

* Doubtless the Yarou-Dzambo.

stretching to the horizon, and unfortunately their sight was so dazzled and weak, that they could not even discern the long black poles, that have been planted at certain distances along these steppes, to guide the caravans. The immeasurable plain seemed to them entirely white, a boundless, trackless sea of snow. How were they to continue their journey? Their strength too was exhausted, and their scanty provisions almost consumed. The situation was a frightful one! D'Andrada, desirous at all events of saving the lives of his two servants, advised them to return to the village of Mana, where they had left the caravan; as the way would be entirely a descent, they might easily reach it in six days, and need not fear losing their way, since they only had to retrace their steps. As for himself, he would seek out some shelter among the rocks, where he might be protected from the wind and snow, and would endeavour to await the arrival of the caravan. He had still barley for eight or ten days, and would put his trust in Providence. This plan having been agreed on, they spread their cloaks, and lay down to try to get a little rest.

As soon as day dawned, D'Andrada urged his two servants to set off, as the smallness of their stock of food made it necessary that they should not lose a moment; but whether from fear, or from attachment to their master, they burst into tears, and declared they would not go without him. D'Andrada did all he could to encourage them, but he could not conquer their reluctance, and was at last obliged to set off with them, though he greatly dreaded having to return to the village where he was threatened with being taken prisoner. They passed once more all the places where they had endured to no purpose so many sufferings, and "the way appeared to me," says D'Andrada, "much easier, as it was a continua descent; but my servants suffered much from the blisters on their feet, which hindered their walking. We dragged ourselves along for three consecutive days and a half. Towards the end of that day we heard something like the voice of a man, crying in the desert, and though we could not see him, we directed our steps towards the place whence the voice seemed to come, and met a peasant, who gave us some good news." Firstly, the companion of D'Andrada, the brother who had remained at Mana, on account of the bad state of his health, was quite well again, and ready to set off with the caravan; secondly, the authorities of the district had become more kindly disposed towards the missionary, and instead of wishing to make him prisoner, had sent him some provisions, barley, meal, honey, and some furs to protect him from the cold; and as they had considered it an impossibility for him to cross that vast desert plain in this season, they had sent off a messenger to bring him back, and guide him to a safe place, where he might wait for the caravan.

Father d'Andrada, greatly comforted by these good tidings, gave himself up with confidence to his guide, and after another three days' march, reached a mountain gorge inhabited by shepherds, who received the party into their tents with frank and cordial hospitality. The caravan was not long in coming up with them, and then D'Andrada had the happiness of meeting the brother whom he had left so ill perfectly restored to health. As to himself, some days of rest and good milk diet sufficed to restore his strength. "I felt, indeed," he says, "better than I had ever been, and the only indisposition that remained, was the extreme weakness of my eyes, which could not bear the light at all."

The caravan had to stop at this encampment for six weeks, when the snow melted, and it resumed its march, following the path pursued with so little success by Father d'Andrada, but which was now in a more practicable state. A courier, according to custom, preceded the caravan, to announce its coming to the sovereign of Thibet, and inform him of various particulars concerning the travellers, and D'Andrada must certainly have been pointed out as the most distinguished person of the party, for three horses were sent to meet him,

10*

that he might make his entrance in a somewhat dignified manner. "Three days before our arrival, three horses were sent to us, for myself, my companion, and a servant, and they came in good time, for at our entrance into the town the people thronged around us, and the women rushed to the windows to gaze at us, as if we had been wonderful curiosities. The king did not show himself, but the queen was upon a kind of balcony of her palace as we passed, and we bowed profoundly to her, and then went on to a house that was ready to receive us. The king imagined we were merchants, and that we brought him some valuable jewels, and could not conceive that any motive but the desire of gain could have tempted us to undertake so painful a journey; when he was undeceived on this point his satisfaction in our arrival appeared wonderfully diminished, and he put off for three or four days the granting us an audience. He inquired, however, what was the real motive of our journey, and I replied that we had not come to Thibet to buy or sell, since we were not traders; that I was very grateful for the favours that had been granted me, but earnestly begged for an hour's audience, during which I would explain to him the reasons that had brought me to his dominions, and I assured him beforehand they were such as would give him great satisfaction."

The king soon sent for Father d'Andrada, received him very kindly, and conversed a long time with him by means of an interpreter, a Mussulman of Cashmere. The missionary stated that he had undertaken this long and perilous journey to find out whether there were, as it was said, still Christians in Thibet; that formerly preachers of that true religion had penetrated into the country, but that it was to be feared that by this time the faith they had planted must be much weakened and possibly corrupted. He had come, therefore, to explain once more the principles of true Christianity, and to destroy the superstitions that had grown up in their stead.

The king appeared to comprehend very little indeed of this speech, perhaps partly because the interpreter, being a Mussulman, had no mind to exert himself in the interests of Christianity. Father d'Andrada perceived this, and threatened, if he were not more accurate in his interpretation, to have him punished, and employ a pagan.

The king prolonged the conversation in some measure, in order that the queen, who had come and hidden herself behind a curtain, might listen to it; and at last her majesty, being tormented by curiosity, sent to the king to say that she must absolutely see these men, and soon after made her appearance; she put many questions to them, and she was subsequently present at all the audiences granted them.

It is much to be regretted that father d'Andrada did not keep any record of these conversations with the king and queen of Thibet; they could hardly have failed to be of some interest. All that we know, is that the missionary succeeded in gaining the sympathy and goodwill of the prince and of the principal personages of the city, and that he was authorised to present himself at court whenever he chose, with the assurance of being always welcome. He also had an abundant allowance of provisions sent to him daily—rice, mutton, flour, butter, grapes, wine. The grapes were of two sorts—the one small and black, but very sweet, the other large, white, and sour. They come from a place ten or twelve days' journey from the city.

These details may help us to verify the town which Father d'Andrada calls *Caparangua*, but which is not to be found under that name in any map, and indeed, during our stay in Thibet we never heard such a name mentioned. We know the kind of grapes he speaks of; there are many at Lha-Ssa, and we were told they came from Ladak and Hamil. The town of Caparangua, therefore, may have been situated between Cashmere and Ladak, towards the northern extremity of the chain of the Himalayas.

Father d'Andrada could not make a long stay at Caparangua, as he had promised to rejoin the Great Mogul, whom he had left to undertake this journey. He feared too that if he did not profit by the good season, he might find the roads blocked up by snow, and he therefore begged the king to grant him his dismissal; but his majesty pressed him much to remain, and would only agree to his going on condition of his taking an oath to return in the following year. D'Andrada, who had remarked that both the court and the people were very favourably disposed to receive the light of the Gospel, joyfully gave the promise, and obtained also five conditions, drawn up in a written document, to which the king gave his assent. This paper is given by Father d'Andrada, as follows:—

"We, king of the great kingdom of Thibet, having felt great pleasure in the arrival of Father Antony d'Andrada, a Portuguese, to teach the holy law in our dominions, and regarding him as our master, grant to him full and perfect liberty to preach freely and teach our people the said law, and we forbid all persons from disturbing him in its exercise.

"We command, moreover, that a piece of ground shall be given to him whereon to build a church. We consent, that if there should arrive in our country any foreign merchants, the said religious man and his companions shall take no part in their traffic, in order that they may do nothing that might be incompatible with the dignity of their functions.

"We promise, besides, to give no credit to any reports that may be raised concerning them by the Mussulmans, being very that sure they who follow a law full of errors, would find a sweet satisfaction in vexing those who profess the true religion.

"We, furthermore, most earnestly solicit the Grand Provincial of the Indies to send us the said Father d'Andrada again, that he may instruct our subjects.

"Given at Caparangua, and sealed with our arms."*

* Relation, p. 26.

This is the form in which Father d'Andrada gives the document, and he also mentions that the king gave him several letters of recommendation to the princes of Cashmere, Agra, and Lahore, and gave orders that he should travel in Thibet "without being subject to the taxes and impositions by which the people are crushed." In return for these benefits Father d'Andrada presented to the king a fine painting on copper representing the Virgin and the Infant Jesus. "It was easy to see," he says, "that the king and all his court were sorry for our departure; and in bidding us farewell, he reminded us that we were to come again as soon as possible, because we '*carried his heart with us.*' He had us escorted not only to the frontiers of his kingdom but even across the desert, and gave orders privately that we should be everywhere provided with as much meat, rice, and butter as we required. Three days after our departure we were overtaken by three men, who brought us from the king some baskets containing more than a thousand peaches, which, though small, were of extremely pleasant flavour. The men told us that these peaches had been sent to the king from a town distant about fifteen days' journey." These peaches are, at Lha-Ssa, an object of considerable traffic; they have an exquisite flavour, and come, like the grapes, from Ladak : so that this circumstance tends to confirm the conjecture we have formed as to the probable situation of Caparangua.

The return journey of Father d'Andrada was performed with far less fatigue and suffering than the former one, and after having paid his respects to the Great Mogul, he went to Agra, where he was very anxiously expected by his brethren. He related to them the various incidents of his adventurous expedition, the good reception he had met with from the Thibetans, the deeply religious character of that people, and their readiness to receive the Christian faith. When the missionaries of Agra saw the decree of the king, and learned that Father d'Andrada had promised to return to him, they were inspired with the most fervent desire to accompany him, and to devote all their zeal to this mission; and the Provincial of the Indies, desirous of cherishing the germs of salvation deposited in a land so long the prey of Buddhist superstition, hastened the return of D'Andrada, and gave him four other missionaries as associates.

This new colony of apostles set forth in June, 1625. "We had," says D'Andrada, "many obstacles to surmount, although such as were not to be compared with those of our first journey, and we reached Thibet in the course of the month of August. Our return gave the king apparently much pleasure, for he sent men four days' journey to meet us, with horses and many presents, and orders that we were to be honourably received in all the places we should pass through. When we got to Caparangua we were lodged in a house next to that of the king's son. Some days afterwards, being obliged to go in person to an important war, he sent for us and desired us to give him our blessing. The expedition lasted six weeks, and when the king came back, he declared his resolution of having himself instructed in all the principal points of the Christian religion, and only desired to wait till we should have acquired the language of Thibet."

In one of his letters, dated the 15th of August, 1626, Father d'Andrada has left us some curious details, concerning the manners and customs of the Thibetans; and they are almost precisely such as we found them, more than two centuries afterwards, and have endeavoured to describe in our "Travels in Thibet," &c. We coincide too with his observation, that with this people the religious sentiment is extremely powerful, so much so, indeed, as to absorb almost all others. They seem to attend to industry, agriculture, and commerce only just sufficiently to satisfy the most rigorous exigencies of material life, and to regard this world merely as a place of passage, through which to accomplish a sad but short pilgrimage towards a better. This feeling is so deeply implanted in their minds, that the word for man in general in their language signifies "traveller;" and the earth counts for so little in their estimation, that, instead of saying, "What country are you from?" they say, "Under what part of the sky do you walk?"

Perhaps we may attribute to the strength of the religious sentiment, the prodigious number of Lamas to be seen in Thibet. There is no family that has not several among its members, and out of three brothers, two will generally embrace the religious vocation.*

The king of Caparangua used to be much attached to the Lamas before the arrival of Father d'Andrada; but by degrees he withdrew from them to approach more nearly the Christian missionaries; he used to like to hear them explain the principal points of Christian doctrine, and he learned the Catholic prayers, and repeated them with much devout feeling. "He often comes to us," writes Father d'Andrada, "though otherwise he goes into the house of no private person; and whenever he comes, he enters the church to say his prayers, and often repeats to us that as soon as he shall be sufficiently instructed he will have himself baptized and embrace the Christian religion."

This prince had, in fact, openly expressed his inclination for the new doctrine and his sympathy for the missionaries; and when they began to build their church and made a grand ceremony with it, he himself laid the first stone, and presided over a festival so entirely unusual among the Thibetans. These public manifestations did not fail to terrify the Lamas, and they had a public meeting, in which two of the principal members of the hierarchy, one the brother, and the other the uncle, of the king, were charged in the name of Buddha to use all their influence to turn him from Christianity, and induce him to abandon his resolution of getting himself baptized. They represented to him how shameful it would be if stran

* See vol. II. of the "Travels in Tartary and Thibet."

gers, who had come to the country only a few months ago, should persuade him to forsake the ancient faith of his fathers to embrace a new one of which he knew little or nothing. They pointed out also the serious dangers to which such a course of conduct would expose his royal authority; for as he was at war with several petty neighbouring sovereigns, he might have reason to dread irritating his own subjects against him, or setting at defiance a body so numerous as the Lamas, and whose power over the minds of all classes of the people was so irresistible.

The threats of a revolution did not, however, appear to shake the resolution of the king; and the Lamas, seeing him inaccessible to fear, tried the method of persuasion. They invited him to come and pass some time in their monastery, hoping that retirement, meditation, and prayer would effect some change in his sentiments. The prince consented to go and reside for two months with his brother, who was Grand Lama of the most renowned Buddhist monastery in the country. When it was supposed that he was sufficiently armed against the seductions of the strange religion, a proposal was made to Father d'Andrada for a public conference to discuss the respective merits of Buddhism and Christianity.

The conferences that took place were numerous, and chiefly concerning the nature of God and the system of the metempsychosis; and, according to D'Andrada, the Lamas admitted the Trinity in Unity, and their name for the first person signified *source* or *origin;* for the second, *book;* for the third, *intention,* or *love.* The dogma of the Incarnation was one of the main articles of their creed.

With respect to the metempsychosis, the Lamas held that God, having created all things in the beginning, created nothing more afterwards, and that only revivals and transformations now took place. The world contained a certain fixed number of souls, which, according to their good or bad actions, migrated into bodies more or less perfect. D'Andrada objected to this, that in that case reason and free will must be supposed in the inferior animals; and a Lama replied, that animals were endowed with intelligence, and consequently capable of good and evil actions. The wolf commits a sin when he kills a sheep, the cat when she eats a mouse, the spider when he strangles a fly. "Do you not see," he added, "that the tiger prefers flesh to grass, whilst a sheep would die of hunger by the side of a dead body? Who teaches animals to fly from human creatures, who would take or kill them?"

D'Andrada merely tells us that to any one armed with the weapons of the true faith, it was easy to refute, in a victorious manner, the arguments of the Lamas; but it is to be regretted that he has not left us more exact information concerning these interesting conferences. "The natives of Thibet," he says in conclusion, "are mild and pious in disposition; and during several months that I spent with them I never heard any kind of dispute. They have their rosaries almost always in their hands, and like to talk of heavenly things; they are very courteous, and treat strangers with the greatest kindness. Their women are continually employed in spinning or weaving, and some even cultivate the ground. The queen divides her time between prayer and work, and her favourite occupation is spinning. The men perform little manual labour, and in the summer are mostly at war or engaged in practising archery and the management of various weapons, or in wrestling, in which they are very adroit." The only thing the missionaries found to object to in this country was the thinness of the population, at least in comparison with that of Hindostan, which is very dense. But if the towns are less populous and less mercantile they are more adapted to apostolic labours, being far less corrupt and vicious. "This kingdom is also," says D'Andrada, "the entrance to many others of the same religion and speaking nearly the same language." Unfortunately, Father d'Andrada's narrative breaks off here, and we have no further information concerning the rising mission; though the Tartar history of the period affords ground for the conjecture that its success at first was considerable, but that this early success was what eventually caused its ruin by exciting the jealousy of the Lamas. The sovereign who had protected the missionaries lost his life in a revolution occasioned by his attachment to Christianity. There is every reason to believe that he had actually become a Christian, or at least that he had entirely renounced Buddhism, and that he had openly declared his determination to be baptized.

This prince, according to the Tartar historians, was named Tsan-Pa-Han, and it does not seem impossible that by some mistake in transcription it was altered into Caparangua, and used to designate the town in which he lived; for no such city as Caparangua is to be found in any geography. The dominions of this Tsan-Pa-Han were situated to the west of Lha-Ssa, and comprehended a great part of Thibet, as far as the sources of the Ganges; and Tartar historians say that this king wished to destroy the law of the Lamas, which he had forsaken, and to substitute for it a foreign religion; and that for that reason the *Typa*, or first minister of his kingdom, came to an understanding with the Telé-Lama, or Buddhist sovereign-pontiff, who reigned at Lha-Ssa, to oppose his projects; and they called in to their assistance a Mongol prince of the Koukou-Noor, a personage entirely devoted to the Lamas. He levied a considerable army, and advanced into Thibet, where a sanguinary battle took place, in which Tsan-Pa-Han was defeated and killed; and the Mongol prince occupied Thibet with his army, and was proclaimed *Han*, or sovereign, by the Talé-Lama, who exercises immense authority over the Buddhist populations of High Asia.*

It was doubtless in consequence of this revolution that the missionaries were compelled to abandon that part of Thibet, into which they had penetrated with so much toil and difficulty; and it is known that D'Andrada returned to Goa, and died by poison on the 6th of March, 1634.

* Recueil des Lettres Édifiantes, vol. xxiv. p. 11.

CHAPTER VII.

Revolutionary character of the Chinese.—Secret Societies.—Insurrection of the Sect of the White Lily.—Edict against Secret Societies.—Persecution of Christians.—Memorial in their favour.—Fall of the First Minister.—Doctor Paul.—The Mantchoo Tartars attack the Empire.—Their Chief swears to exterminate the Dynasty of Ming.—First successes of the Tartars.—Death of the Emperor Wang-Lié.—Curious Petition of the Christians.—Jesuits summoned to Pekin to make Cannon.—Discovery of the Monument of Si-Ngan-Fou.—Testimony of Father Semedo.—Progress of Conversions.—Sincere Piety of the Neophytes.—Admirable Conduct of a Christian General.—Death of Dr. Léon.—Biographical details concerning that illustrious Christian.—Dr. Paul First Minister.—He favours the Christians.—Commissions the Jesuits to Reform the Calendar.—Fathers Schall and Rho arrive at Pekin.—They are placed at the head of the Board of Celestial Literature.—Death of Dr. Paul.—Abject condition of his descendants.

THE revolution which in 1626 occasioned in Thibet the fall and death of Psan-Pa-Han, does not seem to have been an isolated fact. This event was doubtless intimately connected with that formidable insurrection which at the same epoch convulsed the Chinese empire, and was destined to bring about the overthrow of the dynasty of Ming, and to substitute for it the domination of the Mantchoo Tartars.

Strange notions have been taken up by Europeans of what is called the immobility of Asiatic nations; and learned writers have entered into very elaborate investigations of the question how the Chinese government could have subsisted without alteration for 4000 years. Many very erudite and ingenious solutions of the problem have been offered; but the fact they have taken so much pains to account for, happens to be not true, and no fact at all—a misfortune that has happened to other philosophical explanations. The Chinese have changed their maxims, renovated their institutions, tried various political combinations; and though there are certainly some that they never have tried, their history presents nearly the same phases as the governments of men of other nations.

China has assuredly no need to envy other countries for their facility in effecting revolutions, civil wars, and the tragical overthrow of dynasties; on the contrary, she might perhaps awaken envy in certain parties among ourselves for her skill in that department.

What would our European amateurs of revolution say if they should find that in the art of overthrowing society, they were after all mere children compared with the Chinese? And yet it undoubtedly is so; and the history of these people is little else than the narrative of a long series of catastrophes, that have shaken and disorganised the empire from its summit to its foundations.

One rather singular feature in the character of the Chinese, and which perfectly accounts for the numerous revolutions among them, is their decided taste for secret societies.

Whilst the preachers of the Gospel, animated by pure and ardent zeal, were traversing the provinces, founding missions, and seeking to establish the kingdom of Jesus Christ throughout the empire, there were other missionaries, inspired by a very different spirit—the spirit of disorder—who were labouring to overthrow the government, and recruiting all over the country their army of ambitious malcontents.

The vast association called Pé-Lien-Kiao, or sect of the White Lily, was organised in all the cities of the empire, and its ramifications extended also into the country. It had its chiefs, its watchwords, its secret nocturnal meetings, its secret printing and distribution among the people of the most violent diatribes against the government and the mandarins, and it only waited for a favourable moment to burst out openly into the insurrection that had been so long in preparation. The mandarins in the meanwhile were watching and endeavouring to paralyse the movements of the conspirators.

SECT OF THE WHITE LILY. 237

In 1622 one of the most dreaded chiefs of the sect of the White-Lily was arrested in the province of Chan-Tong; and immense agitation was created amongst the members of the association, for the government had given orders to the magistrates to force from this chief, by all imaginable tortures, the betrayal of the principal agents in the conspiracy. He remained, however, resolutely silent concerning his accomplices; but as they could not feel quite certain that his resolution would not be overcome by the cruelty of his tormentors, they resolved to succour him, and at the same time to save the society from ruin. They therefore suddenly attacked and captured the tribunal where he was detained, ransacked it from top to bottom, killed several mandarins, delivered Ly-Kong, and carried him about in triumph amid the acclamations of his friends.

After such a demonstration as this they could not draw back. Ly-Kong and his partisans declared themselves in a state of insurrection—appealed to all the discontented throughout the empire, and with the assistance also of the vagabonds and thieves, whom there was no difficulty in collecting, organised a little army, and after pillaging several villages, where they did not meet with the smallest resistance, they seized two towns of the third class, and fortified themselves in them as well as they could. The alarm was now given at Pekin, which was not very far distant; and the government hastened to send considerable bodies of troops to quell the insurrection before it should assume a too formidable aspect. Several battles took place with varying results. The rebels, bold as they were, were hardly strong enough to resist the amount of regular military force brought against them from all directions, and they abandoned the posts they had seized, and retired towards the province of Nankin, drawing after them bands of disorderly persons, who were proceeding to join them, and as they passed along the imperial canal, they captured and pillaged several large junks, that were carrying tribute from the provinces to Pekin.

The government, justly alarmed at the popular effervescence which was manifesting itself in various parts of the empire, gave orders to the mandarins, great and small, to make the most active exertions to discover the partisans of the White Lily, and when they had discovered them, to show them no mercy; and the enemies of the Christians eagerly seized on this occasion to renew their accusations against the missionaries and their neophytes. Under the pretence that they were in the habit of holding secret assemblies, they affected to confound them with the partisans of the insurrection, and from that time the Christians were given up to the hatred and malevolence of their persecutors.

The assessor, Kio-Tchin, who had in the preceding persecution displayed so much animosity against them, unfortunately occupied at this period the eminent position of prime minister, and he composed and published in all the provinces of the empire, a thundering manifesto against secret societies. He represented that their object was the subversion of all authority, and their means the preaching disobedience to the magistrates and the emperor; and after having drawn a most lugubrious picture of the calamities brought by such societies upon the government and the nation, he pointed out to the especial reprobation of all honest people the sects of the White Lily and of the Lord of Heaven, or Christians. As a proof, he said, that the members of these two associations had equally detestable purposes, and were animated by the same spirit of insubordination to the emperor's orders, it was well known that those strangers who had come to propagate in the central empire the fatal sect of the Lord of Heaven had been expelled by a decree of the sovereign, but that, without paying any regard to the expression of the imperial will, they had continued to inhabit their former residences, and to spread with the same audacity the poison of their bad doctrines. The minister's manifesto concluded with the following words. "The law of the Lord of Heaven is false; it deludes men, it encourages them to hold secret assemblies. In former years, the magistrates presented to the emperor some memorials against the partisans of that sect, and severely prohibited their religion; and now those who profess that bad doctrine are guilty of not obeying the will of the emperor. According to the laws of the empire, it would be necessary to pursue these people with rigour, and punish them severely; but being ignorant and insignificant persons, they do not deserve all the severity of the laws. As for the foreigners, let them be compelled to quit the empire, and let the native Chinese be imprisoned for a month and suffer the cangue; and they shall be afterwards taken before their respective tribunals, and exhorted upon their obedience to the emperor, and the avoidance of bad doctrines."

The Mandarins knew well, even without any such expressions as this of the minister's sentiments, that they would be doing what was very agreeable to him if they persecuted the Christians to the utmost. The opinions of Kio-Tchin were sufficiently notorious, and it was no secret that the best way now to get on at court was to declare yourself an enemy of the worshippers of the Lord of Heaven. The missions were now invaded by emissaries from the tribunals, who ransacked the chapels, and even the private oratories, and carried off the books, images, crosses, and all objects of devotion, to make them serve as materials for accusation. All the Christians who could be seized were loaded with chains and dragged to prison, and the greatest severity was shown to the catechists, whose business it was to examine the catechumens, and preside over the prayers and religious exercises in the absence of the missionaries. In the mission of Nankin alone, no less than forty persons became on this account the victims of the mandarins or their satellites. They were insulted and treated in the most shameful manner, to induce them to confess imagin ary crimes, and acknowledge themselves members of the White Lily Society, and partisans of the insurrection. An old man named André was so cruelly mangled by the rattan, that he expired in the tribunal in the presence of his judges, or rather his executioners.

During this new persecution, the missionaries were obliged again to quit the country, or to hide themselves in the most solitary places, in the deepest recesses of woods, or in caverns of the mountains, and there were some who could find no place of refuge but a cemetery, and who had to live in tombs, under the protection of the dead.

Although, however, the terror was general, the Christians were not wholly given up to the mercy of their persecutors. Dr. Léon maintained at Hon-Tcheou-Tou an attitude of dignity and courage; he opposed the departure of Father de la Roque, the superior of the mission, and desired him to remain in his house and perform in perfect freedom the duties of his ministry. Having summoned the Doctors Paul and Michel, he drew up, in concert with them and with Father de la Roque, a statement of the wide differences existing between the members of the White Lily Society and the worshippers of the Lord of Heaven. The manifesto of the *Colao* Kio-Tchin was then rigorously attacked by him; the accusations it contained against the Christians proved to be entirely false, and such as could only have proceeded from hatred and malice; and as soon as the memorial was finished, Dr. Paul set off to carry it himself to Pekin, and undertook to exert to the very utmost his influence among the grand dignitaries of the Court to get it presented to the emperor.

The prime minister, when he heard of the arrival of Dr. Paul in the capital, easily divined the purpose of his journey and by means of spies gained information of the memorial to be presented to the sovereign. He judged, therefore, that there was no time to lose, and immediately drew up an act of accusation specially directed against the Doctors Paul, Michel, and Léon, representing them as the heads of a secret society, the object of which was to overthrow the government and ruin the empire.

This affair might have proved disastrous and completely ruined the missions, but that Providence did not permit it to do so. At the very moment when Kio-Tchin thought himself most secure in his power, it was suddenly overthrown by one of those terrible and unexpected strokes to which the Mandarins of the Celestial Empire are constantly exposed. The disgrace of their chief persecutor was like the dawn of a brighter day to the missions of China, and the hope became brighter still when Dr. Paul was soon afterwards raised to the dignity of prime minister.

The imperial power, however, which could thus launch its destructive thunderbolts at the first men of the state, was itself to be attacked and undermined. The arbitrary administration of the eunuchs, and the exactions of the Mandarins had so exasperated the people of China and weakened the bonds of authority, that the spirit of revolt kindled by the secret societies was soon openly manifested from one end of the empire to the other. The dynasty of Ming, after having destroyed the Mongol power, founded in China, at the commencement of the twelfth century, by Tchinguiz-Khan, seemed now itself to have run its appointed course, and to have reached the term of its existence. It was no longer capable of struggling against its domestic enemies, and at the same time repelling on the frontiers the aggressions of a warlike and enterprising people.

The Mantchoo Tartars, long a mere tribe of wandering herdsmen, following their cattle about the banks of the rivers Amour and Sangari, had for some years past been issuing from their obscurity, and assuming a more important character; and the chiefs of the Eight Banners, after having carried on a fierce war amongst themselves, had at length united, in obedience to the strongest among them, to found a monarchy.

The government of Pekin, always accustomed to treat neighbouring states in the style of absolute sovereignty, had seen with no good will the progress of the Mantchoo power, and neglected no means of impeding its measures and frustrating its alliances; and it even at length presumed to seize and put to death a chief whom the Mantchoos had chosen for their king.

Fortunately, however, for the Tartars, this prince left a son old enough to succeed him; and to show that he was worthy to do so, he began his reign by avenging the death of his father. Scarcely had he been recognised as their head by the warriors of the Eight Banners than he organised an army, and making a sudden irruption into the province of Leao-Tong, he seized on Moukden, and struck terror into the whole country. He might have even continued his course to Pekin, from which he was not far distant, and demanded from the emperor an account of the assassination of his father; but he seems to have been capable of controlling his passions, and contented himself with sending an ambassador with a respectful letter, in which he begged the emperor to attribute to the transports of just indignation and grief the irruption made into his dominions; attributed the death of his father to the ministers, and professed himself ready to evacuate the territory he had captured, if the emperor would undertake that justice should be done on his guilty subjects. The Son of Heaven, either by mistake or contrivance, never saw the letter himself, but merely had it laid before his ministers, who had of course no desire to satisfy the offended sovereign, or to carry his complaints to their master.

The king of the Mantchoos, then irritated, with good reason, at the manner in which he was treated, swore to effect the ruin of the emperor and his ministers, and despatched to the court of Pekin a bold declaration of his grievances, and others of which the Mantchoo Tartars in general had to complain, ending with these laconic words:—"To avenge these seven injuries, I am about to reduce and subjugate the dynasty of Ming." In order to put his threat into immediate execution, he mounted his horse instantly, and without losing a moment, besieged and took the towns of Leao-Tong, and having ravaged that province, he passed into that of Pe-Tchi-Li, and advanced to the very gates of Pekin, after having carried fire and sword along his whole route. But, notwithstanding his great success, he appeared to be satisfied with having shown the Chinese what the Mantchoos were capable of; and he returned now to his own country laden with the spoils of two rich provinces, and having audaciously assumed the title of Emperor of China, with the significant addition of Tien-Ming, that is to say, "Order of Heaven."

The imperial government now understood, somewhat too late, how wrong it had been to think so slightingly of these Tartars, hitherto peaceably occupied in the care of their flocks and herds; and it resolved, without allowing them time to grow more powerful than they already were, to send an immense army to crush them at once, in order to avoid the danger of having hereafter to contend, at the same time, with enemies from within and from without. An imperial force of 600,000 men, marched to Mantchuria, but in the very first battle, it was defeated, and left on the field no less than 50,000 men.

The Chinese infantry, exhausted by long marches, could not stand a moment before the fiery Mantchoo cavalry, who pursued the fugitives to the very walls of Pekin; but again, Tien-Ming, instead of profiting by the opportunity of the signal advantages he had gained to lay siege to the capital of the empire, returned a second time, as if over-awed, to his own dominions. He seems to have understood, that before undertaking so great a conquest, he must take time to organize his own people, and especially to subject completely to his authority the Eight Banners of Mantchuria.

In the meantime, the emperor Wan-Lié died, after a reign

of forty-seven years, during the earlier part of which he governed with wisdom and ability; and he deserves that a history of Christianity should record his name, since it was chiefly to him that Father Ricci and the other missionaries owed the favour they enjoyed in the empire. As we have seen, he received them into his palace, granted them for a long time a pension to subsist on, permitted them to preach the Gospel freely in the capital and the provinces, and gave them a fine and extensive piece of ground, in the environs of Pekin, for a cemetery. History reproaches him with having allowed himself to be governed by his eunuchs, and with having in his old age abandoned to them his authority; and it was in these latter years that the persecutions of the Christians, of which we have spoken, broke out, and in which many of the missionaries were driven from the empire. But Wan-Lié did not live to see the terrible revolution that he had in some measure prepared by his excessive weakness, and which resulted in the complete destruction of his family, and the subjection of his country to a foreign yoke.

Wan-Lié was succeeded by Tai-Chan, who reigned only four months, and left his power to his son Tien-Ki, who, had he longer held the reins of empire, would have been able to restore order to China, and as it was, he roused the sinking courage of his subjects, and inspired them with the hope of subduing the insurgents and repulsing the Tartars.

As Tien-Ki received favourably all proposals made to him, with the view of effecting improvements in the state of his army and rendering them a more equal match for their enemies the Tartars, it was thought this would be a good opportunity to get the missionaries, who had taken refuge at Macao, recalled, and to restore to freedom those who were hidden in the provinces. As they had been banished by a decree of the emperor, the declared will of the sovereign alone could permit them to re-appear, and such a declaration it was by no means easy to obtain. The attempt was made, nevertheless, for an affair must be desperate indeed for a Chinese to give it up as hopeless. The cleverest of the Christian converts discussed the matter among themselves, and at length their fertile imaginations hit upon the following plan. A memorial was to be addressed to the emperor on the subject of the contest with the Tartars; the Christian doctors undertaking the composition of the piece. A moving picture was drawn of the horrible calamities entailed by the war, the ravage of the country, the slaughter of men, the destruction of towns, the ruin of commerce, arts, and industry, which had now been going on for years, without its being possible to stop the course of these disasters, notwithstanding the enormous sacrifices of men and money made by the empire. At the conclusion of this dismal description, allusion was made to the fault committed by the Chinese government, in driving out the European strangers, men virtuous, learned, capable of conducting with success the most important affairs, and possessing in a supreme degree the knowledge of mathematics, and doubtless of many extraordinary inventions that might have done good service to the state, if these men had still, as formerly, inhabited the Celestial Empire. It was then suggested that, possibly, these European strangers might not be all gone; that so many persons would hardly, in so short a time, have traversed so vast an empire, by paths so difficult; and the petitioners prayed that the emperor, in his wisdom and solicitude for the welfare of his people, would order that they should be diligently sought for, and if any could be found, have them brought to Pekin, to give their advice as to the mode of carrying on the war with the Tartars, and also to preside over the casting of cannon,—an art in which, it was added, they particularly excelled.*

This curious document is attributed by Adam Schall, to

---

* Porrecto supplici libello, quo facultatem adeundi curiam in eaque commorandi rogabat, ad exhibendam artem quam quæ se ferebat tormentorum æneorum.—*Historica Narratio Missionis Sinensis, ex litteris P. Adami Schall*, cap. l. p. 4.

Father Lombard himself; but, according to Alvarez Semedo, the Chinese doctors were the authors of it. It appears that the missionaries were not much pleased with this stratagem. "Our Fathers," says Semedo,* "made great opposition to the means that were taken to re-establish them, seeing that they were entirely ignorant of the military art, and thought it would have been better to have found some other pretext; but Dr. Léon, who was one of the principal actors in the comedy, replied to their objections:—'My Fathers, do not make yourselves uneasy. If they propose to make warriors of you do you make use of the title as the tailor does of his needle, which is of no use to him but to pass his thread through; when the stuff is sewn, and the garment finished, he leaves it, having no longer occasion for it. Only come back by the emperor's order, and you may afterwards easily change the warlike weapon for the studious pen, and instead of fighting you can write, for the defence of Jesus Christ, against the superstitions of the Infidels.'"

At last the memorial was drawn as Dr. Léon, who well understood the art, desired; and it was presented, and by the help of our friends, placed in the hands of the emperor, who replied as we wished, and sent it to the minister of war, who not only verified it, but added that he believed, certainly, that our Fathers could, by the secrets of their mathematics, so enchant the Tartars, that they should be unable to make use of their weapons. And then it was ordered that the Fathers should be immediately sought for; but it needed not to go far to find them, since those who got the order knew perfectly well where they were.†

This happy event was for all the Christians in China a cause of great joy, and it was certainly not very difficult to find the missionaries. Father de la Roque, the superior of the mission of Han-Tcheou-Fou, was hidden in the environs of the town, in

---

* Alvarez Semedo, p. 355.
† Histoire universelle du grand royaume de la Chine, p. 864.

a house of Dr. Léon, and he was now officially desired to present himself at court, with two brethren of his own selection. The Fathers Dias and Lombard, the Superior-general of the missions of China, having received a similar notice, hastily made their preparations, and returned to Pekin, where they entered publicly as in triumph, and followed by an immense concourse of people. They went first to the office of the minister of war, who had summoned them, and he received them with every expression of sympathy, and offered them a residence in the Palace of War. The missionaries, however, excused themselves from accepting this favour, alleging that as they had not yet rendered the state any service, they could not deserve it, and would prefer resuming their former abode, where they had a church and a house adapted to their mode of life.

Their restoration to their old residence too would appear to the public as a virtual repeal of the decree of banishment. When they found themselves once more installed in Pekin, the missionaries did not make great haste to began casting cannon, and fabricating implements of war, wherewith to exterminate the insurgents and the Tartars; but, rejoicing to see once more their beloved neophytes, gave themselves up with fervour to their apostolic labours.

Whilst the missions of China were thus unexpectedly restored to animation, it pleased Providence to permit that their progress and prosperity should be still farther promoted by a most remarkable discovery. It was just at this period that there was dug up at Si-ngan-Fou the remarkable stone monument spoken of in the beginning of this work, and which offers such convincing proof that Christianity was flourishing in China in the seventh century. As Father Alvarez Semedo was in China at the time of this discovery, and examined at leisure this important inscription, we will here refer to what he says on the subject.

" In the year 1625, as they were digging the foundation of

an edifice to be erected near the city of Si-ngan-Fou, the capital of the province of Chan-Si, the workmen struck upon a stone tablet, more than nine spans long, by four broad, and rather more than one thick. One of its extremities terminated in a pyramidal form, the slope of the sides of which was about two spans from the summit to the base. On the face of this pyramid was a cross, well formed, and terminating in *fleur-de-lys*, like that which is engraved on the tomb of the Apostle St. Thomas, in the town of Meliapour, and such as were formerly used in Europe.

"This cross was covered and surrounded by clouds, and had three lines written beneath it horizontally, and in characters commonly used in China, and so clearly and distinctly engraved that they could easily be read. The entire surface of the stone had similar characters inscribed upon it, only not of the same size, and there were others of a foreign kind that could not be made out.

"No sooner had the Chinese discovered and cleaned this precious treasure of a venerable antiquity, than, urged by the curiosity that is natural to them, they ran to the house of the governor, to give him information of the discovery. He came quickly to the place where the stone was, examined it with attention, and had it raised upon a handsome pedestal, and covered with a roof supported on pillars, to protect it from the injuries of the weather, and leave it, nevertheless, free to the observation of spectators, who seemed as if they could not sufficiently contemplate so august a monument of the religion of their ancestors. He desired, moreover, that this valuable memorial should be preserved within the enclosure of a Bonze temple, and near to the place where it had been found.

"It would be impossible to calculate the number of people who came from all directions to see this stone, some admiring it for its antiquity, others for the novelty of its characters which to them appeared foreign; and as the light of the Gospel and the knowledge of our religious doctrines are now diffused nearly throughout the empire, a pagan, who was an intimate friend of Dr. Léon, having heard of the mysteries alluded to in the inscription, thought to oblige him by sending him a copy of it, and did so, though the friends were at a distance of six weeks' journey from one another; the Christian Mandarin living in the town of Han-Tcheou-Fou, where our Fathers almost all took refuge in the last persecution.

"Three years afterwards, in 1629, some of our Fathers travelled into the province of Chan-Si with a Christian Mandarin named Philip, who wished to have them in his company during a mission with which he was charged to that country. They were not there long before they built a church and a residence for the missionaries, at Si-ngan-Fou, the capital of the province; where God had brought to light so precious a testimony of the possession formerly taken in His name of this flourishing kingdom by the preachers of His law, and had permitted his testimony also to be made use of for the confirmation of His people and their restoration to their ancient rights.

"Happily for me I was one of the first of those destined to advance the affairs of this new church, and this humble residence; and I esteem this so much the more fortunate for me that it has enabled me to view and examine this inscription at my leisure.

"Among the Chinese letters there are several that represent the names of priests and bishops who flourished at that time in the empire. There are others that were not so immediately recognised as Greek and Hebrew characters, but they form only the names of the same persons. I went to Cranganor in India to consult Father Anthony Fernandez on the interpretation of these letters, knowing that he is versed in the books of the first Christians converted by St. Thomas; and he assured me that these were Syriac characters, and resembled those still in use."*

* Histoire Universelle du Grand Royaume de Chine, p. 289.

The discovery of this monument of Si-ngan-Fou made a great sensation in all the provinces of the empire, and contributed not a little to the success of the missionaries. The Christians, who had of late had to endure so many insults and outrages, were now enjoying high consideration from both the Mandarins and the people, and especially since the most illustrious of their neophytes, Dr. Paul, had been raised to the rank of Calao, or prime minister. Seeing a worshipper of the "Lord of Heaven" at the head of the government was to the Chinese a most powerful argument in favour of the religion. At this period conversions were very numerous, and several new missionaries came to partake the labours of the old; new churches were built, and notwithstanding the troubles that disturbed the empire the number of converts was rapidly increasing. In 1627, it was calculated that there were thirteen thousand Christians dispersed through seven of the provinces; namely Kiang-Si, Tche-Kiang, Kiang-Nan, Chang-Tong, Chan-Si, Chen-Si, and Pe-Tche-Ly;* and in ten years more they had increased to forty thousand. This number may indeed be considered insignificant in relation to the enormous population of China; but if it is remembered that these results were obtained in less than forty years, in spite of immense difficulties in gaining access to the interior of the country, of innumerable obstacles and of sanguinary persecutions; and if also it is taken into consideration that this amount of success was obtained among the most anti-religious people on the face of the earth, it cannot be said that it was not satisfactory; and it may be received as evidence of the possibility by zeal and perseverance of fertilising the soil most ungrateful and most unpromising to the cultivator.

During the first year of the preaching of the gospel in China, the neophytes were not recruited in the higher ranks of society. We have related that the first Christian convert

* Martino Martinio, de Statu et qualitate C'ristianorum in Sina, p. 16.

of China was a poor dying man, found by Father Roger in the fields, where he had been abandoned by his family, and who breathed his last almost immediately after he had received baptism. In the frivolous estimation of the world this was not a brilliant beginning, but the gaining of the soul of this poor man was a conquest as precious in the sight of God as that of the rich and powerful Calao. The Church, in receiving the unfortunate with peculiar tenderness, proclaims aloud the holy equality of all the children of God, and declares herself the mother by adoption of those whom the world rejects. But she also receives with tenderness the great ones of the earth, and it is right and reasonable that the preacher of the gospel should sometimes attach himself by preference to those whose elevated position may probably enable them to exercise efficacious influence on those below them. In the words of St. Bonaventura,* "The conversion of a rich man is often more useful than that of a poor one, since the religion of the poor man is only profitable to himself, but that of a rich and powerful one is advantageous to the multitude. The conversion of the Emperor Constantine was of more service to the Church than that of a great number of persons of inferior ranks."

These were the considerations that induced Matthew Ricci to make such constant efforts to establish himself at Pekin; and the missionaries who succeeded him pursued the same end, and exerted themselves to illuminate with the light of the gospel the highest classes of Chinese society, whence it might the more easily enlighten the people; and notwithstanding the violent persecutions by which they were assailed, they made numerous converts in those classes. Dr. Paul was, as we have said, a man of the highest distinction; the Doctors Léon and Michel were Presidents of Supreme Courts; and in addition to these three grand dignitaries, there were among

* Questione 23, in determinationibus questionum circa Reg. Sancti Francisci.

the Chinese Christians of this period fourteen Mandarins of the first class, ten who had taken Doctors' degrees, eleven Licentiates, and three hundred Bachelors. In the imperial family the conversions had been especially numerous, for more than a hundred and forty members of it had been baptized; and though these princes had no official share in the government, the dignity of their birth could not but give them a certain amount of influence. Forty of the principal eunuchs attached to the service of the Emperor had also been converted to Christianity; and the Chinese neophytes, whether Mandarins, men of letters, princes, or people, were sincerely attached to the religion they had embraced, fulfilled its duties with fidelity, and studied its doctrines and the practical obligations which result from them with much earnestness. There was nothing to compel them to renounce the easy self-indulgent habits of scepticism and idolatry, to adopt a faith that must exercise restraint over all their bad passions. No worldly interest could possibly be the motive of their conversion, neither wealth nor rank could be obtained by their becoming Christians; but, on the contrary, nothing was more probable than that they would, in consequence of that act, incur the hatred of their relations and friends who had remained in idolatry, as well as the persecution of the government; and it might be even imprisonment, torture, exile, or death. Men magnanimous enough to trample upon all considerations of human interest, can have no other motives for a change of religion than those of conscience, God, and eternity. All the details that have been preserved to us concerning the Chinese neophytes show them to have been regular and pious in their conduct, and to have fulfilled with equal fervour their duties towards God and their neighbour; and their constancy and fortitude in times of persecution afford an additional proof of the sincerity of their faith and their attachment to Christianity.

One very remarkable improvement that appeared to have

been effected in these men by their change of faith, was the fraternal charity towards one another so strikingly displayed by the converts. A spring of kindness, generosity, and disinterestedness seemed to gush forth in hearts formerly hard, cold, selfish, and covetous; and the sight of a Chinese forgetting himself, to become anxious for the welfare and the interests of his brethren, was perhaps as beautiful a miracle as any effected by the gospel.

One day a Portuguese ship, from Macao, bound for Japan, was wrecked upon a rock not far from the coast of Fo-kien, and the whole crew perished, with the exception of twelve persons, who had the good fortune to save themselves in the boat. The sky was covered with heavy clouds, and the sea tempestuous; and after being driven about the whole night, they were at last thrown on the shores of China, where they were immediately surrounded by an insolent multitude, who, instead of offering them food or clothing, overwhelmed them with abuse. The satellites from the nearest tribunal soon came up, and as at that period the Dutch, lying in ambush in the island of Formosa, often committed shameful acts of piracy on the coast of Fo-kien and Tche-Kiang, the unfortunate shipwrecked men were taken for these sea-robbers, and thrown into prison. As the people were freely allowed to gratify their curiosity by gazing upon them, there was continually a mob gathered about them, without any one thinking of offering any solace to their misery; but it happened afterwards that some Christian neophytes of the neighbourhood went to pay them a visit, and having remarked that they prayed with a rosary, they perceived that they were Christians, and being touched with compassion did what they could to console them. It was forbidden indeed to treat them otherwise than as enemies; but their charity and ingenuity found means nevertheless to assist the unfortunate prisoners and provide for their wants. In order to furnish them with clothing, for instance, the Christians used to go into the prison with one garment over another, and, before going away, manage adroitly to slip off the under one, so that the keepers did not perceive that they had made any change;* and they afterwards exerted themselves so successfully with the Mandarins in their favour that they were sent back to Macao.

The happy influence of the Christian religion in transforming the character of the Chinese, besides being manifested in the ordinary affairs of life, inspired a nobleness of feeling in grave and difficult circumstances that had hitherto been unknown to them.

Whilst the Mantchoo Tartars were making perpetual incursions on the territory of the empire, the province of Leao-Tong, bordering on Mantchuria, was placed under the military government of a Christian Mandarin, named Soung.

He had gained, in various engagements, considerable advantage over the Tartars, and might have rendered more signal services to the state if he had been better seconded by the government; but no money was sent to him to pay his soldiers; for having made a rule to himself never to send bribes to the men in power he had scarcely anything but enemies at the *Ning-Pou,* or War Office. It was of no use for him to explain in writing the state of insubordination into which his army was falling for want of pay; he could get no kind of answer.

As he was much beloved by his soldiers, he repressed for a long time the spirit of sedition that was secretly springing up among them, though as yet it manifested itself only in murmurs; but at length their patience was exhausted, and they mutinied, took possession of a town, and pillaged the inhabitants.

By this act of violence the soldiers understood very well that they had ruined their general, and that the only chance of safety for him lay in his declaring himself openly against

---

* Alvarez Semedo, p. 351.

the emperor; and they omitted nothing to drive him to this desperate step, promising to follow wherever he should lead them, and swearing never to lay down their arms till they placed him on the imperial throne. A revolutionary spirit was at that time prevalent over the whole country, and there were already several pretenders to the throne.

General Soung saw as well as his troops that his fall was inevitable, and that if he wished to save his life he had no choice but to accept their offer; but he was a Christian, and he could not reconcile treason with his principles; on the contrary, he expressed in the most energetic terms to his captains the horror with which he regarded the crime proposed to him; and when he afterwards regained his ascendancy over the army, he had the courage to punish the authors of the mutiny.

This noble conduct, which excited the admiration of the whole empire, found only censors at Pekin; and as soon as the news of what had taken place reached the court, a courier was despatched from the War Office, to order Soung to come immediately in person to Pekin and render an account of his conduct to the emperor, whilst at the same time he was superseded in his command, and a successor appointed to the military government of the province. At this intelligence, consternation spread throughout the army, and with one voice they counselled their general not to obey the order to go to Pekin. "Remain in the midst of us," they said; "we shall know how to defend you against the attacks of those who envy you;" and whilst the soldiers were holding this language, the Tartar sovereign, being informed of what was passing, offered him an asylum in his territories, and assured him of protection if he would come over to him. But in the midst of such pressing temptations the Christian general listened only to the voice of his conscience. He endeavoured to persuade his soldiers to imitate his fidelity, and then, tearing himself from them. he went heroically to place himself in the hands of enemies, who, incapable of being touched by such magnanimity, pitilessly condemned to death* a man so worthy to live.

Only a few days had elapsed after the glorious death of General Soung, before the Christians of China had to deplore the loss of another of their most illustrious neophytes, Dr. Léon. As this eminent person never ceased, up to the last hour of his life, to express his devotion to the missionaries and to the cause of Christianity, we think it right to enter into a few biographical details concerning him.

Dr. Leon was born at Han-Tcheou-Fou, the capital of the province of Tche-Kiang, and having passed through his academical studies with remarkable success, obtained in his own province the diplomas of the two first literary degrees, and then went to Pekin to receive that of Doctor, which is never conferred anywhere but in the capital of the empire. He was in the exercise of an important office there when he became acquainted with Father Ricci; and the young Doctor, endowed with a lively and penetrating intellect, knew well how to appreciate the great qualities of the learned and virtuous European. The desire of increasing his knowledge and acquirements first led him to cultivate an intimacy with the missionaries, whose character and talents he greatly admired. The study of geography had a special attraction for him; but it did not make him forget the higher importance of that of religion.

In the rather affected expression of Semedo, he " cultivated the knowledge of God conjointly with that of humanity, and marrying heaven to earth, learned at the same time the laws of Jesus Christ and the situations of the kingdoms of the world." The doctrines of Christianity were so attractive to him, that he delighted in assisting the missionaries in the correction of the catechism that they were about to publish; and though as yet he had not attained to faith, he was never tired

---

* Father Dorléans, Hist. des Deux Conquerants Tartares, p. 40.

of admiring the consistency and harmony of Christian truths. He used to say that if the religion was not true, it was at least admirably contrived so as to satisfy all the requirements of human reason, and it was his admiration for Christianity that inspired his lively and sincere attachment to the missionaries. He aided them with his counsels and his authority; he was the first to encourage the building of a church at Pekin, and he even carried his devotion to the cause so far as to purchase a piece of ground for it at his own expense.

Our Doctor, however, was still a pagan; but his good works and the uprightness of his heart in his search for truth, procured for him that special grace of God by which truths are made to germinate in the soul. His intelligence when kindled by light from above perceived the divine glory of the religion of Jesus Christ, and understood the true relations between man and God; he became a Christian, and earnestly demanded baptism, but some delay was made in granting him this favour, on account of the attachment which, like other Chinese, he had to the practice of polygamy. A serious illness that brought him to the brink of the grave, induced the missionaries nevertheless to confer upon him the sacrament of regeneration and that for the dying at the same time; and the water of baptism and the holy oil of extreme unction together operated such a change in him as to make him cry out that he was no longer the same man. His body had recovered its health, and his soul was endowed with strength sufficient to enable him to conform without any restriction to the law of God.

A short time after this miraculous transformation, Dr. Léon returned to Han-Tcheou-Fou, to the bosom of his family; and he had no sooner arrived, than he hastened to remove the numerous little idols of gilt wood which adorned his household temple, and to burn them in the interior courtyard of his house. One of his relatives, who witnessed this action. was greatly scandalised, and reproached him keenly with what he called its impiety. But the doctor, having explained with his customary eloquence the motives of his conduct, the relative was so much struck by what he heard, that he determined to study a religion apparently so far superior in clearness to the confused doctrines of the Bonzes and Doctors of Reason.

The neophyte Léon, who was already inspired by the ardent zeal of an apostle, affectionately questioned his friend, and unfolded to him in a methodical manner the truths of Christianity; and thus had the happiness of communicating to another soul the convictions by which his own was so profoundly penetrated. Father Trigault, who was then at Han-Tcheou-Fou, completed the instruction of the fervent catechumen, who was soon admitted to baptism, Dr. Léon acting as his godfather in the ceremony, and bestowing on him the name of Michel.

These two had been connected from their infancy by the closest ties of friendship; they had studied together, and passed with equal success through their academical career, and on the same day, after a brilliant competition, they both gained the Doctor's degree. To the bonds of kindred and of friendship were now added the still more sacred one of the same Christian faith, and during the whole remainder of their lives, they continued to be the firmest pillars of the new Church of China. During the tempests that threatened its existence, their house at Han-Tcheou-Fou afforded the missionaries a secure and hospitable refuge from the fury of persecution; and in calmer, happier days it became a focus of Christian propagandism, an "upper room," whence the disciples of Jesus Christ went forth anew to the conquest of souls.

Doctor Léon, both in his private and public life, constantly and zealously employed his influence, as a mandarin and a man of letters, to diffuse around him the light of the gospel, and advance the work of the propagation of the faith; and his character was especially remarkable for the decision and candour which prevented his ever attempting to enter into any compromise with the numerous superstitions by which Chinese life is perpetually environed. He was no respecter of persons, and he never hesitated to proclaim his convictions, without regard to the opinion of men, whenever his conscience demanded it; and neither the mandarins, the men of letters, nor the public at large could ever succeed in intimidating him.

A short time after his conversion to Christianity, he was sent in quality of Prefect to a town of the first class; and, when a mandarin takes possession of a new office of this kind, it is customary for him to go first into the pagoda of their palace, prostrate himself before the idols, and implore their protection. Dr. Léon betook himself in state to his palace, according to the prescription of the Book of Rites, followed by a numerous suite, and with music playing and banners displayed, advanced in solemn procession to the pagoda; but as soon as he found himself in presence of the idols, he turned to the satellites of his palace, and pointing to the gilded statues, commanded the soldiers to overthrow them, drag them out of the pagoda, and set fire to them.

"This palace," said he, "is henceforth my house, and I will not have in it idols in which I do not believe." The satellites remained open-mouthed and petrified with astonishment at this unexpected command; but it was given with such an air of authority, that after the first moment of consternation, they set to work to obey it, whispering to one another that, doubtless, their new Prefect was a worshipper of the Lord of Heaven.

Dr. Léon was willing to admit that the irresistible impulse towards a religious faith of some kind may lead men, up to a certain point, to prostrate themselves blindly before idols; but to remain obstinately attached to vain superstitions, or sunk in scepticism after having become acquainted with the doctrines of the gospel, was a thing he could not understand. He was persuaded that those who were capable of serious reading could not fail to become passionately devoted to the sciences as taught by the Europeans, and afterwards by means of the sciences to be brought to the knowledge of the true God. He had a profound conviction of the immense influence of books, and the value of literature, and he was continually urging the missionaries to labour diligently in the translation of the good books of the West, being persuaded that that would prove the most efficacious means of propagating the faith among the Chinese, who have always had so high an esteem for literature and men of letters.

Preaching by means of books was always, in his eyes, a matter of so much importance, that for the thirty years of his life that followed his conversion he devoted himself to that mode of apostleship with unheard-of zeal, and his daily occupation consisted in composing works with this object, or translating those of Europe with the assistance of some missionaries sufficiently versed in the Chinese language. So assiduous and unremitting was he in this kind of labour, that, according to Semedo, in town or country, at home or on a visit, and even at the gayest festivals, he was never without some book in his pocket; and even while he was being carried along in a palanquin, on the shoulders of his servants, he used continually to read and write, although, having lost one eye and having his sight very weak in the other, he could not do so without much inconvenience, and holding the paper quite close to his face.

These persevering habits of study, united to a very superior intellect, had enabled Dr. Léon to become so well skilled in most branches of European knowledge, that there were few subjects on which he would not speak to good purpose, and with genuine erudition. He was well acquainted with the first six books of Euclid, and had translated them into Chinese, and he had also carried his researches into various branches of mathematics far enough to compose seven volumes on those subjects. He had translated a great number of works on astronomy, as well as those of Aristotle, and those that were in use at that time in the celebrated Faculty of Coimbra. His time was so fully occupied, and he wrote on such a variety of different subjects, that at his death he left more than twenty volumes of manuscript quite ready for the press. The various curiosities of Europe that the Chinese in general were so delighted with had few attractions for him; but he seemed quite to thrill with joy at the sight of a new book, would seize on it and read it with avidity, and as age advanced upon him he was often heard to lament that he could no longer labour so assiduously at the translation of foreign works. When he went to visit the missionaries, his first anxiety was to know what books they were engaged upon, and he took great pleasure in correcting their style, and aiding them with his extensive literary experience. "I can with truth declare," says Father Semedo, "that out of fifty books, both religious and scientific, many in several volumes, which our fathers translated into Chinese, there was scarcely one that did not pass through his hands, either for revision and correction, or to receive from him a preface and additions of various kinds. No more acceptable present could be offered him than that of a book lately translated into Chinese."

The extraordinary zeal for books that was manifested by Dr. Léon, did not proceed from pure literary and scientific enthusiasm, but he saw in them the most efficacious means for the conversion of his countrymen. The propagation of Christianity in China was his ruling passion, and occupied him incessantly; but when he considered the vast field to be cultivated, and the small number of evangelical labourers to work in it, he could not help lamenting the deficiency to the missionaries, and complaining that so few assistants came to them.

"You are now old," he would say simply, "and the Chinese language presents many great difficulties. Will you have the time and the capacity to form those who shall come hereafter?"

One day the superior of the Portuguese Jesuits wrote to him to offer him some of the most beautiful rarities of Europe; but he replied that he desired nothing so much from his kindness, as that he would send to China a great number of preachers of the gospel.

As he was so anxious for new missionaries, it will be easily believed that he was affectionately solicitous for the welfare of the old. Their health, their studies, their progress in the language, their apostolic labours, all interested him profoundly, and he used even to visit their private apartments, to see that they were furnished with all things needful; and in the winter carefully examined their clothing, to ascertain that they were sufficiently protected from the cold. When they were suffering from illness, he used often to prepare their medicines himself, (the literary men of China are always, more or less, physicians and druggists,) saying that many medicines failed of their effect from want of sufficient care in their preparation.

On the arrival of a new missionary, he used to make many inquiries concerning his character, and exert himself to gain his confidence and sympathy, and though a warm friend to them all, he showed perhaps the most especial kindness to the young ones. He seemed quite distressed at the trouble the strangers had in learning his native language, was delighted when they began to stammer Chinese, and did all in his power to help them over the difficulties, giving them lessons in the art of conversation, as well as of compliments and etiquette, so important to any one who desires to be well received in that country. Subsequently, when they were more advanced, he laid down a plan of study for them, and pointed out the books that they would find most profitable. What a treasure must this amiable and learned old man have been to the young missionaries, transported thus suddenly into a new world, where they had to become completely transformed, and to adopt not only a new language, but entirely new habits and manners! We have seen how intrepid Dr. Léon was in his devotion to the missionaries in time of persecution; and we have mentioned the remarkable memorial that he addressed to the emperor, to induce him to permit the return to Pekin of those who had been exiled. But the mandarins, envious of the fame and popularity of Dr. Léon, made use of this last circumstance to effect his downfall. They accused him at court of having kept up close and secret relations with strangers, and favoured their plots and intrigues in the empire; and, moreover, of having declared himself a partisan and propagator of a religion opposed to the laws of the state and the maxims of the sages of antiquity. This last accusation was urged with so much malicious pertinacity that Léon was disgraced.

The privation of the mandarinate was, however, a matter of small concern for this high-minded Christian, and he found ample consolation in the thought that he had lost his own position in endeavouring to secure that of the missionaries. He did not, either, remain long out of office; for when his friend Dr. Paul was made Colao, neither the important political interests to which he had to devote his attention, nor the cares of office in a peculiarly complicated and difficult position of affairs, made him forget for a moment the interests of religion, nor relax in his efforts for the propagation of the faith. It was with the view of raising the credit and authority of the missionaries, that he got them entrusted with the task of reforming the Chinese calendar; and convinced that he could not be better seconded in such a project than by his friend Dr. Léon, whose knowledge, ability, and courage he had ample means of appreciating, he got him re-established in his office of Vice-President of the Court of Rites.

Dr. Léon was not ambitious, and a quiet, retired mode of life, divided between study and prayer, had far more charms for him than the often fruitless agitation of a public position; but he received the news of his nomination, nevertheless, with pleasure, as it would probably enable him to be of more service to the missions, especially with the co-operation of a Colao so fervently devoted to the cause. He set out, therefore, for Pekin; but the length of the journey and the severity of the winter, in addition to the infirmities of his advanced age, were too much for him, and he fell ill, a very few days after his arrival, of a malady which made such rapid progress that his life was soon despaired of by the physicians.

The Heavenly Father of the family now called to Him for his reward the faithful servant who had so well fulfilled his task.

It may be imagined with what faith and piety this excellent Christian received the last sacraments of the Church; and the three missionaries then at Pekin were with him in his last moments, as well as the most distinguished neophytes of the capital, with the Colao, Dr. Paul, at their head. When he approached the sick man to recommend himself to his prayers, Dr. Léon, collecting all his remaining strength, took his hand affectionately, and thanked him for all the attentions he had shown him, particularly in the recent appointment. "My brother," he said, "I am passing to the life eternal, and I go content, since I see our missions and our Fathers protected by your authority. You have called on me to second you in an affair most important to the welfare of Christianity, but my sins have rendered me unworthy to participate in such a work; suffer me, however, from my death-bed, to confide to you the future destinies of our dear mission." After these words, which were heard with deep emotion by all present, Dr. Léon breathed his last. It was on the 1st of November, 1630. "His memory," says Father Alvarez Semedo, who knew him well, "will live eternally in the hearts of our Society, and his virtues will not be forgotten by the more high-minded among the Chinese nobility."

In receiving the last breath of Dr. Léon, the prime minister of the emperor had also received as a sacred inheritance his zeal in the cause of the Christian missions. At this period the government was much occupied with the reformation of the calendar, which was full of errors, and which, as we have said, was now entrusted to the European missionaries, whose astronomical science was greatly superior to that of the Chinese and Mussulmans. Dr. Paul addressed a memorial on the subject to the emperor, who approved the contents and gave orders to summon to the court any two among the missionaries who should appear most capable of fulfilling the duties of the office assigned them. The choice fell upon the Fathers Jacques Rho, and Adam Schall, the former of whom, an Italian by birth, and a skilful mathematician, had been obliged to stop at Macao, on account of the persecution raised against the Christians in China, and he had protected that town in 1622 from an invasion of the Dutch, by teaching the inhabitants how to make use of their artillery, and afterwards secured it from future attempts by new fortifications. When he had made his way into the Celestial Empire, he learned in a short time to write and speak the Chinese with as much facility as an educated native could have done; and two years after the discovery of the famous inscription in Si-Ngan-Fou he went to that city to found a mission.

Father Adam Schall, a native of Cologne, came to China in 1622, and was also sent to the mission of Si-Ngan-Fou where he occupied himself with the apostolic ministry, and the study of the sciences most nearly connected with astronomy. He acquired such great popularity in a very short time, that for the church whose erection he superintended he received as many subscriptions from infidels, who admired his mathematical abilities, as from the converts to Christianity. It was indeed on account of their scientific reputation that these two missionaries were summoned to Pekin.

Immediately on their arrival at the capital they were placed at the head of the "Board of Celestial Literature," and Dr. Paul hastened to present to the emperor all the works on astronomy and physical science published up to that time by the missionaries of China. From the moment of their entering on their functions, the Fathers Rho and Schall had to maintain a constant struggle with the government astronomers, who could not see without jealousy strangers placed thus at the head of their academy; and they wrote pamphlets and circulated libels to depreciate the astronomical methods of Europeans. The literary class, who knew nothing whatever of the subject of astronomy, were precisely those who were loudest in their clamours. The emperor, being supported by his prime minister, did not allow himself to be influenced by these intrigues, and Dr. Paul suggested to him an excellent test of the respective scientific pretensions of the rivals. An eclipse was expected to occur in a short time, and the Chinese and European astronomers were ordered to make their calculations separately, and send the result of their labours to court. As the Fathers had made their observations with the closest attention, their statement was found, when the eclipse took place, to be verified in every point, while that of the astronomers of China was quite at fault; but though thus publicly convicted of ignorance and incapacity, they did not on that account make any abatement in their pretensions to superiority; and only conceived from their defeat a still more virulent hatred against the missionaries.

In the meantime occurred the death of Dr. Paul, the most illustrious and distinguished of all the Chinese who embraced the Christian religion. Though a statesman and a celebrated author, he was remarkable for modesty and sincerity, two virtues that are by no means conspicuous in the character of his countrymen. It was related of him that one day the emperor asked of his ministers assembled in council some explanation of a difficulty in legislation that perplexed him. No one solved the problem satisfactorily; but when, at the close of the meeting, one of his colleagues asked Dr. Paul what was his opinion on the point in question, he immediately gave him the required answer with the utmost clearness, and with great erudition. Every one was astonished that he had not made a parade of his knowledge in the presence of the emperor, and asked him why he had not spoken thus before the council; but he replied, "As I was not personally interrogated, I wished to leave to others the merit of the reply."

The duties of his high office never made Dr. Paul forget those incumbent on him as a Christian. He had in his palace a small oratory fitted up with taste and simplicity, to which he gladly retired in moments of leisure, to devote himself to prayer and meditation; and regularly every morning, before going to preside in the Court of Rites, he was in the habit of giving half an hour to pious exercises in his oratory. In his last moments he was consoled by the presence of Father Adam Schall, for whom he had the tender regard of a son.

During our own residence in China, we went one day to visit his tomb, in the environs of Schang-Hai, not far from the banks of the Blue River. It was an immense tumulus, of a pyramidal shape, rising in the midst of a field now overgrown with creeping plants and brambles; and around this great hillock enclosing the remains of the celebrated Scu-Colao, we found lying on the ground some fragments of a pillar and of sculptures which had formerly constituted a portion of a triumphal arch and of a funeral monument now crumbled to dust. There is not so much as an inscription to indicate the name of him to whom the monument was erected. We should ourselves have passed the place without notice, had not a neophyte of Schang-Hai who accompanied us, stopped us and said, "There is the burial place of the famous Christian Scu, Grand Colao of the last emperor of the dynasty of Ming." We knelt down on a mutilated fragment of granite, and whilst we were repeating a prayer for the deceased, we saw passing a little way off some Chinese peasants, who, from the wretched tattered state of their garments, and from their legs being covered wi h blackish mud, we conjectured to be returning from their labour in the rice fields. They stopped, and gazing at us with an air of half stupid astonishment, not unmixed with malice, said, "See, there is a master of the worshippers of the Lord of Heaven; he is praying for the dead!" The peasants who spoke thus were the descendants of Dr. Paul! The family was still very numerous, but had long fallen into apostacy and the most abject misery. They had their abode in a group of poor hovels that we saw a little way off, and which still bore the name of *Scu-Kia-Wei*, that is, hamlet of the family of *Scu*. It was a most distressing spectacle! A few years ago,* when the modern Jesuits returned to the mission of China, they had the happy thought of purchasing a piece of ground in this very hamlet of Scu-Kia-Wei, to form their first establishment; and they built their chapel by the side of the tomb of Dr. Paul. If we do not mistake also, they had afterwards the happiness of bringing back to the Christian faith the descendants of him who protected with so much zeal at the commencement of the seventeenth century the apostolic labours of the former children of St. Ignatius.

* In 1842.

CHAPTER VIII.

Father Schall fabricates a Harpsichord for the Emperor.—Christianity in the Imperial Harem.—The Tartars summoned to the Assistance of the Empire.—Father Schall establishes a Cannon Foundery.—Gratitude of the Emperor.—Progress of the Insurrection.—Ly-Koung the Chief of the Rebels.—He attacks Pekin.—Tragic Death of the Emperor.—Character of this Prince.—The Insurgents at Pekin.—Adam Schall before the Revolutionary Tribunal.—First Act of the Government of Ly-Koung.—Submission of the Lettered and the Magistrates.—Heroism of General Ou-San Koui and his Father.—Ou-San-Koui swears to exterminate Ly-Koung.—He invokes the Tartars.—Rout of the Insurgents.—Terrible Conflagration at Pekin.—The Catholic Mission is saved.—The Mantchoos Masters of the Capital.—Character of their policy.—Memorial of Father Schall.—He is appointed President of the Board of Mathematics.—The Government Astronomers.—The Mantchoos favour the Missionaries.—Father Martini and a Tartar Chief.—The Tyrant Tchang-Kien ravages and depopulates Sse-Tchouen.—Adventures of Fathers Buglio and Magalhans.—Father Schall at Pekin.

The Chinese astronomers now recommenced their cabals against the missionaries, and still hoped, by means of calumny and falsehood, to ruin them in the opinion of the Emperor and the country. But Providence did not suffer them to succeed in their attempts; and their jealousy and hatred only served to betray their own intrigues, while the missionaries rose higher than ever in public estimation.

It was the thirteenth year of the reign of Tchoung-Tching, when one day there was found by chance in a corner of the palace the famous spinet which Father Ricci had brought to the court, and which had had no small share in bringing him into favour. After exciting enthusiasm for a short time, the instrument had afterwards fallen into oblivion, and it had suffered considerable damage from time, during the reign of Wan-Lié, Tai-Chan, and Tien-Ki. The Emperor Tchoung-Tching had the good fortune to recover his great grandfather's favourite instrument, and he commanded Father Schall to repair it, and make it again as good as new. There were few arts or sciences to which these zealous men were entirely strangers; and Father Schall set to work, restored the old instrument, or rather made a new one, and composed for it some musical airs, somewhat adapted to the whimsical taste of the Chinese.

Animated by the hope of becoming the means of converting the imperial court to Christianity, this learned mathematician could pass from astronomy to musical instrument making, from religious controversy to painting and sculpture, and be in fact all the while occupied only with the glory of God and the salvation of souls, for everything he did tended to these ends. When he sent the new harpsichord to the Emperor, he offered, at the same time, a magnificent album representing the principal incidents in the life of Jesus Christ, with an explanation in Chinese characters, and to this he added a representation of the adoration of the three Magi in wax, with the figures carefully coloured. These things pleased Tchoung-Tching so much that he had them installed in a place of honour in his private cabinet, and allowed the ladies of his palace to visit them at pleasure for ten days.

The potentates of Asia are known to be in general sunk in the most degrading sensuality. They keep within their palaces a considerable number of women decorated with the titles of queens of the first, second, and third class; and they have also in attendance upon them crowds of girls from families of distinction, as well as legions of eunuchs. The Emperor of China, had, at the period of which we are speaking, two thousand women in his harem, and eunuchs to the frightful number of ten thousand, who, besides being employed in the service of the palace, filled various important offices in the administration. This class of men, though not as liable as others to the seductions of sensual pleasure, are devoured by ambition and addicted to intrigue to an almost incredible extent, passing their whole lives in contriving methods of influence, and insinuating themselves into important offices in the administration.

It does sometimes happen, however, that amongst these degraded beings are found exceptionable natures of the noblest order, accessible to every pure and generous feeling; and some of this character having embraced Christianity, the faith of Christ made its way even into the harem of Tchoung-Tching.

The palace of the Emperor of China is situated in the centre of Pekin, and surrounded by three strong walls, in the two first enclosures of which are lodged the troops of the emperor's guard, the ministers, the eunuchs, and a considerable number of officers civil and military. The third, which is much more spacious than the others, contains, besides the imperial residence, lakes, gardens, and parks of astonishing magnificence. There dwells the Son of Heaven, inaccessible to all but the eunuchs and women of his palace; and when once the latter have entered this brilliant prison they leave it no more, and all their relations with the external world are broken for ever. How difficult it was to introduce the light of the Gospel into this jealously guarded seclusion may be imagined; but the Spirit of God "bloweth where it listeth," and no human power can prevent its entrance.

The ladies of the palace, whose lives are extremely monotonous, of course did not fail to seek a little amusement by frequenting the hall in which the Emperor had had displayed, for the gratification of their curiosity, the wax-work figures and bas reliefs presented to him by Father Schall, and there was amongst the eunuchs a very worthy Christian named Joseph, who explained to them minutely the subjects of the representations; and what was at first but a frivolous amusement, the gratification of an idle curiosity, soon became the means of imparting religious truth. Many of these ladies were, by the grace of God, so powerfully affected by what they heard, that Joseph began to occupy himself in earnest with their religious instruction, and was authorised to administer to them the rite of baptism. Three of these new Christian women bore the title of queens of the first class, and they received the names of Agatha, Helena, and Theodora; and as these pious neophytes could not go out of the palace to attend any religious service, they made themselves amends by devoting a longer time to prayer in their apartments. They liked also to devote their hours of leisure to the embroidering altar cloths, and making ornaments and artificial flowers, which they sent to the mission, happy in being able to contribute to the magnificence of ceremonies which they were never to witness. By the year 1639, there were thirty-eight of these Christian ladies in the imperial palace.*

Whilst religion was thus making considerable progress, and had even begun to exercise a salutary influence on the court, the revolutionary spirit by which China was then agitated was gaining ground; insurrections were multiplying in all parts of the empire; and the Emperor, finding himself vigorously attacked by the Mantchoo Tartars, sought to turn their valour to his advantage, by calling in their aid against the insurgents. The courtiers admired this policy, and thought it extremely clever to "make use of the foreigner's whip to chastise domestic enemies."

The Tartars on their side lost no time in responding to the Emperor's appeal; they attacked the rebels, beat them in various engagements, and in the intoxication of their success allowed it to transpire that they meant to give the law to the Chinese, conducting themselves everywhere more like conquerors than auxiliaries. The government of Pekin then, when it was too late, bitterly regretted having called in these dangerous friends. Already the report was rife that the victorious Tartars were coming to besiege the capital; and the Emperor, now that the danger was imminent, was meditating

* M. Martinio, Brevis Relatoi, &c., p. 89.

at the same time the defence and the desertion of the city. One day, one of the principal ministers came to Father Schall, and began to talk to him of the perplexities of the government, and its fears of an approaching invasion of the Tartars. He spoke of the means of defence, and the advantages there might be in employing cannon of great calibre if they were skilfully cast. The minister had, in fact, been sent to sound Adam Schall, and see whether this all accomplished man was not also acquainted with the art of making cannon.

The learned missionary, unaware of the trap that was laid for him, did really make some judicious remarks on the art of casting cannon; and thereupon the minister immediately produced a decree of the emperor, charging *Tang-Jo-Wan* (Adam Schall) immediately to set about the organization of a cannon foundery. Various other decrees were also found to be in readiness, by which brass, iron, and all necessary materials were placed at his disposal, and he was authorized at the same time to claim the services of all the workmen he should require. In vain did the poor missionary protest that he knew nothing whatever of the art of making cannon more than what he happened to have read in books, and there was a great difference between theory and practice. All his protestations were vain, and the only answer the minister gave him was the formal order of the emperor.

Adam Schall, therefore, was obliged to resign himself to his fate, and set to work; and the foundery was built close to the palace, in order that the court might be able to amuse itself by watching the proceedings. As soon as the brass was melted, and when preparations were being made for running it into the mould, the workmen who had been placed under Father Schall's orders made arrangements to offer a solemn sacrifice to the Spirit of the fire. The missionary hastened, however, to put a stop to their superstitious practices, and arranged instead a Christian altar, on which he placed an image of the Virgin and Child, and then, wearing

12*

surplice and stole, he addressed his prayers to God in presence of an immense crowd praying for a benediction on the work he had undertaken, in the hope that it might tend to his glory. The success was complete; and historians say that twenty excellent cannon were cast, the greater number of which were bored for throwing forty-pound shot.

Father Adam Schall met with many admirers, but also awakened much envy. When the larger guns were finished, he cast some culverins, which might either be placed upon carriages, on the shoulders of a couple of men, or between the humps of a camel; and during the two entire years that this foundery occupied his attention, Schall had to carry on a perpetual war against state robbers, who never failed to demand three times the amount of material that was really necessary for the manufacture of a gun. The pestilence, also, which suddenly attacked the capital, gave him great embarrassment, twenty-five out of the thirty workmen he had trained being carried off by it.

The Emperor Tchoung-Tching showed his appreciation of so great a service by sending two inscriptions to the residence of the missionary, written in vermillion by his own hand. One was a grandiloquent eulogy on the science and virtue of Father Schall, and the other a public tribute of admiration for the Christian religion, the doctrine which, it said, kept men away from harm and conducted them to God. Nothing, in the eyes of the Chinese, could have been so signal a mark of imperial favour as this. Copies of the two inscriptions were despatched to the provinces, and did not fail to augment the influence of the missionaries and to encourage the neophytes. At Macao, indeed, as soon as the two documents were received, the event was treated as a great national fete; the guns of the citadel were fired as a salute of the happy news, and for eight entire days music and shouts were heard in all the principal quarters of the town.

The cannon and culverins that the Emperor had cast were,

however, unable to defend him against the insurgents, whose number and power daily increased. From north to south the whole empire was overturned, and the clang of arms was to be heard everywhere. Each province produced a chief who proclaimed himself the Son of Heaven, and who aimed at nothing less than the foundation of a dynasty. Numerous Tartar squadrons, under the pretence of defending the emperor, fought on their own account and increased the disorder. At Pekin, the soldiers, regardless of discipline, ran about on the ramparts; the citizens shouted in the streets; the Mandarins fled or concealed themselves; the principal eunuchs kept up secret communication with the insurgents, with the Mantchoo Tartars, and with the government ministers, all being ready to rally to the flag of the conqueror, whoever he might be, and to proclaim that terrible motto of revolutions, *Vae victis.*

The most important among the insurrectionary chiefs was a certain Ly-Koung. Formerly at the head of a band of highway robbers, he had gathered around him vast numbers of vagabonds and scoundrels; his success had been rapid and prodigious, and his dominion had already extended over six provinces, the inhabitants of which, although not absolutely accepting his authority, had refused to obey that of the Emperor. Ly-Koung, determined to put an end to the long struggle by a decisive stroke, at last collected all his forces and marched them towards Pekin, knowing that with a despotic and perfectly centralised government the seizure of the capital is the conquest of the empire.

But although Ly-Koung had a numerous and warlike army at his disposal, he did not consider it prudent to venture an open attack upon Pekin. To take this large town was no easy matter, for, besides its great extent, it was thoroughly fortified with thick ramparts, and well supplied with artillery. The circumference of the royal palace alone was more than a league; it was defended by three walls, as many ditches, and a quantity of detached forts that could only be taken separately. These difficulties induced the chief of the insurrection to call treason and fraud to his assistance, for both can be combined with the utmost facility in a Chinese character. With money and valuable presents, he bought over the principal eunuchs and the more important officers of the court; and when these preliminary arrangements, which did not occupy much time, were completed, he sent the most gallant and devoted of his captains to Pekin, disguised as merchants, and accompanied by numerous clerks taken from the most trusty of his soldiers, instructing them to open shops, retail the valuable goods they took with them, and conduct themselves, in a word, as men more intent upon their traffic than on the chances of war.

When Ly-Koung had thus skilfully arranged matters, he advanced his army up to the walls of Pekin. The Emperor had not suspected the proximity of the danger; for the courtiers, bribed by the rebels, had concealed it from him, bringing him nothing but the absurd prophecies of the astrologers. No sooner was the presence of Ly-Koung and of his numerous army announced, than the monarch saw himself abandoned by all who had surrounded him; and no one dared to approach him, even to give him advice. Regaining his energy in this trying hour, the Emperor mounted his horse, put himself at the head of a few soldiers, and galloped to the gate where the insurgents had presented themselves. He was betrayed, however, by those who ought to have defended this post, and was met by a discharge of artillery from the very cannon that he had had cast only a few days previously, and from which he had expected so much. His horse was killed under him, his followers fled, and the unhappy prince was left to return on foot and alone to his palace. He rushed to the apartments of the Empress, and telling her that all was lost, entreated her to put an end to her life. He entrusted his three young children to the care of a faithful attendant, and then catching sight of his daughter, the only one of his children who had reached the age of adolescence, and dreading the horrors that might await her, he raised his sword to kill her; but the poor girl fled from death, and the father only cut off one of her hands. The unfortunate monarch, now almost bereft of his senses, and not knowing what to expect, ran out of his palace into the vast park that surrounded it, ascended a small hill from which he had been in the habit of watching Father Schall casting the cannon that had just been turned against him, and after pausing a moment, he pierced his arm with the point of his sword, and wrote in blood upon the corner of his tunic the following words: " Health to the future Emperor Ly-Koung! Do not hurt my people! Do not employ my ministers!" Approaching a large tree he wrote upon the bark, " When the empire falls the Emperor dies." And then unfastening his girdle he hung himself to one of the branches.

Thus, at the age of thirty-six, perished this prince, once the head of the greatest empire of the world; and with him the dynasty of Ming, which had occupied the throne for 266 years, came to a termination. Gifted with great intelligence and an excellent heart, Tchoung-Tching was yet so weak as to allow himself to be domineered over by the eunuchs, and was ruined by them; but although devoted to the Buddhist worship and to the superstitions of the Bonzes, he never failed to protect the Christian religion and the missionaries. His grandfather, Wan-Lié, had formerly received Christianity at court in the person of Father Ricci, and Tchoung-Tching continued to show it the same favour; he eulogised the religion, and saw with pleasure the progress it made.

Father Schall, to whom we are indebted for almost all the details that we have just given, states in one of his letters, that he had read a prophecy in an old Chinese book of all that happened to Tchoung-Tching; the revolution that shook the empire, the invasion of the Tartars, and the peculiar death by which the Emperor perished. There are certainly to be met with in China, books of prophecy of a very remarkable nature, in which the past, present, and future history of all the dynasties is set forth. The Chinese implicitly believe in these prophecies; and this may perhaps account for the frequent occurrence of the events they predict, in, it must be confessed, a somewhat enigmatical manner.

The day after the Emperor's death, the insurgents, to the number of 300,000 men, entered Pekin, destroying, like some fierce torrent, every thing they came near. The chief rushed at once to the Imperial Palace, vainly seeking the Emperor; and as he had promised an enormous sum to whoever should find him, the corpse was at last discovered, and was subjected to the utmost indignity. The conquerors filled the town with carnage, and cut the throats of every one they met, man, woman, or child, though an order was at last issued by the chiefs putting an end to the sacking of the town. In the midst of this horrible butchery, the house of the missionaries was protected in a most providential manner. While the streets of Pekin were running with blood, Father Schall retired with his companions into the chapel, and there, at the foot of the altar, awaited what might be his fate with prayer and resignation. The insurgents presented themselves at the doors, and Father Schall threw them open. After having examined the whole building without hurting any one, or even stealing any thing, they tranquilly retired, leaving the pious family of Christians thanking God for the protection He had accorded them. Directly afterwards, they found, fixed up over the principal door, a writing, imperatively forbidding any one from doing the smallest injury to the house of Tang-Jo-Wan (Adam Schall). The author of this document could not be discovered.

After the first massacre in the streets, the public places, and even in the interior of the houses, the insurrectionary government endeavoured to regulate the assassinations a little. They established a sort of Committee of Public

Safety, presided over by the brother of Ly-Koung, before which all suspected persons—that is, any who might, it was supposed, still be attached to the fallen dynasty—were brought; and, after a few trifling formalities, put to death; the sabre and gallows were permanently in the ascendant. One day, three of the satellites of this tribunal came to Adam Schall, *inviting* him to come before the brother of the new Emperor. The object of such an invitation could not be doubted. "Where are your chains?" Adam Schall said, with calmness and dignity; "my hands and my neck are at your disposal. Invitations are no longer sent; we are in a time of violence and oppression." With these words, the missionary followed the ill-omened messengers.

Adam Schall found the avenues to the judgment hall blocked up with numbers of ill-looking figures, who received him with ferocious exclamations. "Here comes the great chief of the law of the Lord of Heaven!" "See the master of the Christians!" It was evident from these cries, intermingled with fierce shouts of laughter and signs of joy, that the band of ruffians imagined that they had got hold of the possessor of immense riches.

The president of this tribunal was surrounded with armed executioners, and all the strange and horrid implements of torture, in the invention of which the infernal genius of the Chinese is so skilful.

In front of the tribunal, there was a sort of theatre where a troop of courtesans were going through their performances, and singing lascivious songs, for the amusement of the judges; but as soon as Father Schall entered with his calm and majestic aspect, a wonderful change seemed to be produced in the minds of these bloodthirsty men. The president ordered away the singing girls, respectfully approached the missionary, and, taking him by the hand, invited him to be seated, at a table provided with rice, tea, wine, and numerous refreshments. After having been received in the most conciliatory manner, and assured that no harm would be done to the mission, Father Schall was sent back in peace, much to the displeasure of the troop of miscreants, whose faces darkened and whose hands clenched at seeing so rich a prey escape.

During this anxious time, Father Schall was the soul of the Christian community at Pekin; and while the general confusion occasioned by the insurrectionary army had dispersed the other missionaries, and sent them for safety to the more tranquil provinces, he had always remained with his dearly beloved flock, thinking it more especially his duty, now that the wolves had come to devour it, not to leave it without a pastor. His zeal and solicitude extended to all the neophytes, and he never abandoned them for a moment, going from one to another day and night, to carry consolation and encouragement to all; exhorting them to rely upon Providence for protection, and to look, through the miseries and dangers of this world, to the salvation of souls and the eternal future life.

Ly-Koung no sooner saw himself master of Pekin, than he installed himself with great ceremony in the imperial palace, and solemnly proclaimed himself the Son of Heaven, the Emperor and Sovereign of the Central Kingdom. Once possessed of the imperial throne, he sent despatches to all the civil and military Mandarins, ordering them to make returns of their names and rank, in order, he said, that he might assign them various offices in his new government. Many of the principal magistrates of Pekin, faithful to the memory of their sovereign, and hating the tyrant Ly-Koung, armed themselves with a barbaric courage imitating the sad example set them by the Emperor Tchoung-Tching, and rather than stoop to solicit the favour of a usurper, put themselves to death; some cutting their throats, some strangling themselves, and others throwing themselves into wells. The number of these Catos of the Celestial Empire, was, it is said, very great; though a large majority of the Mandarins, not deeming it advisable to show themselves so zealous for the memory of Tchoung-

Tching, hastened to send in their names to the new emperor, hoping by a prompt obedience to get into favour with the government. They had reckoned without their host, however, for Ly-Koung, despising their servility, instead of giving them places condemned them to pay very large sums of money, varying according to the importance of the offices they had held, saying that as he was now heir of the empire, they must restore to him what they had stolen from his predecessor.

All the servants of the fallen dynasty who had shown so much eagerness to rally round the new government, found themselves mercilessly fined ; and all who could not pay in time were decapitated. Numbers were executed daily without Ly-Koung being satisfied ; and even the children of the men thus put to death were ordered, under the same penalty, to pay the fine that their fathers had not been able to meet. Thus perished the greater number of those avaricious Mandarins,. who, by their abominable exactions, had excited the discontent among the people that eventually precipitated the empire into such a frightful revolution.

The insurgents remained masters of Pekin for thirty days, and this was time enough for them to subvert everything, and cover every quarter of the capital with ruins and blood ; the cruelties practised by Ly-Koung also, did not prevent his having many adherents. In China, indeed, even more than in Europe, men are to be found who have a marvellous readiness to enrol themselves under any banner, and who necessarily become the instruments of any *de facto* government. Power, however acquired, seems to fascinate and attract them in an irresistible manner. The learned men of Pekin hastened to prostrate themselves at the feet of the chief of the insurgents, giving him at once the title of the Son of Heaven. " The mathematicians," Adam Schall says in one of his letters, " were the first to spread their sails to catch this new wind. *Primi tunc vela capiendo novo vento explicuerunt mathematici.*"

The importance of the almanack in China is well known.

The Emperor sends it as a token of his power, not only into every province of his own dominions, but also to the tributary kingdoms; and not to accept the Emperor's almanack is to declare open rebellion against him. Scarcely had the insurgents entered Pekin than the members of the mathematical tribunal, who had before predicted the unclouded fortunes of the deceased Emperor, organised a deputation, and going in procession to the provisional government, offered a new almanack to Ly-Koung, in which the name of Ming had been erased in favour of his own. They declared that the stars were certainly propitious to him, and that Heaven had pronounced in his favour. They prayed him to appoint the happy day on which he would solemnly, and according to the rites, assume his seat on the imperial throne, and distribute to the universe his new calendar; according to what was the most ardent wish, they said, of every good citizen. Ly-Kouang, though wishing nothing better, deemed the representatives of Celestial literature too pressing in their demands; and thought it advisable to wait a little longer before sending out the almanacks; he dismissed them, therefore, to their homes, well satisfied, no doubt, with the result of their mission, to prepare very likely a second address in favour of the Tartars who were about to drive the insurgents from Pekin.

The fallen dynasty of Ming still possessed one faithful and devoted servant in the midst of the universal defection of people, magistrates, men of letters, and soldiers, and the name of the brave general Ou-San-Koui is still popular in the Celestial Empire. His heroic conduct has been for upwards of two hundred years sung by the poets and celebrated in all the theatres; and there is not a village in China, where the peasants are ignorant of the name of Ou-San-Koui, the model of fidelity to unfortunate princes. It is gratifying to find, even in China, an instance of a noble character held in honour by a population little in the habit of appreciating anything great, generous, or disinterested.

When the insurgents made themselves masters of Pekin, Ou-San-Koui held a strong place at Leao-Tong, in the northern part of the empire, and he had sworn that while he lived this place should never come into the power of the enemies of the Emperor. Ly-Koung after having spent some days in arranging the revolutionary government, as well as he could, got together his forces, with a view of besieging Ou-San-Koui. He knew that while any power remained in the hands of this brave and incorruptible warrior he would form a point round which the partisans of the fallen dynasty might rally; and indifferent to the opinion of the literary men, he determined not to send out his almanack until he should have conquered Ou-San-Koui. He advanced his army therefore to Leao-Tong, and not even thinking his numerous battalions a sufficient guarantee of success in attacking a place occupied by Ou-San-Koui, resolved to try an appeal to the heart of the brave defender of his country; and having obtained possession of his aged father at Pekin, he had him pinioned, and led out in front of the walls of the town defended by his son, and then sent a messenger to Ou-San-Koui, informing him that his father was there, and would be put to death with the most horrible torture, if he did not relieve him by a prompt submission. At this news, Ou-San-Koui flew to the ramparts, and seeing his venerable father in the hands of the torturers, in violent agitation, though without showing any signs of weakness, he threw himself on his knees, and conjured his father to pardon him if he left him in the hands of the infamous Ly-Koung. "My duty," he cried, in a firm voice, though evidently deeply grieved, "compels me to think more at this extremity of the safety of the empire than of the life of my father. Oh my father," he added, "life is precious, and it might be granted to you by this wretch; but if bought by submitting to this traitor, it is dishonoured." The father replied with calmness and magnanimity, "My son, do your duty, I am ready to die; your father is proud of the senti ment that animates you." At these words, the cowardly Ly Kouang ordered this noble old man to be put to death with the most frightful torture.

Ou-San-Koui seeing the corpse of his murdered father, swore, in his righteous indignation, to exterminate the oppressor of his country, who had now become also his father's assassin. We have already mentioned that Tchoung-Tching had called in the assistance of the Mantchoo Tartars against the rebels of his empire; and Ou-San-Koui, seeing that his own troops were incapable of contending with the formidable army of Ly-Kouang, sent a courier to the Tartar chief, to ask for a reinforcement. This chief repaired immediately to the town defended by the Chinese general, and concerted means with him of inducing the enemy to raise the siege. The Tartar army was in a great measure composed of cavalry, and to its dashing assistance Ou-San-Koui owed the brilliant success obtained over the Chinese troops accustomed only to make war by tricks and stratagems. The Tartar squadrons came up at full gallop, and with the impetuosity of a torrent fell upon the insurrectionary army, routing it completely. The panic was so great indeed, that its flight never ceased till it reached Pekin, while the Tartar horsemen massacred them in such numbers, that more than a hundred thousand men remained upon the field of battle, though Ly-Kouang himself escaped, and reached Pekin. The town, surrounded with high and strong walls, plentifully provided with cannon and munitions of all kinds, as well as with provisions and men, was now able to stand a long siege; but the Emperor of the revolution had been so terribly shaken by the charge of the Tartar horse, that he thought it better to continue his flight as far as the province of Chan-Si, from which he had originally started when on his march to Pekin. Before providing thus for his own safety, however, this brave warrior took the precaution of advising his companions in arms to set fire to the imperial palace and the entire town.

Ly-Koung's soldiers nevertheless were not so careless of their interests as to burn Pekin, where so much wealth was accumulated. They infinitely preferred pillaging it, and then returning loaded with spoil to their worthy chief at Chan-Si. But though they set to work with all possible diligence, the Tartars arrived before they had done, and they were obliged to decamp with the utmost speed, the Mantchoo cavalry pursuing them and cutting them to pieces in the fields and highways. It is said that on the route from Pekin to Si-ngan-Fou there were to be seen scattered about pieces of silk, embroidered garments, and utensils of all kinds, and of great value, so that one might have supposed that the country had been traversed by bands of merchants whom fear had compelled to abandon their goods.

The province of Chan-Si is one of the largest, as it is one of the richest in China, and its capital, Si-ngan-Fou, was the focus of the insurrection that overturned the empire. There was then a flourishing mission in this town of which Father Nicholas Trigault had been the founder. Father Adam Schall had had charge of it for several years, and had only left it when he was summoned to Pekin by the emperor's order to revise the calendar and organise the academy of mathematicians and astronomers.

Whilst Pekin was a scene of devastation, of fire, and blood, several of the principal Christians, who placed little reliance on the protection of the Tartars, wished to emigrate to Chan-Si, and solicited Father Schall also to adopt this resolution.

"You see," they said, "that Pekin no longer offers you the peace and tranquillity so necessary for the work of God; return then to your first mission, where your former Christian family is awaiting you, and whither that of Pekin also will accompany you. The sheep will follow the shepherd wherever he goes." But Father Schall gently resisted their entreaties, and would not abandon the capital, though continually exposed to a thousand perils. He thought that God had not permitted the mission to be founded in a manner almost miraculous for him to renounce thus, under pretext of flying from danger, all the advantages it might present. He therefore placed himself entirely in the hands of Providence, and resolved, whatever might come of it, to remain at Pekin; and the Almighty soon rewarded the faith and pious trust thus manifested, and proved that the apostle had not counted in vain on His protection.

Whilst the Tartars were pursuing the plunderers along the route to Chan-Si, some bands of insurgents who had been hidden in Pekin set fire to the city. The twelve gates of the ramparts were surmounted by great kiosks of carved wood painted in brilliant colours; at a given signal these were all set on fire, and the flames soon communicated to the palaces of the grand dignitaries, the tribunals civil and military, the academies, supreme courts, and principal quarters of the town. The incendiaries had taken care to place in readiness large quantities of powder, and the capital of the Chinese Empire was soon one vast blazing pile, hurling its ruins from time to time into the air with terrific explosions. The imperial palace was the first public building devoured by this terrible conflagration.

In China the pagodas, tribunals, and all great public buildings are of wood, with colossal carved work painted, and almost covered with gilding and with the brilliant varnish to which Europeans have given the name of lacquer; and these edifices are extraordinarily rich and magnificent in their decorations. The imperial palace was supported on seventy columns resting on marble bases; and as soon as the fire had consumed these columns the whole palace fell in with such a tremendous crash that it was heard all over Pekin, and caused the utmost terror.

Whilst the whole of this vast city was thus becoming the prey of the flames, the habitation of Father Schall remained untouched. Three incendiaries had entered it, but the Father saluted them politely and gently, and begged they would not do any harm. They were just about to cross the threshold again, when a band of furious insurgents broke a large opening in the outer wall, and were rushing in through it with lighted torches; but the courageous missionary ran to them, saying, "That way of entering people's houses is the way of thieves, and not of soldiers. Go back, and I will open the door for you, that you may not disgrace yourselves thus." These words had the effect of calming these misguided men, and they retired without executing their sinister project. The fire went on, however, with frightful rapidity; nothing was heard but the crash of falling houses, the cries of victims, and from time to time the violent explosions occasioned by the gunpowder concealed in the great buildings. Pekin was one huge furnace, and the leaves and branches of the stately trees that encircled it beyond the outer wall were completely calcined, while far and wide over the country every trace of vegetation was burnt up and destroyed, so that it had the same sombre appearance as in the depth of winter.

In the midst of these scenes of desolation Father Schall was performing prodigies of charity. As he knew that in catastrophes of this kind the Chinese easily abandon themselves to despair, and frequently commit suicide, he traversed the town from end to end, and entered such houses as had not yet been destroyed. In many of them, as he himself has related in his letters, he found whole families hanging; and he was sometimes able to save some of the unfortunate creatures, who were not yet dead, and whom he took to his own house, which providentially still remained uninjured, though for days together it was surrounded by flames, and strewed continually with burning brands. Even his library and his mathematical and astronomical instruments were preserved completely uninjured.

Had the fire reached his library, the loss would have been irreparable, for there were preserved the valuable works of

Father Ricci and the other missionaries, as well as numerous writings of his own on astronomy. But God did not permit this misfortune; and the fire, after it had raged all around, stopped at the walls that enclosed these literary, scientific, and theological treasures, so that Father Schall had not to regret the loss of so much as one instrument or a single volume. This extraordinary fact did not of course pass unnoticed by the Chinese, and the fame of it was spread even to the most distant provinces of the empire. It was said that Heaven had protected, at Pekin, the books of the Christian doctrine and the astronomical labours of Tang-Jo-Wan (Adam Schall.)

The Mantchoo Tartars, after having vanquished and put to flight the revolutionary bands of Ly-Koung, collected their forces into one body and marched upon Pekin, which was now little else than a heap of ashes and ruins; but it was still regarded as the capital of the empire and the seat of government; and an attempt had been made to reorganise it, after the expulsion of the insurgents.

Up to this time, the Tartars had been supposed to be fighting with the brave Ou-San-Koui in the cause of the dynasty of Ming, of which there still remained one representative, in the person of a young son of the deceased emperor, now living in profound seclusion in a southern province. Tchoun-Té, the chief of the Mantchoo race, did not, however, conceal his intention of installing himself at Pekin with his victorious army with the purpose of founding there a Tartar dynasty. His companions in arms had traversed, as conquerors, a great part of the Flowery Kingdom, had tasted of the enjoyments of Chinese civilisation, and had little inclination now to return to the banks of the Songari and Saghalian rivers, resume their monotonous nomadic life, and devote themselves to the care of their flocks; for they felt themselves capable of becoming the shepherds and keepers of the Chinese nation.

It was with these ideas that they advanced upon Pekin, and

their projects of conquest were doubtless no mystery; for before they entered the town, they were met by a numerous deputation, composed of the chief magistrates and citizens and the most influential of the men of letters, who congratulated them on their victories, and accompanied them as in triumph into the city. On the way, Tchoun-Té addressed the principal members of the deputation, and asked them whether they were receiving him as a guest, or whether they wished in future to be governed by the Tartars,—a question to which he received no very precise answer. But when the procession reached the enclosure of the Yellow City, or Imperial Palace, there was a universal acclamation of "*Wan Suy! Wan Suy!*" —Ten thousand years! Ten thousand years!—the cry by which the head of the State is ordinarily saluted in China.

After this fervent and spontaneous expression of public feeling, the politicians of Pekin could exclaim, "The Tartar Empire is constituted."

General Ou-San-Koui, indeed, made some protests, but they were too late. He had given masters to his country when he thought only to give her defenders.

The Mantchoo prince survived his triumph but a very short time; for only a few days after his entrance into Pekin, he was seized by a violent malady of which he died, but not before he had proclaimed his son, the young Chun-Tchi, emperor, and appointed three of his brothers regents, earnestly recommending them to remain united, if they wished to secure the brilliant prosperity of their race. The princes who were to act as guardians to the young monarch were great warriors and profound politicians, especially the eldest, whose name was Ama-Wang, and who, uniting the sagacity and ability of a statesman to the finest qualities of a soldier, may be regarded as the true founder of the power of the Mantchoo Tartars in China. He knew how to govern the Chinese with the utmost firmness and energy, without allowing his yoke to press too heavily on them.

It was his plan to mingle and fuse the two nations together, so that they should form but one; though in the years immediately succeeding the conquest he applied himself particularly to establishing the authority of the conquering race.

Such was the character of one of the first acts of the new government. The Tartar troops were so numerous that they could not be contained in the interior of the city at the same time as the Chinese population, and an edict was therefore issued, by which the latter were ordered to evacuate the town, and betake themselves to the outside of the wall of enclosure, three days only being allowed for them to effect the migration. The Chinese submitted without resistance to this harsh proceeding from those who, but a few days before, had inquired whether they were disposed to grant them hospitality; and with respect to the period allowed for the removal of their household goods, the incendiaries and plunderers had made that part of the command extremely easy of execution, for the majority of the unfortunate people of Pekin had nothing to take away but their hungry bodies and some tattered clothing.

The order to emigrate was a terrible blow to Adam Schall, for he saw in it the destruction of his beloved mission. How could he leave what it had cost him so many years of labour and solicitude to establish? It would be to hazard the loss of all the privileges that had been obtained, and to retrograde to the point at which affairs had stood before Father Ricci gained any footing at all in Pekin.

Father Schall believed that there was no time to be lost if he wished to prevent the disaster with which the mission confided to him was threatened. He therefore took his pencil* and drew up a memorial, in which he declared that he was a European, devoted to a religious life, and that for several years he had been preaching to the people of China the law of

---

* Chinese writing is performed with a small brush or hair pencil instead of a pen.

God; that he possessed in the capital a temple, sacred images, and a great number of books, and all things necessary for the exercise of his apostolic functions, and that three days were insufficient to enable him to transport his establishment elsewhere. That being besides charged, by order of the deceased Emperor, with the office of reforming the calendar and correcting the numerous errors that had crept into it, he had in his house the various writings and important calculations made for it engraved on wooden blocks ready for the press, and that to carry these about from place to place would be to run the risk of destroying them and causing much detriment to the public service. He therefore entreated the glorious strangers, now masters of the empire, to suffer him, a stranger like themselves, to remain and reside permanently in the capital.

With this document, composed with the utmost care in his very best Chinese style, Father Schall betook himself to the seat of government, where a kind of senate of Chinese and Tartars, in equal numbers had been hastily got together. Around this Areopagus he found, what is always to be found in the antechamber of a new power, swarms of suitors and supplicants. They were all kneeling on both knees, holding up their petitions in both hands and uttering most profound sighs; but no one was taking the slightest notice of them with the exception of a few of the satellites, who now and then, when the crowd became too great, dealt about amongst them a pretty liberal allowance of thumps with their rattans and bamboos. Father Schall having, since the fall of the Ming dynasty, no longer any official character, presented himself in his ordinary dress and knelt down like the rest; but his long beard and his majestic aspect soon made him remarked. The president of the assembly, having cast upon him a very benevolent look, made a sign for him to approach and present his petition. After having rapidly glanced over the contents of the paper, he asked the missionary to what temple he alluded. "To the edifice to which the Christians go to adore the true God, the creator of all things," was the reply. "Why do you not give it the name of Miao?" (pagoda.) "In order to distinguish our religion from others." The president then spoke to him of the calendar, and asked him whether he held any office in the tribunal of mathematics. "I am at the head of that tribunal," replied Father Schall. And at these words the president invited him to rise, spoke to him with the utmost affability, and desired him to come again on the following day. He then commanded that two mandarins, in their state robes, should accompany him back to his house, partly to do him honour, but partly also to examine his establishment and see whether every thing was exactly as he had stated.

On the following day he was received with every mark of veneration, and a decree presented to him authorising his remaining in Pekin, and to this was added an edict addressed to the Tartars, enjoining on them to treat Tang-Jo-Wan with respect and not to disturb any thing in his house; and he was told to fix this edict on his door. It was obtained in good time, for when Adam Schall returned to his house he found it filled with Tartars, who came with the intention of installing themselves in it and turning him out of doors; but as soon as he had read the edict which he carried, they all retired and sought an abode elsewhere. The establishment outside the town, in the cemetery where Father Ricci was buried, was preserved by the same means.

We have seen with what zealous haste the astronomers and mathematicians presented a new calendar to the chief of the rebels on the very day of his entrance into Pekin, and they were now no less anxious to be in time with the Tartar government. The same deputation set off again with the same ceremony; and when they were asked what they had to offer to their master, they replied, "We bring the ancient calendar of the Celestial Empire, now happily become yours, fully revised and corrected."

"We know," said the Tartar, "that your calendar is full of mistakes, and we have been told that it has been put in order by Tang-Jo-Wan, the celebrated astronomer from the West. Let Tang-Jo-Wan be called." That was not at all what the officers of "Celestial Literature" desired. They had intended to supplant Adam Schall, whose superiority had long been a grievance to them, and they had now the vexation of hearing him proclaimed as the reformer of their calendar.

In the month of September of this year, 1644, an eclipse of the sun took place, which afforded to the Tartars an incontestable proof of the knowledge of the European missionaries and the ignorance of the pretended official astronomers of the empire; after having found that only the calculations of Tang-Jo-Wan were correct, they appointed him master and president of all that concerned celestial literature. This decree was drawn up, presented by the Court of Rites, and duly signed by the young Emperor Chun-Tché, in the month of February, 1645.

The office to which Father Schall had just been appointed by the new Tartar government was one of the most considerable and most coveted that it had to bestow; and the monk, now become a grand dignitary of the empire, would thenceforth be able to employ the influence of his position to advance the work of the propagation of the faith. The credit which he enjoyed at Pekin would enable him to protect his brethren scattered over the provinces, and to struggle successfully against the persecutions of the mandarins.

During times of trouble and confusion, the missionaries had doubtless to suffer, like others, the evils that war necessarily brought with it; but on the whole they were well treated by the Tartars, and as far as their apostleship was concerned they had not much cause to regret the change of dynasty.

Father Martini, to whom Europe was indebted at that epoch for the best and earliest information it obtained concerning events in China, was at a mission in the province of Tche-Kiang, when the rumour was spread of the approach of the Tartar army.

At this news, a panic terror seized on the people, and the Christians rushed to take refuge in the residence of Father Martini, who received them kindly, tried to reanimate their courage, and taught them to rely on the protection of God. When the Tartars were about to enter the town, Father Martini had a placard placed upon his door with an inscription in large characters to the following effect: "A doctor of the Law of God, from the Great West, dwells here;" then he placed in the vestibule of his house tables covered with Chinese and European books, telescopes, and various mathematical and astronomical instruments, and above the principal table a beautiful figure of the Saviour. The Tartars were much struck with this display, and their chief sent for the missionary, and treated him with great consideration.

The Tartars, as they gained ground in the empire, began to impose on the Chinese the obligation of shaving their heads, and adopting the Mantchoo costume[*]; and this proceeding, which at first seemed a mere caprice, had in fact a deep political purpose. By this token of submission or its absence, it became easy to recognise those who were or were not attached to the new government; and the uniformity of costume could not but contribute to fuse together the two races, and disguise from observation the enormous numerical superiority of the Chinese over the Tartars. The foreign domination too would appear less odious when the eye should be no longer wounded by the external diversity of conquerors and conquered.

The Chinese, however, made a most energetic resistance to this decree, and this outward mark of servitude seems to have

---

[*] The leaders of the insurrection which is at the present moment convulsing China have adopted a similar policy, and oblige their partisans to let their hair grow, and return to other ancient Chinese fashions abolished by the Mantchoo Tartars.

been felt as more intolerable than the servitude itself. Men who had appeared indifferent enough to their national indepen dence, and made no great exertion to secure the safety of their heads, fought for their hair and the fashion of their garments with all the courage of despair. Many of them actually chose to die rather than part with their locks.

When the Tartar chief requested Father Martini to cut off his hair and conform to the Mantchoo mode in his garments, he willingly complied, as he felt no particular anxiety about the fashion of his attire, and did not share the Chinese pas sion for length of tresses. The operation of shaving his head was therefore performed on the spot in presence of the Tartar, and with a certain amount of solemnity; and when Father Martini laughingly observed that his Tartar head did not now agree very well with his Chinese person, the Mantchoo took off his own official tunic, his cap and his boots, and having invested the Jesuit with these articles of his toilette, had him conducted to his home by a military guard of honour.

The new government soon brought the north of China into a tolerably tranquil state, but the agitation was still very violent in the south and west. The province of Sse-Tchouan, one of the richest and finest in the empire, had fallen under the power of a famous rebel chief, named Tchang-Hien, whose ravages and cruelties exceeded all belief. When he marched upon Tchang-Fou, the capital of the province, the terrified inhabitants fled at his approach and hid themselves among the mountains; and this precipitate flight alone saved them, for no sooner had the tyrant entered the town than he ordered the indiscriminate massacre of whatever men, women, or children were left in it; and then, in the midst of a hideous mass of bleeding corpses, had himself proclaimed emperor. Some time after these frightful murders, Tchang-Hien learned that the greater part of the inhabitants had taken refuge in the mountains, and he sent soldiers in pursuit of them. Many were found and brought back, and amongst them two missionaries, the Fathers Buglio and Magalhans, who, some years before, had founded the mission in the capital of Sse-Tchouan.

The missionaries were dragged with chains round their necks into the presence of the ferocious tyrant, who had just had himself proclaimed Emperor by an army of robbers, and they could not doubt that he was about to murder them. But to their great astonishment, no sooner had the sanguinary Tchang-Hien cast his eyes on them, than he ordered their chains to be taken off, received them with extraordinary honour, speaking to them in the most affable manner, and promising that as soon as he should be in peaceable possession of the empire, he would build in all the provinces magnificent churches in honour of the Lord of Heaven. In order to show them too that he was in earnest in these promises, he immediately assigned to the missionaries a stately mansion, in which they were allowed to fit up a chapel, and devote themselves in perfect liberty to the duties of their ministry.

Such benevolence on the part of a man who was the terror of the whole western country was perfectly unaccountable, but the missionaries profited by these unexpected favours to labour diligently for the conversion of the infidels. They baptized several, and amongst others the father-in-law of Tchang-Hien, who maintained himself for some time in his usurped authority, and even governed the province in an equitable manner, to the astonishment of the people, who were accustomed to think of him as a kind of wild beast.

The moderation of Tchang-Hien, however, was not of long duration, and he soon abandoned himself again to the bad impulses of his ferocious nature. Having learned that in various places people had revolted against his authority, he ordered massacres which, as detailed in the annals of China, cannot be read without shuddering.

The insubordination of a single individual would generally entail the destruction of all the inhabitants of the street or the quarter in which he lived. A Buddhist monk having had the imprudence to censure his administration, all the Bonzes of the province, to the number of 20,000, were slaughtered. The inhabitants of a town, in which the population was estimated at more than 600,000, were pitilessly murdered, without a single one being allowed to escape. "Soon," say the Chinese annals, "a river of blood covered the earth. The tyrant had the dead bodies thrown into the river, in order that the inhabitants of the countries by which it was watered might be warned, by the spectacle of its waters changed into gore and the mangled bodies floating on them, of the frightful fate that awaited themselves."*

This miscreant was preparing to march upon the province of Chan-Si to conquer it, but, before setting out, he wished to deprive the province of Sse-Tchouan of the power of revolting during his absence, and the method he adopted to effect this purpose was the ordering a general execution in all the districts, and after having selected the troops necessary for his expedition, he had the rest massacred to the number of 140,000. The sight of blood and quivering limbs seemed to afford the monster a positive enjoyment; he liked to be present at these horrible spectacles, and himself to suggest to the executioners refinements of cruelty.

The soldiers were tortured in various ways, quartered, flayed alive, slowly cut into small pieces, and often he would not suffer them to be killed out of their misery—but left them in their mangled state to die in more lingering agonies.

One day he ordered his troops to send their wives into a neighbouring plain, under pretence that he was going to distribute to them a certain amount of pay, for them to subsist upon during the absence of the army. He himself would go to them he said, and accordingly he betook himself to the appointed spot, attended by his numerous harem; and when the unfortunate women arrived he had their throats cut.

* Histoire Générale de la Chine, vol. II. p. 94.

These almost incredible details are reported by all the historians of the time, who add that Tchang-Hien left the great province of Sse-Tchouan almost entirely depopulated.*

The Fathers Buglio and Magalhans could not remain under the government of such a monster; but not daring, without his permission, to quit the residence he had assigned them, they addressed to him a petition, asking leave to go and seek elsewhere a place less exposed to the tumults of war, where it might be possible for them to fulfil in peace the duties of their sacred ministry. The tyrant was so irritated at this request, that two hours after he sent for the servants of the missionaries, reproached them with having suggested to their masters the idea of flight, and immediately condemned them to be flayed alive. At this news the horror-struck missionaries rushed to the tribunal in the hope of saving the lives of their unfortunate converts; they declared that these men had nothing to do with their resolution, and they did not even know of their project of leaving the province. The monster, instead of granting the pardon for which they besought him, ordered the missionaries themselves to be dragged to the place of execution; they were about to be torn to pieces, when the son of the ferocious Tchang-Hien seized the arm of the executioner, already raised to strike, and snatched his victims from him. The tyrant allowed himself to be disarmed by the supplica-

---

* "This bloodthirsty tiger exercised his fury even upon the animals which had escaped in the general massacre of the inhabitants; and entire herds of horses, oxen, and sheep, were slaughtered by his order. Nothing now remained to be done by the destructive monster but to reduce the province to such a condition that it could never more be inhabited; and he tried to effect this by pulling down palaces, the walls of the towns, public and private edifices,—nothing was spared, but the whole was reduced to utter ruin by the troops. 'I will,' (as he afterwards caused it to be published through the army,) 'I will annihilate even the very name of that province, that my vengeance may be eternal. I will find elsewhere palaces, and my soldiers houses more convenient and magnificent; let them feel no regret in seeing all these absolutely destroyed. Since the province is to remain for ever a desert, what would be the use of trees and forests? Let the fire complete my vengeance, and a universal conflagration consume all that can be destroyed by flames?'"—*General History of China*, vol. xl. p. 25.

tions of his son, who knew and loved the missionaries; but nevertheless the Fathers Buglio and Magalhans were confined in a dungeon, where they suffered all kinds of ill-treatment. They had been pining for a month in their gloomy prison, when they were brought out to be dragged into the presence of Tchang-Hien, and had now no doubt that their last hour was come, for the sanguinary monster was at that moment directing a frightful execution, and already the capacious hall where he sat was streaming with human blood and covered with corpses. The executioner was approaching Father Magalhans, when a sentinel cried out that the Tartar cavalry were advancing towards the town. The tyrant did not appear to give faith to this news; nevertheless he rose, and accompanied by some soldiers went to see if there was really any danger, and soon found himself in the presence of some horsemen of the Tartar advanced guard. The ferocious Tchang-Hien fell at the first attack, pierced through the heart with an arrow; the army of the insurgents was immediately seized with a panic terror, and the missionaries, taking advantage of the confusion, which was general, escaped from the hands of the executioners, and hastened to take refuge in the Tartar camp. But in flying from one danger they fell into another; for, being taken for spies, they were attacked by a party of horsemen, and fell severely wounded. One of the arrows passed right through the arm of Father Magalhans, and Father Buglio received a deep wound in the right thigh, in which the head of the arrow lodged; but the poor missionaries tried to console each other, and to dress each other's wounds. Whilst Father Magalhans was endeavouring to tear out with his teeth the iron which was deeply buried in his companion's flesh, some other horsemen fell upon them; one of the Tartars had seized Father Magalhans by the hair, and was already preparing to cut off his head, when his chief, having by chance observed the long beard of the missionary, stopped the soldier's arm, and asked Magalhans if he knew Tang-Jo-Wang (Adam Schall). "He is my elder brother," answered Father Magalhaas. At these words, the horsemen surrounded the two missionaries, and removed them to the tent of the Mantchoo Tartar general, who on hearing who they were and what had happened to them, had their wounds dressed, caused them to be nursed with the greatest care, kept them in his own tent, and when they were cured, took them with him to Pekin, where they found Father Adam Schall in possession of the favour of the Tartar sovereign, and enjoying considerable influence with the new government. They then discovered to whose influence the missionaries of the provinces were indebted for the kind treatment they had received from the Tartars.

The missions of China had indeed enjoyed greater liberty ever since Father Schall had been at the head of the department of mathematical and astronomical science. But the duties which daily devolved upon him, besides that they were not always in perfect harmony with his habits as a priest, left him very little time to devote to the immediate interests of his sacred ministry. The daily presentations at the imperial palace, the visits to be paid or received, his presence at official ceremonies, the establishment of a great Mandarin with a numerous train of servants and retainers, all this was very oppressive and often very unseemly for a missionary. Father Schall, who was far less a courtier than priest and an apostle, soon discovered this, and hastened to address a memorial to the young emperor Chun-Tché, in which he explained to him that his sacred office laid on him the obligations of prayer and preaching, which his conscience forbade him to neglect, but which he could not, nevertheless, always reconcile with the functions of his new office; he therefore entreated to be released from the honorary and ceremonial requirements of his appointment; and the Emperor yielded to his request. According to ancient custom, the newly elected members of the mathematical college had to give up their first year's emoluments to the president; but Adam Schall disinterestedly sacrificed this privilege. He renounced all the pomp and luxury with which his predecessors loved to be surrounded, and much reduced the number of those door-keepers, or rather *Cerberi*, who blocked up the avenues to the tribunals, extorted money from the people, and prevented them from having access to the Mandarins; but notwithstanding all these reforms, this dignity was, as we shall presently see, the source of the greatest trouble and the most intense anxiety to Father Schall.

The high official position which the Jesuits have sometimes occupied at Pekin has, in many circumstances, been a great assistance to them in promoting the success of their mission; but it must also be granted that it has frequently been very injurious.

The mathematical college was composed of seventy members and a hundred supernumeraries; and when a place was vacant, Father Schall, as president, had the privilege of appointing to it. All disappointed candidates, as well as their relations and friends, therefore became the bitter enemies of the Christian religion and its ministers. It is not in general well for the Christian clergy to mingle too much with the affairs of this world: the exercise of the office of a Mandarin by a priest is not likely to tend to the glory of God, or to the promotion of man's salvation. This is true in all countries, but especially in China, where the inhabitants, naturally avaricious and jealous to excess, cannot reconcile themselves to seeing foreigners fill important offices to the exclusion of the native literati.

CHAPTER IX.

Legend respecting the origin of the Mantchoo Tartars. — Father Schall and the King of the Coreans. — Rash Enterprise of the Regent of the Empire. — Ama-Wang listens to the advice of Father Schall. — Influence of that celebrated Missionary. — The Claimants of the Ancient Dynasty. — Their Friendliness to Christianity. — Dissensions among the Chinese Claimants. — They are Destroyed by Ama-Wang. — Death of that Illustrious Tartar. — Majority of the Young Emperor. — Application of Father Schall. — His Advice to the Emperor. — Intimacy between Father Schall and the Emperor. — Chun-Tché loves and favours Christianity. — Progress of the Missionaries. — Construction of a beautiful Church at Pekin. — Zeal of the Christians. — Religious Associations. — Titles conferred by the Emperor on Father Schall and his Ancestors. — Sickness of Chun-Tché. — Exhortations of Father Schall. — Death of the Emperor. — His Funeral.

THE new Chinese empire soon became firmly organized by the energy, and, we may also say, by the capacity of the Mantchoo Tartar race.

These men, who until that time had thought of nothing but keeping flocks and herds, and hunting and fishing, in their vast forests and broad rivers, were found better calculated than had been imagined to become good governors of provinces and wise rulers; and their firm belief in their future high destiny contributed much to enhance and confirm their success. They were persuaded that their nation, having miraculously descended from heaven, was destined to accomplish great things on earth.

The true conqueror of the empire, Ama-Wang, uncle of the young Emperor Chun-Tché had formed an intimate friendship with Father Schall, and liked to converse familiarly with him; and in one of these conversations he one day related the miraculous way in which his family derived their origin from the stars. "Ten generations," said he, "have now passed away, since three young girls descended from the skies to bathe on the banks of the Songari; their names were Argila, Changura, and Fégula. Some magnificent red fruits, coming they knew not whence, were found on the banks of the river close by Fégula's tunic, and she, perceiving them and admiring their beauty, ate of them. Her two companions, after rising from the stream, reascended into heaven; but Fégula could not follow them: she had become pregnant, and had no longer power to quit the earth. She gave birth to a beautiful male child, suckled it, and then placed it in a little island formed by the waters of the river. She directed it to await there the coming of the person who was to be its guardian, and who would, ere long, come to the island to fish; and having said these words, she arose up into the sky whence she had descended.

"It happened as Fégula had foretold; the child grew up into a prodigiously strong and valiant man. He had sons and grandsons, who, by degrees, became powerful in the land. After five generations, a terrible war broke out, which annihilated them; they were all put to death with the exception of one, who fled across the desert. When overpowered by weariness and unable to continue his journey, he sat down on the ground, at the risk of dying by the hands of his pursuers. But the divine Fégula was watching over him; she directed the flight of a magpie, which perched on his head. The enemy, thinking that the magpie was perched on the trunk of a tree, departed; and thus, by the help of heaven, was rescued the heir of that race which Fégula had brought into the world.* He became the progenitor of the Mantchoo Tartar nation; and from him descended in a direct line the founder of the dynasty which now fills the imperial throne of Pekin."

The Mantchoo Tartars believe this legend, and this convic-

---

* It was in remembrance of this miracle that the Mantchoo Tartar government forbade, under the severest penalties, the destruction of magpies' nests in Pekin.

tion of their divine origin contributed not a little to inspire them with that perfect confidence which is often an earnest of success. Being also by nature very superstitious, they contrived to find in every thing an omen of their future greatness. Thus the reform of the calendar and the improvements in astronomy, which had been in progress for so many years, had been completed at the very moment when the Tartars had made themselves masters of the empire. This was evidently an excellent omen; and they thence concluded without hesitation that their empire was to last forever. This fortunate coincidence of the reform of the calendar with the foundation of the empire gave great celebrity to Father Schall. The name of Tang-Jo-Wang became highly popular both at court and in the provinces; for it was, in some degree, associated with the fortunes of the new dynasty. The young Emperor Chun-Tché sent Adam Schall a marble tablet, on which was an inscription, paying homage to the Lord of Heaven, and celebrating the knowledge and virtue of Tang-Jo-Wang. The Emperor was proud of the fact that, on the very day on which the Tartars entered triumphantly into the walls of Pekin, the new calendar was presented to them. "Let none be surprised," said he, "that I should honour Tang-Jo-Wang, and show him the most peculiar favour; for immediately that heaven had granted me the empire, this extraordinary man was also sent to me, and I receive him as a gift from heaven."

At this period the king of the Coreans was at Pekin. Having fallen into the hands of the Mantchoos at the termination of the war, he had been brought to Moukden, the capital of Mantchuria; and the Tartar chief had promised to set him at liberty when he became master of the Chinese Empire. As soon as Chun-Tché was proclaimed Emperor, he kept his word to his illustrious captive, and he, before he should return to his own dominions, desired to return his thanks to his deliverer.

During his stay at Pekin the King of Corea* became acquainted with Father Schall. He was fond of visiting the father in a friendly manner, and used to receive him in his own palace with the utmost cordiality; he endeavoured also, by this instructive conversation, to improve the noble Coreans of his retinue, hoping that they would carry into their own country valuable information on the subjects of astronomy and mathematics, sciences in which they had yet made no great progress. The missionary, on his side, did not fail to take advantage of this frequent intercourse, to instruct his new friends in the truths of the Christian religion, not doubting that they would afterwards scatter the seed of the true faith over the land of unbelievers. By degrees, they contracted so close an intimacy with each other, that it was not without the deepest regret they separated.

As the King of Corea had a taste for Chinese literature, Father Schall sent him, some days before he left Pekin, a copy of every work written by the Jesuits on scientific and religious subjects; and to these he added a celestial globe and a beautiful picture of our Saviour. This present pleased the king so much that he wrote, with his own hand, a letter to Father Schall in the Chinese character, to express his gratitude. Here is a translation of this curious document.

"Yesterday, whilst I was looking at the unexpected present you have sent me, the image of the Saviour, the celestial globe, the books on astronomy and other subjects, which contain all the science and wisdom of the European world, I was filled with joy, and my imperfect language cannot express the warmth of my gratitude.

"In looking over some of these valuable books, I perceive that they contain doctrines calculated to improve the heart

---

* Corea, called by the Chinese, Kao-Li, is a great peninsula situated between China and Japan. Its length from north to south is about 200 miles, and its average breadth 60. Although under the same degree of latitude as Italy, the climate of Corea is very cold.

and adorn it with every virtue. These sublime doctrines have been until now unknown in our country, where the light of intelligence is but dim and obscure. The holy picture possesses such majesty, that, when it hangs on the wall, one need only look at it to feel the soul at peace and purified from every stain. The globe and the books of astronomy are works so necessary in a kingdom, that I know not how I can have been so fortunate as to have obtained them; there are, certainly, some of the same kind in my dominions, but it must be confessed that they are full of errors, and that for centuries they have been more and more departing from the truth.

"Since you have thus enriched me, why should not my heart rejoice? When I return to my own country, they shall be respectfully placed in my palace; I shall have them engraved and printed, that they may be circulated among studious men and lovers of science. By this means my subjects will be enabled to appreciate the good fortune which has led them out of the desert into the temple of erudition, and the Coreans will know that it is to the learned men of Europe they are indebted for such a blessing.

"And we two natives of different kingdoms, coming from countries so distant, and separated by the great waters of the ocean, we have met in a foreign land, and loved each other as if we were united by the ties of blood. I cannot understand by what hidden power of nature all this has happened. I cannot but confess that the souls of men are united by knowledge, however distant they may be from each other on the earth. I now think of nothing but the happiness of being able to carry away with me these books and this sacred picture into my own country. But, when I reflect that my subjects have never heard of divine worship, and that they may offend the majesty of the Lord of Heaven by erroneous practices, my heart is full of uneasiness and anxiety. For this reason, I have been thinking, if you will permit me, of sending back the sacred picture, for I should be guilty of a great crime if that reverence should be omitted that is due to it.

"Should I meet with anything in my own country worthy of your acceptance, I shall send it you as a mark of my gratitude; it will be a trifling gift in return for the 10,000 I have received from you."

By expressing at the end of his letter an intention of sending back the picture of the Saviour, the King of Corea only acted in accordance with the rites of Chinese politeness; it was a mere formula of propriety and modesty; for when a present is received containing various articles, it is considered good taste to return what is most valuable. Father Schall begged the king to keep the picture, and at the same time asked if he could not take with him one of the catechists, to preach the religion of the true God to the Coreans. The king replied, "That he joyfully accepted the whole present," adding, "I should like to take with me one of your European companions to instruct us; nevertheless, whoever you may send shall be considered as your representative."

Although so well disposed to receive the true faith, the King of Corea could not at that time obtain preachers of the gospel, since their number was still inconsiderable in China, and the policy of the Mantchoo Tartar emperors afterwards forbade all communication between the Coreans and Chinese. The subjects of the two countries were to have no intercourse except at fixed periods, and by means of mutual embassies, the members of which were counted and appointed beforehand; and they were allowed to remain and carry on trade abroad only for a very limited time. Some monks of the Order of St. Francis made afterwards many attempts both by land and sea to penetrate into Corea, but always in vain, until the time when a member of the Corean embassy himself came to search for the precious seed of the Gospel, in order to sow it in his own country. We shall have occasion to speak of this again in the course of our narrative.*

The young Emperor Chun-Tché was growing up in the palace of Pekin, whilst his uncle, the true founder of the empire, was organising the administration of the provinces and struggling in the south against the partisans of the old régime, who, sometimes on one side, sometimes on the other, made continual attempts to effect a counter-revolution. Chun-Tché was remarkably intelligent for his age. Though he was still a mere child, he employed himself assiduously in public affairs, and showed an energy and capacity very displeasing to those whose interest it was to see the regency of his uncle prolonged. Ama-Wang, though sincerely attached to his nephew, nevertheless loved power; and, accustomed for many years to be sole master of the empire, he was uneasy at the rapid progress of the young Emperor; was displeased to feel the reins of government escaping from his hands, and foresaw that he should soon have to obey his ward. In order to protract as much as possible the duration of his absolute authority, it was his desire to withdraw himself from the controul of the precocious sovereign, which was already becoming burdensome. For this purpose he resolved to lay the foundation of a great city not far from the capital, whither he might retire with the Mandarins and the six supreme courts, leaving young Chun-Tché at Pekin with the population of traders, men of letters, and Bonzes. The execution of this grand plan required enormous sums of money, and he fairly emptied the treasury, besides loading the people with additional taxes, and seizing labourers out of every family, who were condemned to work

---

* We have already spoken of an expedition of the Japanese into Corea, early in the seventeenth century. The leaders of the expedition were Japanese princes converted to Christianity. Several Jesuit ministers followed them into that country, and many of the Coreans were baptized. "Still more affected," says Charlevoix, "by the examples of virtue their conquerors gave them than persuaded by the sermons of the ministers of the Gospel."—*History and General Description of Japan*, vol. L. p. 609.

gratuitously, and enrolled by thousands for this kind of forced labour. So blind was Ama-Wang rendered by an excessive love of authority, though otherwise a wise man, and endowed with many fine qualities!

During this time, the partisans of the fallen dynasty tried to organise themselves, and emigrated in numbers towards the southern provinces, where it was said, there dwelt a branch of the Ming imperial family. The people, exasperated by the exorbitant impost with which they had just been loaded, openly expressed their discontent, and the Mantchoo race had some cause to fear the loss of an empire that was only just acquired. Ama-Wang was so dreaded, that no one dared to warn him of the danger, or exhort him to renounce his insane intentions. But there was one man in Pekin, who, moved by profound pity at the misery of the people, and dreading to see the flames of civil war rekindled, had the courage to make himself heard, and to break the deceitful silence which prevailed around the powerful Ama-Wang. This man was the Catholic missionary Father Adam Schall. Supported by the influence and authority conferred on him by his title of President of Celestial Literature, he dared to address to the prince-regent an admonition, in which, after having made known to him the alarming signs which were appearing in the heavens and on the earth, he said that, to restore peace to the people, the unfortunate project of founding this great city must be resigned, for that the execution of it would be the overthrow of the empire.

The works had been for some days carried on with activity, and the future magistrates of the city were assembled at the palace of Ama-Wang, when the admonitory letter of Father Schall was delivered. The regent began to read rapidly and aloud this courageous remonstrance; but overcome by anger he was unable to finish it. "Why," said he, "has Tang-Jo-Wang the audacity to speak to me in this way?" "The European," answered one of the ministers present, "has not exceeded the limits of his authority or the duties of his office; if you think that he has gone too far, if you blame him, he will henceforward keep silence, and the empire will lose the benefit of his advice." Ama-Wang became calm and began to reflect seriously. The next day he sent for Father Schall, and told him he had done his duty as a worthy President of Celestial Literature, by sending this warning full of prudence and wisdom. The plan was abandoned, and orders were given for the works to cease and the labourers to be sent back to their families. This event made a salutary impression on the minds of both Tartars and Chinese, and reflected great honour on the Christian religion and its ministers.

On the same day when the proclamation appeared announcing that Ama-Wang had abandoned his project, there were still, in the prisons of Pekin, more than 700 unhappy creatures, who had been torn from their labours and their industry to be sent to the new city; they lay groaning and crowded together in frightful dungeons, when suddenly their chains were broken, and they were restored to liberty. As soon as they found that this happiness had been obtained for them by Tang-Jo-Wang, a preacher of the religion of the Lord of Heaven, they ran in crowds to the church of the mission, and, prostrating themselves, struck the earth with their foreheads in token of gratitude. The surrounding streets were filled with these poor workmen, who stretched out their arms towards the church, and thanked the "Saint of the West" in a loud voice for having restored them to liberty.

How sweet must have been the emotions of Father Schall, when he heard from his cell the thanksgivings of this multitude of men whom he had restored to their families, and in some measure to life. The Jesuits have sometimes been blamed for having endeavoured to please the court of Pekin, by too much devotion to the arts and sciences, but it seems to us, that if those who thus censure them would consider all the good effected under their influence they would be induced to do them more justice. A single act of charity often does more for the propagation of the faith than the most eloquent sermon.

The name of Tang-Jo-Wang was now in every mouth. Great and little, Chinese and Tartars, all were unanimous in his praises. The most important men in the government seemed to regard it as an honour to go and visit him, and hear him discourse on the sciences and religion. These visitors certainly did not all embrace Christianity, but the celebrity of the illustrious missionary contributed much to the glory of God and the salvation of souls. Several of the friends of Father Schall were appointed governors of provinces, and the remembrance of their former relations with the chief of the religion of the Lord of Heaven, induced them to favour the Christians under their jurisdiction. Tang-Jo-Wang was known throughout the empire, and the name was often for the missionaries themselves as a shield to protect them from the darts of their enemies. One day Father Francis Ferrari was dragged before the Mandarin of his district, and was just about to be condemned to flagellation, as a propagator of bad doctrines, when some person in the tribunal exclaimed that he was the companion of the celebrated Tang-Jo-Wang. At these words the Mandarin rose from his seat, made a thousand apologies, and ordered that he should be reconducted to his house with a guard of honour, and we have already seen that the mere name of Father Schall saved the lives of the Fathers Buglio and Magalhans, when they fell pierced with arrows in the midst of a Tartar squadron.

Whilst the missionaries were enjoying in the north of the empire the favour and protection of the Mantchoo Tartars, their fellow labourers for the gospel scattered about the provinces of the south were kindly treated by the members of the old Chinese dynasty, who were making vain efforts to regain their power. We have seen the tragical end of Tchoung-Tching, who hung himself on one of the trees in his own park, after endeavouring with barbarous tenderness to put his daughter to death. This unfortunate monarch had left three sons, the two youngest of whom had been massacred by the ferocious bands of the revolutionary chief, Ly-Koung. The eldest, who was eighteen years of age, succeeded in making his escape, and wandered a long time, under various disguises, through the southern provinces. Having at length found means to place himself in the house of a rich man as a servant, he adopted that melancholy expedient, and afterwards, it is said, devoted himself to the cultivation of letters and poetry. He composed satirical songs against the usurpers of his throne, and sang them himself to the accompaniment of the guitar, endeavouring to console himself thus for the loss of a crown. His master, however, wanted a servant and not a poet, and treated him with so much severity, that the unfortunate prince was obliged to seek an asylum elsewhere.

He went to an old Mandarin, whom the Emperor, his father, had formerly overwhelmed with favours, and hoping the remembrance of the imperial munificence would obtain for the poor fugitive prince a hospitable reception. He does not seem to have known how little gratitude is to be expected by those who are no longer in a position to confer benefits. The former favourite of the dynasty of Ming had no mind to compromise himself, and pitilessly shut the door on the heir of his royal master, for fear that if the prince were discovered he should himself be involved in his ruin. The poor exile then resumed his wandering life among the mountains of Chan-Si, till, worn out by hunger and misery, he determined to go and seek an asylum with his maternal grandfather, an inoffensive old man, whose poverty, seclusion and grey hairs had induced the Tartars to spare him. The prince made his way to the humble habitation, situated in a deep gorge among high mountains, and found his aged relative with a young woman at his side, who started at his approach. It was his own sister, she whom the Emperor Tchoung-Tching had vainly endeavoured to put to death before destroying himself, but whose ill-directed stroke had merely cut off her hand. These two young people had grown up together in the palace of the most powerful sovereign of Asia, in the midst of luxury, riches and pleasure, and doubtless had dreamed of nothing but a brilliant destiny for their future lives; and now they were fugitive wanderers, meeting by chance in a wild country, where they were seeking a refuge from the bloody terrors of revolution.

It may be supposed how affecting was the meeting; a source at the same time of profound grief and soothing consolation. The venerable white-bearded old man, the young princess mutilated by the desperate act of an affectionate father, and a young prince, the heir of the greatest throne in the world, seeking shelter together in a little cottage hidden in the woods in the midst of mountains, must have formed a singular group.

All the members of the fallen dynasty had not shown the same resignation in submitting to the usurped power of the Mantchoo Tartars. Several petty princes, the nephews or cousins of the Emperor Tchoung-Tching, had resorted to arms, and rallied around them the partisans of the Chinese nationality; and one of them, who had assembled rather a considerable force in the province of Kouang-Si,* had had himself proclaimed emperor under the name of Jun-Lié. He had his court completely organised, and an Empire of the Restoration was thus seen rising by the side of that acquired by conquest.† It will perhaps be remembered that the first attempts at Christian propagandism in the seventeenth century were made in this province of Kouang-Si, and it was there that Fathers Roger and Ricci, after innumerable difficulties, succeeded in building a house and a church at Tchao-Tcheou, near the

---

* It is in this same province that the present insurrection in China commenced, the object of which is—as the former one was—to drive out the Mantchoo Tartars.

† Jun-Lié was proclaimed Emperor in 1647, in Kouang-Si, and his authority was soon recognised also in the provinces of Ho-nan and Fo-Kien.

Flowery Tower, afterwards called the Tower of the Strangers. We have related the struggles and vicissitudes of this first Catholic mission; but by labour and perseverance, Christianity had at last been firmly planted in Kouang-Si, and at the period of which we are speaking, the province contained several preachers of the gospel and a considerable number of neophytes.

The members of the fallen Ming dynasty who had taken refuge in this province had formerly known Father Ricci at Pekin; they had listened to his religious instructions, read the books that he had published, and had been witnesses of the progress of the Christian faith; but standing, as they did then, at the summit of grandeur, surrounded by the dazzling pomp of imperial power, they had closed their eyes to the light, and had felt perhaps little inclination to humble themselves at the foot of the cross. But now that the throne of their ancestors had fallen, and that they were in danger of losing for ever their kingdom in this world, although fighting valiantly to regain it, they thought at the same time of preparing for themselves a place in that of eternity. The mercy of God is infinite, and effects, sometimes by a wonderful combination of circumstances, the salvation of His elect.

The missionaries, scattered over the Central Empire, had the prudence not to entangle themselves during these revolutionary times with any political party. As those resident at Pekin had at once submitted to the government of the Mantchoos, those of Kouang-Si had faithfully obeyed the Emperor Jun-Lié; and allowing others to fight sanguinary battles for the possession of empire, they laboured zealously for the peaceful conquest of souls. In the north, Father Adam Schall, the friend of the Tartars, enjoyed the favour of the Emperor Chun-Tché; and in the south, Father Andrea Koffler, being attached to the Chinese dynasty, was honoured by the friendship of the Emperor Jun-Lié and his court. He was so fervent and persevering in his efforts for their conversion, that he succeeded in conferring baptism on several princes and princesses, and among others on the Empress herself and her young son, with the consent of Jun-Lié. The Empress took the name of Helena, and gave to her son that of Constantine; two magnificent names, but which, alas, in this instance, did not realise the hopes to which they gave rise. These illustrious neophytes were, nevertheless, pious and sincere in their devotion to the duties of the religion which they had embraced; and they appeared to pursue the conquest of the kingdom of Heaven with more earnestness and confidence than the re-conquest of the Chinese Empire. The Empress Helena, desirous of offering to the Sovereign Pontiff the homage of her filial piety, entrusted Father Boym, a Polish Jesuit, with letters for Alexander VIII., who then occupied the chair of St. Peter. But the missionary had hardly left the coast of China when political events occurred which completely ruined the hopes of the dynasty of Ming and frustrated the generous projects of the Empress Helena for the propagation of the Christian faith.

The reaction which had taken place in Kouang-Si, in favour of Chinese legitimacy, had made progress enough to occasion serious uneasiness to the victorious Tartars, but, fortunately for them, another prince of the dynasty of Ming had divided and weakened the Chinese party by having himself proclaimed emperor at Nankin. The enemies of the Mantchoos thus lost their centre of operations, and knew not round which standard to rally, but passed from Nankin to Kouang-Si and from Kouang-Si to Nankin as fortune appeared to favour the one or the other claimant. The state of affairs was soon still further complicated by the appearance of a third pretender, who had, in fact, the most legitimate claim of all, being the son of the last emperor, and the true heir to the throne.

We have already mentioned that this young prince had sought an asylum in the house of his maternal grandfather, where he had found his sister. He appears to have been living in tranquil retirement and obscurity when he learned that two of his relations were endeavouring to rouse the partisans of the family, and to recover the empire on their own account. The news had an electric effect upon him; the imperial blood boiled once more in the veins of the young man; and he who had submitted to the usurpation of strangers could not think without indignation of that of his own relations. The thought of seeing one of his own subjects seated on the throne was more painful to him than that it should be occupied by a Tartar conqueror. He bade adieu therefore to his sister, and proceeded at once to Nankin, where he announced himself as the son of the Emperor Tchoung-Tching, and the sole heir of the dynasty of Ming. This unexpected apparition completed the confusion of the Chinese party; and some declared themselves for, and some against, the imperial prince. But the pretender who had been proclaimed at Nankin refused to acknowledge his legitimate sovereign, and gave orders to arrest him as an impostor, and throw him into prison.

Immediately on the arrival of this news at Pekin, the Tartar government, thinking that there was no time to lose, resolved to profit by the anarchy that reigned in the enemies' camp, to strike a decisive blow and exterminate in a single campaign all the rival claimants. The able and intrepid Ama-Wang put himself at the head of a considerable army, marched upon Nankin, crossed the Yellow River without hindrance, and encamped his troops on the banks of the Yang-Tse-Kiang. After several fierce encounters, the Tartars passed the great river and took the town of Nankin by storm. Two of the pretenders who had been asserting their rival claims fell alive into the hands of Ama-Wang, who sent them to Pekin, where they were put to death along with their principal partisans.

Whilst the Tartar government was ridding itself of its enemies by these bloody executions, the indefatigable Ama-Wang was pursuing his victorious course. From Nankin he fell, swift and terrible as the thunderbolt, upon the third pretender at Kouang-Si. The dynasty of Ming, restored for a brief period, fell at the first shock of the Tartar cavalry. The Emperor Jun-Lié was killed in his palace with his young son Constantine, and the Empress Helena was carried off captive to Pekin, where she found, in the exercise of her religion, a great source of consolation for her misfortunes. Father Schall often went to her, to afford her the benefit of his ministry, and the letters of the missionary inform us that this princess endured the rigours of her unhappy fate, with a heroism truly Christian.

Ama-Wang returned to Pekin covered with glory, and amidst the acclamations of the whole city, for the Chinese as well as the Tartars were full of admiration for the valour and eminent qualities of the first regent; but only a few days after his brilliant triumph, this illustrious man, the conqueror, the pacificator, and the first organiser of the empire, was struck down by death.

At the death of Ama-Wang, the young Emperor Chun-Tché had attained his fourteenth year, and was consequently, by the laws of the empire, of age. The council of regency made some attempts to retain the young monarch still some time in tutelage; but it was obliged to yield to public opinion, which loudly demanded that Chun-Tché should assume as soon as possible the reins of government. This young man had indeed been early remarked for his precocity and for mental qualifications far above his age. He was full of intelligence, activity, and courage, and was remarkable for the precocious maturity of his reasoning powers, and his immovable firmness of character. He had formed a strong attachment to Father Schall, and in the long conversations that he held with him, used to like to hear him speak on serious and useful subjects; and his frequent intercourse with that eminent missionary could have hardly failed to develop the valuable qualities with which he was endowed by nature. When after he had attained his majority, it became known that the regents intended nevertheless to retain the supreme authority in their own hands, a political movement took place hitherto unexampled in Pekin.

The ministers, the presidents of the Supreme Court, and all the mandarins of the capital, betook themselves in solemn procession to the imperial palace, and laid down at the gates the attributes of their dignity, declaring that they would not take them again unless the young Emperor should himself assume the reigns of government, and exercise supreme authority. Chun-Tché, then declaring that the regency existed no longer, boldly assumed his position at the head of the empire, and convoking the Tartar princes and grand dignitaries of the state to a solemn meeting, addressed them in a speech, the ability and energy of which excited the admiration alike of the old Chinese politicians and of the Tartar warriors. It was remarked, too, that it contained a warm eulogium on the European Tang-Jo-Wang.

Father Schall, who in the honour and anxiety of his influence over the young Emperor, never lost sight of the sacred object of his mission, had availed himself of the present friendly disposition of his majesty to address to him two petitions. The first, for the restoration of the ramparts of the city and the imperial palace, burnt by the revolutionary bands of Ly-Koung, was received with great applause and immediately granted: the second concerned a matter more delicate and difficult. The Empress-mother being greatly addicted to the superstitions of Buddhism, had endeavoured to inspire the young Emperor with the same sentiments, and had succeeded but too well; so that immediately after the death of Ama-Wang, the Bonzes had hastened to throng around Chan-Tché, and not content with obtaining from him a promise to raise in the empire a considerable number of towers in honour of Buddha, they desired that he should declare himself publicly and officially their disciple. They had even carried their audacity so far as to predict that if he did not yield to their wishes he should die in the eighth month of that year.

Father Schall, distressed to see the young Emperor falling into such a deplorable course, plainly expressed in this petition the opinion he entertained of the Bonzes and Buddhist superstitions. "It would be shameful," he said, "to place the destinies of the empire in the hands of men who are not learned or virtuous enough to give them any pretension to become the preceptors of the Emperor. It is not true that they have any power over demons; and the little flags that they plant on the tops of towers and the roofs of houses are the playthings of the winds, and nothing more. They have no influence upon spirits, who are subject only to the Almighty power of God. These little flags cannot stop them, for they can pass through walls, fly in the air, or make their way even through the bowels of the earth, if God permits it. There is no obstacle for them; bodies can stop bodies only, and spirits can come and go without the Bonzes having any power to prevent it. The Bonzes are equally incapable, too, of a knowledge of future events. Life and death depend on God alone!

The Emperor read attentively the appeal of his "President of Celestial Literature," and then exclaimed to those around him:—"I know that this wise old man has always spoken the truth to me. What a pity that he did not warn me sooner." He had in part already entered into engagements with the Bonzes to build a Buddhist tower, and given enormous sums for the erection of others; and though he seems, after reading the memorial of Father Schall, to have felt some regret at having done so, he would not withdraw his promise without the advice of the Empress-mother. He sent the memorial to her, but she only bowed her head without uttering a word; and though the step taken by Father Schall was not so successful as he desired, and did not obtain the formal sanction of the Emperor, it was approved by the court of rites, which had some cause to complain of the Bonzes, and took advantage of the circumstance to forbid their continuing the erection of the Buddhist towers.

Father Schall continued to exercise great influence over the emperor, who was accustomed to call him *Maffa*, a Mantchoo word that may be translated, " venerable old man," and the zealous missionary employed all the influence he possessed in giving salutary counsels to the young monarch endowed by nature with so many excellent qualities, but too often led into dissipation by the temptations that surrounded him. The official functions of the father afforded him opportunities of speaking of the virtues necessary to the chief of so vast an empire, and of the incompatibility of an excessive love of the chase, of good cheer, and of the pleasures of the senses in general, with the constant solicitude he ought to feel for the happiness and welfare of his people. One day they were talking familiarly of the methods of organizing a good administration, and the Emperor said, " Maffa, whence comes it that the magistrates and prefects of the towns are so negligent in the performance of their duty? I treat them very well. What can be the cause of their neglect?

" Prince," replied Schall, " the mandarins have doubtless remarked that your majesty often acts as if you had no need to occupy yourself with the interests of the empire; and they are endeavouring to make their conduct resemble yours. That is probably the cause of the negligence of the mandarins." The answer seemed to be a little too severe, for the Emperor rose abruptly, and went away, but he was not really offended, for he soon after sent refreshments to Maffa, who was fearing he had gone too far.

Chun-Tché was passionately fond of hunting, and gave himself up to this amusement with all the ardour of an Emperor of sixteen, whose power is such that a gesture often is sufficient to set in motion all the nobles of his empire, and make them rush to gratify his inclinations. This passion for hunting, too, belonged to his Mantchoo race, for not being yet enervated by the luxurious refinements of Chinese civilisation, they retained the taste for the vigorous bodily exercises usually in favour with a pastoral and nomadic people. These grand hunts were made on the scale of great military expeditions, and the Mongul kings, and the chiefs of the eight banners, were invited to attend them. They came to Pekin in caravans, with enormous trains of men, horsemen, and camels laden with baggage; and this army of hunters carried ravage and desolation wherever they went.

One day Chun-Tché had decreed that there should be a hunt beyond the Great Wall, and at this news the inhabitants of the country lying between the capital and Tartary were plunged into grief and consternation; for it announced nothing less than their ruin. Every one knew very well that this hunt would be the cause of destitution and despair to hundreds of families; but no one dared to say so, and already the preparations for this tumultuous fête gave the environs of Pekin the aspect of a vast camp, in which a hostile army was preparing to lay siege to the town.

The Christian charity of Father Schall was, however, so much affected by the thought of what the people were about to suffer, that he went to the Emperor, and said to him at once with the true frankness of an apostle that this hunt would be a public calamity, and that he ought to abstain from it.

The Emperor looked astonished. "I have," he said, "held counsel on the subject with the princes and nobles of my empire, and they have all, without exception, given their assent to it."

"If," said Father Schall, "your majesty previously expressed a wish to have this hunt, no one of them would have dared to speak against it. You should have asked the opinion of the poor people whose country is about to be laid waste; you would not then have found a single one who approved this

14*

armed expedition. I entreat your majesty to allow yourself to be moved by consideration for the public welfare. Instead of proceeding in this tumultuous manner to the Land of Grass, and crushing all the people on your route, it would be better to remain in your palace, and occupy yourself with the administration of your empire." Chun-Tché made no reply to this harangue, and Father Schall retired; but as he was afterwards returning to his mission, he saw numerous squadrons of the Tartar horse moving off, and having asked what that signified, he was told they were returning to the Steppes of Tartary, as the Emperor had countermanded the hunt.

There is an ancient Tartar law by which, if a prince is killed in battle, all the chiefs in the army are condemned to death unless they can prove distinctly that they were occupied elsewhere by order of their prince, so that it was impossible for them to defend him.

In 1653, an expedition had been sent to the south, to quell a considerable insurrection. A Tartar prince was to command the army, and as he was a very valiant man, and eager to gain all the glory of the campaign, he went with a small chosen band in advance of the rest of the troops, in order that no other chief might have any share in his expected victory. He very soon met the enemy and immediately gave him battle, though his force was quite insufficient for such a contest; but, fearing to be accused of cowardice if he waited till the rest of the army came up, he threw himself impetuously on the battalions of the insurgents. He fought a long time like a lion, but was at length overpowered, and fell, pierced with innumerable arrows. He was already dead when the other chiefs came up, fell upon the victorious insurgents, killed more than twenty thousand of them, and put the rest to flight.

The bravery of these soldiers should certainly have pleaded in their favour; but on their return to Pekin two hundred of the principal officers were loaded with chains and condemned to death. They were awaiting in their dungeons the execu tion of the sentence, and though every one was deeply interested in their fate, no one dared to petition for their pardon for fear of weakening military discipline. Father Schall however, came to the assistance of these unfortunate heroes He presented himself before the emperor, and had only read a few words of his petition, when Chun-Tché, much affected interrupted him, saying, "Thou art then the only person, Maffa, to address me in language which so harmonises with the feelings of my own heart. I desired to save the lives of these warriors, but I could not be the first to suggest it; for I am young, and might appear not to understand the importance of strict military discipline. I waited till their pardon should be solicited from me." These unhappy persons were thus all saved, and were merely lowered a few degrees in military rank, that there might be no violation of that law of responsibility, which is in some measure the basis of the organisation of the army amongst the Mantchoo Tartars.

We have mentioned these different instances to show how Father Schall used his influence with the young Emperor. It was always in the cause of charity that he exerted himself; he tried to do good to all, in order to win their confidence, and lead them to the knowledge and practice of the Christian religion. When he was at court and in conversation with the Emperor, it was always said, "Tang-Jo-Wang is with the master; he is labouring for the happiness of the poor people." Chun-Tché would sometimes say to his ministers, "You suggest nothing to me but ambition and vain glory; it is not so with Tang-Jo-Wang; in the memorials he addresses to me, it is his compassionate heart which speaks, and I cannot read them without shedding tears." The Emperor was in the habit of carefully treasuring up these letters of Father Schall in a casket which he took with him in all his journeys, for he used to like frequently to read over the writings of his dear Maffa;—certainly a flattering testimony to the noble character of Father Schall, and we must agree that it was also honourable to Chun-Tché, who, though still so young, knew so well how to appreciate virtue and merit.

It is very pleasing to observe the conduct of this poor priest in a foreign land, in the presence of persons of the highest rank of two altogether different races, one remarkable for urbanity, obsequiousness, refinement, and habits of diplomacy and artifice; the other, on the contrary, half barbarous, rude and warlike in manners, still intoxicated with the conquest of the most extensive empire in the world: yet, whether holding intercourse with the Chinese or the proud Tartars, knowing how to win the veneration and confidence of all by his disinterestedness, his openness, and charity.

Chun-Tché departed from the customs of the Chinese Emperors in being easy of access. Before the accession of the Tartar dynasty, the eunuchs watched night and day at the gate of the palace, and in the morning collected the petitions addressed to the Emperor. It was also at the palace-gate that the astronomers and other literati presented theirs, with this difference only, that they were permitted, and even commanded, to present them not only in the morning, but in the very hour in which they might have observed any phenomena. This privilege was extended in favour of Father Schall: he was permitted to visit the Emperor whenever and wherever he might be; thus it seldom happened that his memorials were presented with the others; and whether the Emperor was in his palace, his gardens, or with the Empress, his mother, Father Schall was always admitted to his presence. It frequently happened that he went in the evening, and the conversation was then often prolonged till the night was far advanced. Chun-Tché had then the consideration to send him home escorted by six of his guards, lest any accident should happen to him in going on horseback through the streets of the capital; and he took care to advise the guards not to go too fast, and not to frighten the horse. Father Schall was always received at the palace as an intimate friend, and treated with the utmost cordiality; and there were cushions provided for him covered with sable, that he might not fatigue himself by sitting cross-legged in the Tartar fashion. The Emperor often passed whole days in his company, taking lessons in astronomy and mathematics, assisting in chemical experiments, or manipulating drugs to make pills with; and he would then invite the father to dine with him. One day when he was on horseback, hunting in the beautiful park adjoining the imperial palace, Father Schall was about to present a petition. "I will read it in the evening, Maffa," said the Emperor, smiling; then, perceiving a hare leap through the underwood, he shot it with an arrow, quite pleased with the opportunity of showing his skill to Maffa.

The Emperor Chun-Tché did not content himself with merely receiving Father Schall cordially in the palace, but frequently visited him in his own house. He liked to go to the mission, without pomp or retinue, without even being announced beforehand; and he always behaved like a friend of the family, conversing with the missionaries, visiting the chapel, the refectory, the young Chinese who were being educated for the priesthood, and the garden, where he himself would gather flowers and fruits, graciously praising their beauty. The different employments of the missionaries, their studies, their religious exercises, all excited his liveliest interest; he inquired about their habits, the rules of their order, and their manner of living in common. Sometimes when he had passed many hours in conversation with Father Schall, he would say to him, smiling, "I have been a long time here, Maffa, and you have offered me nothing to eat or drink," and then he would accept a little unceremonious collation, which he had always the politeness to praise.

An Emperor of China, being regarded as the Son of Heaven, and the representative of the divinity on earth, is literally an object of worship. Any article he uses is, in a manner, sacred, and the "rites" do not permit it to be applied afterwards to common purposes. The characters which compose his name are forbidden, under the severest penalties, to be used in private writings or printed books. The very seat which has been occupied by the Emperors out of the palace, is considered as a precious relic, and, if any one had the audacity to sit down upon it, he would be looked upon as a sacrilegious wretch. This seat is covered respectfully with a piece of yellow satin, and the simple mortals who happen to come into its sacred presence must bend the knee and prostrate themselves as if they were before the emperor in person.

Now Chun-Tché, when he visited the missionaries, was accustomed to sit indiscriminately, sometimes here and sometimes there, according to his fancy; and this became at length very embarrassing and expensive to the establishment, for there was scarcely a seat which his imperial majesty had not thus rendered unfit for use. One day Father Schall knelt down before the emperor, and said, "Sire, there is scarcely a chair here which your majesty has not condescended to occupy, and now, where are we to sit?" "What Maffa!" answered Chun-Tchè, graciously. "Are you too superstitious? Do as I do, and sit wherever you like."* It must be confessed that there was a something of a Henri Quatre in this Tartar.

This frequent and familiar intercourse of Father Schall with the young emperor, who held in his hands the destinies of more than three hundred millions of people, gave rise to the hope of seeing Christianity planted and rooted forever in this land, till then so barren, notwithstanding the long and unsparing labours of the evangelical husbandmen at different periods. The missionaries of China addressed the most fervent prayers to heaven for the conversion of a prince so gifted. They loved to look upon him already as the Constantine of China; and Father Schall, as far as prudence and propriety would allow, neglected no opportunity of introducing into his

---

* History of the Conquerors of China, p. 117.

mind and heart the light of Catholic truth. One day when, during a long walk, he had been explaining the decalogue and giving a brief account of the Christian religion, the Emperor appeared particularly struck and affected by all that he had heard. In the evening he sent for the missionary, and expressed his desire to have in writing a summary of the instruction he had verbally received; and a secretary who was there, pen in hand, was ordered to write under the dictation of Maffa. Father Schall having then said that many books concerning the Christian religion had been composed in the Chinese language and printed, the Emperor expressed a wish to see them, and an officer was immediately sent to the mission to fetch them. Chun-Tché studied them carefully, and found a particular pleasure in reading the gospel and the lives of the saints; and one day, having perused the history of the passion of our Lord, he became much agitated; sent for Father Schall, and begged him to speak about this great mystery. As this solemn and affecting conversation began, the Emperor knelt down in token of respect; the venerable missionary also knelt by the side of his interesting catechumen, and it was thus that he spoke, with deep emotion, of the sufferings and death of the Saviour of men. Chun-Tché very frequently applied himself to the practice of the precepts which he heard or read in the Christian books, but one day when he was learning, with the catechism in his hand, to make the sign of the cross, one of the principal eunuchs having suddenly entered, he blushed and pretended to be busy about something else. Respect for the opinion of men had great influence over a character otherwise full of uprightness, and often prevented him from acting as openly as might have been wished.

The friendship of the Emperor for Father Schall extended in some degree to all the missionaries dispersed through the different provinces of China. Religion being protected and honoured at Pekin, by the head of the state and the great dignitaries of the empire, the gospel labourers were enabled thenceforward to carry on in peace the work of the propagation of the faith. The Chinese had not the persecutions of the mandarins to fear; they were at liberty to be baptized, and to practise their religious duties openly, without fear either of the bastinado, the spoliation of their goods, exile, or death. When men have not sufficient energy and strength of mind to obey the voice of conscience at all costs, and to devote themselves perseveringly to their spiritual interests, notwithstanding the distractions of this present life, it is a great point to be able to say to them: "Do good, fix your thoughts on your eternal felicity, and you will not be unhappy here below." Man is so weak, that nothing ought to be neglected that may lawfully strengthen and support him. It is undeniable that the exceptional position of Father Schall at Pekin had a beneficial influence over the success of the missions. Preachers arrived in greater numbers and penetrated freely into the interior of the empire; they were able without fear to hold intercourse with the people, destroying their prejudices, enlightening and instructing them, and teaching them to know and love the religion of Jesus Christ. Thus the number of converts increased rapidly all through the provinces. There arose on every side, in the cities, in the suburbs, on the banks of rivers, a number of zealous little Christian communities where God was served in spirit and in truth; the religion of the Lord of Heaven was no longer a novelty in China; the gospels, the catechism, the "Imitation of Jesus Christ," the "Lives of the Saints," and many other pious and doctrinal works, were printed and extensively circulated. The cross was painted over the doors of the Christians' houses and graven on the stones of their tombs. Numbers of chapels were open to the faithful for the performance of public worship, and the beautiful prayers of the Catholic church were sung in the Chinese language from one end of the empire to the other. Father Schall has been reproached with his title of mandarin; his connection with the court has been blamed; he has been asked why he thus threw away his time with an Emperor who only wished to satisfy his curiosity, and did not sincerely desire to be instructed in the truths of Christianity, for which he, in reality, cared very little. These reproaches appear to us unjust. If Father Schall was not ab'e to make a Christian of Chun-Tché, he has, at least, the merit of having laboured with zeal and perseverance for that object; and it is certain that by having succeeded in rendering the government favourable to religion, he facilitated the conversion and salvation of a great number of the Chinese.

It was eighty years since Matthieu Ricci had entered China; during that time the number of Christians had much increased, and the Catholic worship had been everywhere organised in a satisfactory manner, but no church had yet been built which could be opened to the public. The Christians had been hitherto too few in number in each locality to possess sufficient means for so important an undertaking; besides which, the protection of the government had not been so far confirmed that Christian worship could be publicly practised without liability to the insults of the infidels, and the persecutions of the mandarins. The converts had been in the habit of assembling in private houses, where they had fitted up chapels and oratories decorated in the Chinese taste, and supported by the freewill offerings of the Christians, to which the catechumens were admitted, and some well disposed pagans.

In 1650, however, Father Schall laid the foundation of a great church, not far from the imperial residence, and on an immense tract of land granted to him by the emperor. The capital was still encumbered with material of all kinds, the ruins of buildings which had been burnt or demolished the year before by the insurgents; so that it was easy to procure wood, brick, and stone, at a very small expense. The work was begun under the direction of Father Schall, and there soon was seen, in the midst of Pekin, an edifice surpassing all others in height. The church was in the form of a Latin cross, and all the details of architecture and ornament were in the European style, ingeniously combined with the Chinese. There was a very handsome high altar, also four chapels in which were hung pictures representing our Saviour, the Virgin, the Apostles, St. Ignatius, and St. Francis Xavier, and the walls were adorned with inscriptions, in great Chinese letters, consisting of the decalogue, the eight beatitudes, and the principal articles of the Christian doctrine. Above the portico there was a large slab of marble, on which was the following inscription in the Chinese and Mantchoo-Tartar dialects:—

"The Christian faith, first brought into China by the Apostle St. Thomas, was propagated anew in the empire under the dynasty of Thang: under that of Ming, St. Francis Xavier, Matthieu Ricci, and several priests of the society of Jesus, preached this religion verbally, and by books in the Chinese language. They laboured zealously, but the fruits of their labour were scanty, on account of the instability of the nation. The empire having devolved upon the Tartars, and priests of the society of Jesus having reformed and published the calendar of the empire, this temple was raised and publicly consecrated to the service of the living God, in the year 1650, the seventh year of Chun-Tché."

A triumphal arch of white marble in form of a porch, and adorned with sculpture representing various allegorical subjects, was built opposite the church. On the side which looked towards the great gate was an inscription, forming a sort of pendant to that we have just quoted; it was expressed in these words:—" In the year of the restoration of the Gregorian calendar, Father Matthew, an Italian, was the first priest of the Society of Jesus who penetrated into the empire and reached as far as Pekin; he published the Elements of Euclid, and a Treatise on Mathematics. He left in the capital and in many of the provinces brethren of his order, natives of different parts of Europe. In the year 1623 arrived, nearly at the same time, Jean Terence, and Adam Schall, who undertook the reformation of the Chinese calendar. Jean Terence having died, was succeeded by Jacques Rho a short time after,- the latter also died,—and the care of this great work devolved on Adam Schall alone. After twenty years of fatigue and struggle with the jealousy of men he published the calendar, corrected and improved by a new method. The affairs of the Christian religion having thus obtained stability, the temple was built. This triumphal arch was raised in token of gratitude, and dedicated to God and the Holy Virgin, in the year of Grace 1652."

On the exterior façade of the triumphal arch were four great inscriptions, in letters of gold, presented by the Emperor, and in praise of Christianity; on the left were four others of smaller size, sent by the sixty-sixth descendant of Confucius. Father Schall set a high value on this homage rendered to religion by the family of that famous personage, who had still such immense influence in the empire after the lapse of 3000 years. The right side of the arch was adorned with a eulogium on the Lord of Heaven, composed by the first minister, president of the Tribunal of Rites, and who had the direction of all matters relating to foreigners and public worship. The erection of this church, surpassing in size and beauty the most renowned pagodas of the capital, produced an excellent effect on the mind of the Chinese. The magnificence of the pictures, the pomp of the religious ceremonies, and the different inscriptions, which formed a sort of summary of the Christian doctrine, attracted daily a great concourse of the infidels. Many who went to visit the temple of the Lord of Heaven only out of curiosity, here found unexpectedly that grace and enlightenment which touched their hearts, awakened their intelligence, and transformed them into excellent Christians. Here was the fulfilment of the desire expressed in a distich, which may be read above the picture of the Saviour and his Holy Mother,—

"*Qua monstrat Salvator iter cum Virgini matre
China diu amissam concita carpe viam.*"*

The zeal of the converts was in some degree excited by the erection of this magnificent temple, which was a great novelty to them, and of which they were very proud. Early in the morning, before the doors were opened, artizans were seen to stop before the church, as they went to work, put down their little loads, and prostrate themselves in prayer before the house of the Lord of Heaven. There was often an immense crowd, for the pagans gladly mingled with the Christians, persuaded that this demonstration of piety could not fail to bring them good fortune. On Sundays, the converts in the environs of Pekin, came eagerly to their dear church, and on the principal festivals of the year the faithful from the most distant missions arrived in numerous caravans, sometimes after having braved the fatigues and inconveniences of a seven or eight days' journey.

Two Christians of advanced age remained constantly at the church, to teach those who might enter and be desirous of learning the Christian religion, and Father Schall himself also gave a course of religious instruction. He took as an assistant in this important duty a convert of fervent zeal, who had gained with distinction several literary degrees, and who bore the title of catechist. This duty is entrusted, in the Chinese missions, to the best informed amongst the Christians, and those of the most irreproachable character. The catechists have always been of immense service to the missionaries in the propagation of the faith; they usually exhort the pagans and give them the first notions of Christianity; and they have also the care of instructing the catechumens. It will be readily understood that the natives of the country, speaking the language, and perfectly acquainted with the strong and

---

* O, China, restore courageously that path long lost, but which is pointed out by our Saviour, and by his Virgin Mother.

weak points of the Chinese character, are better able to insinuate their ideas into the minds of their countrymen than foreigners are, who, having but recently arrived, are but little conversant with their language and manners. One of these catechists, advised by Father Schall, had himself converted, in the city of Pekin, more than 5000 pagans.

China, as we have already said elsewhere,* is pre-eminently the country of associations. The Chinese never remain isolated, but have a remarkable propensity for forming what they call *houi*, or corporations; there is one for every class, for every kind of trade, for every undertaking, and all descriptions of business; even the beggars and robbers all form themselves into communities more or less numerous. It seems a sort of instinct, which brings certain individuals together, and impels them to cast into a common store all the resources they have, in order to make the most of them.

It sometimes happens that the citizens unite spontaneously to watch over the observance of the laws, in certain localities where the authorities are too weak or too careless to keep order.

The missionaries did not fail to take advantage of this remarkable inclination of the Chinese for associations. As soon as Christianity was sufficiently developed in Pekin and the provinces, they formed congregations of both sexes, who assembled once a month, on appointed days. There were three principal ones for men. The first was called the "Brotherhood of the Mont de Piété;" its object was to supply the wants of the poor and needy, and to relieve every kind of suffering amongst the Christians. The second was instituted for the repeating of prayers, and practising certain good works for the benefit of the souls in purgatory; the third had for its object the funeral solemnities, a matter of great importance amongst the Chinese. The pagans were con

---

* Empire Chinois, tom. II. p. 86.

tinually calumniating Christianity by saying that it took no heed of the dead; that the worshippers of the Lord of Heaven completely forgot their deceased relations and friends; buried them without pomp or solemnity, and never went to pay them any honour at their place of burial. It was to destroy the injurious effect of these false accusations, that the Brotherhood of Funeral Solemnities was formed. Three similar societies existed among the women. They assembled separately, on appointed days; members were named whose duty it was to receive deserted infants and have them baptized; to visit the sick, to assist them in their last hours; to distribute alms to the poor, and to attend funerals.

The missionaries were active above all things in introducing exactness and regularity into public worship; this was not difficult amidst a people to whom the observance of the rites is so often recommended, and where masters of the ceremonies are such important personages; and it often happened that more gravity and propriety might be observed in the Chinese churches and chapels than in those of Europe. The Chinese would not allow themselves to laugh or to hold conversations, above all in presence of the Holy Sacrament. During service they sit, rise, or kneel, as the ritual prescribes, and perform every change of posture with as much precision as a community of monks or nuns, and even the pagans, who go out of curiosity to see the religious ceremonies, never fail to conform to that order and propriety of behaviour which they admire amongst the Christians.

The erection of a public church gave a new impulse, not only to the converts of the capital, but also to those dispersed through the different provinces of the empire. Missionaries became every day more numerous, and, thanks to the liberty they enjoyed of preaching the gospel everywhere, religion made rapid progress, and everything gave cause to hope that this population, rendered torpid by indifference, would at length be roused and simultaneously embrace the Christian faith. It seemed to the missionaries that, after the grace of God, everything depended on the conversion of the Emperor, and that the whole nation would not fail to follow so striking an example. For this reason, in every Christian community, this important conversion, which appeared to have every chance of success, was earnestly besought of God. The Emperor was well informed; he was acquainted with religion, and had continually by his side an apostle full of zeal, whose exhortations never failed. He loved and esteemed Father Schall, and delighted to give him public testimonies of regard.

In that same year when the ceremony of the dedication of the Catholic church took place at Pekin, he seized the opportunity to bestow a public honour on the chief of the mission, and after having raised him to a higher position among the functionaries of the state, he sent him a diploma, which was published in the *Moniteur* of Pekin, in order that the distinction conferred on Tang-Jo-Wang might be known over the whole empire.

This imperial document was to the following effect:—

"By the order of Heaven! Decree in favour of Adam Schall.

"When Heaven destines to the world a man remarkable for probity and fidelity, it takes care at the same time to send a sovereign capable of employing and recompensing his services; and it is for this reason that I have wished to mention the merit of such a man, so that he may rejoice to have served me.

"This remarkable man art thou, John Adam Schall, great and illustrious Mandarin.

"Educated from thine infancy in the mathematical sciences, thou hast come here after crossing boundless seas, and hast now lived amongst us for several years. We also, arriving at an opportune time, have been able to hear thee spoken of, and to know thee; and having admired the scientific works that thou hast published, we sought thee to place thee at the head of the Tribunal of Mathematics. At length, notwithstanding thy repugnance, thou didst accept that office. Thy astronomical calculations have always agreed with the Celestial laws; the rules of the ancients were uncertain, and often without foundation: thou hast examined them, corrected them, and now the science that has been confided to thee is extended and purified.

"We have, therefore, judged it proper to confer on thee an office more elevated in dignity, namely, that of Ta-Chan-Sse of the Grand Tribunal, for we wish by this distinction to excite thy zeal, and induce thee to communicate to us faithfully thy discoveries. We place thee, moreover, in the number of our friends, and we promise thee our sincere benevolence.

"The new empire being for us all an occasion of rejoicing, thou must not be deprived of this common joy. We wish on the contrary that thou mayst be able to partake it, and for this reason we add to thy dignity the title of *Tonhoui-Tui-Fou*,* which belongs to the grandees of the empire. We command that faith shall be put in this present writing.

"Courage then! and this benefit, due only to thy merit, will be further augmented.

"The more thy genius and thy knowledge shall be manifested, the more will thy dignities and thy rewards increase. As the recompence of thy favours we wish that thy science, thy probity, and thy fidelity and thy virtue may shine through the whole world."

In the eighth year of the reign of Chun-Tché.

This document placed Adam Schall in the ranks of the first aristocracy of the empire; and the Emperor, afterwards wishing also to ennoble his ancestors, addressed to him two special diplomas conferring titles on his father and mother.

---

* "Wise and penetrating master."

We have said elsewhere,* that the principal civil and military mandarins, who have distinguished themselves in war or in the administration, receive the titles of *Koung, Heou, Phy, Tze,* and *Nan,* corresponding with our duke, marquis, earl, baron, and knight. These titles are not hereditary, and give no rights to the sons of the individuals thus decorated; but, what seems very curious to us, they may be carried back to their ancestors. This custom seems to have been introduced with reference to the funeral ceremonies for defunct ancestors, and the titles addressed to them by the Chinese. An officer on whom rank has been conferred by the Emperor cannot perform the funeral rites of his ancestors in a suitable manner if they have not been honoured with a corresponding title. To suppose the son of higher rank than the father would be to overthrow the hierarchy, and attack the fundamental principles of the Chinese Empire. The idea of a nobility that instead of being transmitted to children goes back to forefathers, who have long departed this life does certainly seem an absurdity to us; but it might be a question worth asking whether there may not be in reality more advantages and fewer inconveniences in allowing the glory of an individual to be reflected back on his parents, rather than in advance upon his children.

The patents of the honours conferred by his Majesty Chun-Tché on Father Schall's parents have been preserved to us, and we will give a translation of them, as they seem to throw considerable light on the manners and opinions of the Chinese people.

"For the father of Adam Schall!

"Men who are endowed with virtue and perfection have commonly received them from their parents. This truth is known to all the world; and thus, if you boast of being the sons of good parents, you ought to reflect your renown and

* Chinese Empire.

your reputation back upon them, since it is from them you have received them. Now Adam Schall, in examining the good qualities that have come to thee from thy father, we find it suitable to confer on him a great favour, and for this reason, at the commencement of the new reign, we have bestowed on him the title of the dignity that thou hast attained. Thus thou, Henry Schall, Father of Ta-Chan-Sse, Prefect of the Tribunal of Mathematics, thou hast distinguished thyself in the kingdom of which thou art an inhabitant, and by thy manner of bringing up thy children, thou hast acquired great celebrity. Thou needest not to have any regret, for thou hast established thy renown on an eternal basis. In considering the merit of thy son, who has been useful to us and to thee, we willingly grant thee the title of 'Man of rare Piety,' with the dignity of Ta-Chan-Sse. We send it thee in this imperial case.

"Courage then; instruct and bring up your children well, since by this means one augments one's reputation. Thy son is entirely devoted to our service and that of the empire. It is not then without a cause that we send thee this diploma, wishing that thy days may be calm and tranquil, whilst thy son here is glorified on thy account.

"For the mother of Jean Adam Schall.

"Every well constituted empire, when it discovers a man of merit, ought by all means to inquire into his origin. In this research I have been indebted to the obedience of thy son for the information I asked. Marie Schaiffart de Merode, mother of Jean Adam Schall, Prefect of the Tribunal of Mathematics, thou hast by thy diligence and solicitude obtained an admirable result. By thy ingenious industry thou didst excite the child to study, and in reality it is more to thy care than to his own labour that he owes his success. It is therefore proper to bestow on thee some title that thy virtue may be known to all. Now, on account of the renovation of our empire we cannot too much praise thee for the education thou hast given thy son from his earliest age, and we grant to thee the title of 'Woman of remarkable Holiness.'

"Courage then! thy son remembering the encouragement that he met with in his studies will glorify the mother who guided his first steps, and rendered homage to thy merit. This homage we also render thee, according to the custom of our country, since thou hast granted us a son who is a glory to the whole empire. Thy praises will be published through all ages, and all will say that thou hast been a mother endowed with rare virtue.

"Given in the eighth year of the reign of Chun-Tché," Father Schall having been subsequently raised to the mandarinate of the first order, the Emperor not only conferred new titles on his father and mother, but extended them to his great-great-grandfather.

It was not long after Chun-Tché had thus showered favour and distinction upon his dear Maffa, that he fell ill, and his malady was so much increased by political anxieties and inward grief that his life became seriously endangered. The empire had not yet recovered from the effects of the revolution; the governors of provinces announced numerous insurrections, sometimes on the part of the rebels, sometimes from the partizans of the old dynasty. The astronomers perceived in the heavens phenomena of evil augury, and did not fail to divulge their dismal prognostications at court and in public. Father Schall seized the opportunity afforded by these circumstances to make another attempt at producing a religious impression on the Emperor's mind, urging him not to remain deaf to these warnings, and endeavouring to guide his soul towards God. He pressed him to resist no further the inspirations of God and of his conscience; he conjured him to devote himself sincerely to the salvation of the empire, and of his own soul. One day, when Chun-Tché lay on his bed, suffering more than usual from his malady, he called one of his principal eunuchs, and said to him, "Go and find Maffa, and tell him there were terrible things in the memorial he sent me yesterday. I know what Maffa wants. He does what no other would dare to do; he exhorts me to correct my faults. I know my fidelity and his frankness; there could not be found in the whole empire a man who would act towards me more uprightly. My health has been bad since the seventh moon; war and sedition are agitating my provinces; Heaven is offended; it is all over with my empire, and I believe there is no help but in my death. I wish, however, that they would not tell me of these evil signs. Whatever I do the stars always announce misfortune to me. Let Maffa come to my assistance, and give me his counsel as to the conduct I ought to pursue. I know that Heaven has constituted me master of my empire, and I have served both the empire and Heaven as well as I could. I have imposed privations on my body; I have clothed myself in coarse raiment, and I have had but one dish on my table. What can I do more? I am willing to do anything, but I do not like them to be continually displaying before my eyes the menaces of Heaven. If the aspect of the stars is terrifying, do not let Maffa tell me anything about it."

Father Schall, in reply, begged the Emperor, through his messenger, not to be cast down, and declared he should be always at hand to afford him cordial assistance and advice in what should appear conducive to his happiness. He added that he would be faithful to his majesty to the last day of his life, and that he would, as in duty bound, pray to God to help him in his various tribulations. As he pronounced these words, the old man could not refrain from shedding tears, and the eunuch then left him to give a report of what had been said to Chun-Tché. "It is very true then," cried the Emperor, "that the heart of Maffa is full of tender affection for me. Go back to him again, and tell him I no longer dread death. Let it come to-day or to-morrow. I do not know what is left for me to do for the benefit of my empire. There is no one in the palace who can tell me so well as he. If he knows any means by which I can still be useful to my people, and deserve the protection of Heaven, let him tell me. I will do exactly what he shall advise me. I have always treated him with sincere and cordial friendship, let him act towards me in the same manner."

A few days only had passed after the utterance of these expressions, when the unfortunate prince, forgetful of the welfare of his empire, of his promises to Father Schall, and even the painful illness that troubled him, was entirely absorbed in passionate solicitude about the funeral of one of his wives. Chun-Tché had formed a short time before a most vehement attachment to a young widow; and though, according to the laws of the empire, the sovereign is forbidden to receive widows into his harem, he had, in the violence of his passion, audaciously trampled on this ancient custom, and not only married this woman, but even given her the second place after his legitimate consort.

He was entirely taken up with her, and as she was fanatically devoted to the Buddhist superstitions, she had insensibly withdrawn the Emperor from Christianity to deliver him wholly to the influence of the Bonzes. She had even made him promise to be always devoted to them, and to give himself up blindly to their guidance.

It happened that this woman whom Chun-Tché loved with so immoderate a passion, and to whom he would willingly have sacrificed his whole empire, died almost suddenly, and the event plunged the Emperor into such profound grief that he abandoned himself to what seemed like absolute insanity. There was great difficulty in preventing his killing himself, and the Empress-mother had been obliged to throw herself upon him and snatch from his hands the sword which he was about to plunge into his body. These violent emotions aggravated his malady; and day and night he was occupied only with the thought of the deceased woman, to whom he now solemnly accorded the posthumous rank of Empress. He ordered her obsequies to be celebrated with hitherto unheard-of pomp; and even renewed in her favour the barbarous custom of the Tartars, abolished since their accession to China, of sacrificing attendants and slaves on the tomb of their princes, in order that they may render them in another life the same service as in this. By the order of Chun-Tché, more than thirty persons put themselves to death with this view on the grave of the posthumous Empress.*

The ceremony was especially remarkable for the enormous concourse of Bonzes, who came from all directions to attend it; in the interior of the palace only there were more than two thousand; and the unfortunate Emperor, whose grief seemed to have overthrown his reason, paid them the most extravagant honours. He had rich embroidered garments distributed to them, and abandoned himself entirely to their caprices. He even went so far as to have his head shaved in their fashion, and to declare himself publicly a disciple of the Bonzes.

The nobles of the empire, the ministers and censors, all memorialized the Emperor on this preposterous conduct, and Father Schall especially exhorted him, with a courage that was truly apostolic, representing to him, in the most independent and energetic manner, the destruction that other sovereigns had brought on themselves by giving way to superstition and losing all controul over their passions. But Chun-Tché had taken his resolution: "Maffa," said he, "I do not understand you. How can you, who are a religious man, reproach me for doing what my religion bids me do? Would you not think I did wrong if I tried to hinder you from the exercise of your religion? Why then do you wish to prevent me from practising mine? I pardon you, Maffa, because I

---

* Histoire des Deux Conquérants de Chine, p. 182.

know you act thus from affection towards my person. I can willingly endure reproaches from a friend."*

The Emperor continued to manifest his grief in the same extravagant manner, and he and the Bonzes gave themselves up to so many absurd superstitions, that he ended by exciting the contempt and ridicule, not only of the Chinese, but even of the Tartars. Ill as he was, he was seen rushing through the streets like a madman to one pagoda or another, prostrating himself before all the idols he met with, and chanting Buddhist prayers. A countless throng of Bonzes, satellites, and eunuchs, accompanied him to spread carpets before him, and stop the pressure of the crowd upon him; and this disorderly troop insulted the passers by, and pillaged and trampled under foot the merchandise they found displayed in the streets. Their plundering propensities were indulged to such an extent that the traffic of the city was in a great measure interrupted, for the traders preferred shutting their shops and remaining hidden in their houses to exposing themselves to the robbery committed by the Emperor's attendants as they proceeded to their devotions. The people began to murmur aloud, and repeated continually the old Chinese adage, "When the circulation of buyers and sellers is interrupted from morning to evening, and from evening to morning, the empire is on the brink of ruin."

Chun-Tché was not in a state to bear all this excitement, and a violent fever soon seized on him, and laid him on what proved his death-bed. Father Schall went to see him, but the sick Emperor only ordered tea to be served to him, and did not speak. When he felt his end approaching, he would not allow any stranger to be admitted to his presence. He appeared for some time to be sunk in profound thought, and then, asking for his pencil, wrote twelve decrees, by which he granted a general amnesty to all prisoners except such as

* Histoire des Deux Conquérants de Chine, p. 185.

were accused of rebellion and parricide; he bestowed additional dignities on the great mandarins, and distributed to others pecuniary rewards; he freed the people from various taxes; showered benefits upon the servants of his household; and, finally, he summoned the four grand dignitaries of the empire, and appointed them regents during the minority of his successor; and after that, he made, in their presence, a sort of general confession, which was inserted in the official paper of Pekin for the edification of all the monarchs and nations of the earth.

Chun-Tché accused himself, firstly, of having governed badly the empire which his ancestors had confided to him, and of not having procured for it a solid peace. Secondly, of not having profited by favourable opportunities for doing honour to the princes allied to him by ties of blood. Thirdly, of not having listened to the counsels that his mother gave him for the good of the empire. Fourthly, of not having rendered sufficient homage to his father, his grandfather, and the warriors who had deserved well of the state. Fifthly, of having been parsimonious in the recompence of his officers and soldiers. Sixthly, of having defrauded the mandarins and magistrates of their emoluments, in order to amass riches and satisfy his cupidity. Seventhly, of having sought after curiosities and gone into foolish expenses on that account. Eighthly, of having treated his subjects like strangers, and not like his children, when they were oppressed by the mandarins. Ninthly, of having admitted into his palace, and favoured, contrary to the advice of wise and prudent men, the despicable race of eunuchs. Tenthly, of having loved to excess the late empress, and grieved for her loss in a manner to render himself troublesome to himself and his subjects.

"I have a son of eight years old," added the dying man, "and though he is not the eldest, his rare intelligence makes me hope he will govern the empire well. Let him therefore be my successor. To you four, whose fidelity is known to me, I recommend him with confidence." Having thus spoken, the dying monarch inclined his head as a token of respect to the four regents, and then asked for his imperial robe, a garment embroidered with dragons in gold. He then folded his arms, crossed his legs, and said, "Now I am going," and shortly after he expired.*

"The Emperor Chun-Tché died at midnight, and at dawn of day, all the Bonzes and their adherents were chased from the palace. Towards noon the deceased was placed in his coffin, and was wept by an immense multitude who had witnessed the ceremony. The next day the four regents placed on the imperial throne the prince of eight years of age, who afterwards gave to his long and glorious reign the name of Khang-hi. The regents, the imperial princes, the generals, the presidents of the supreme courts, all the great mandarins then in Pekin, prostrated themselves three times before the new sovereign, and struck the ground nine times with their foreheads.

"It was a strange thing," says Father Schall, " and certainly worthy of admiration, that the Mantchoo Tartars should have been able in so short a time to combine the various elements of the Chinese nation, and to attach them to themselves so firmly, that there was not the slightest opposition when it became necessary to seat an infant on the imperial throne."*

The day after the death of the Emperor, all the Tartar tribes nearest to Pekin came in great caravans, with their wives and children, to deplore the death of their master. They were divided into eight Banners, and advanced by numerous groups to make their lamentations round the imperial coffin. According to the "Book of Rites," their tears ought to have lasted three whole days, and in the midst of the general bustle and excitement, the governors of the city do not seem to have considered that the grief of these strangers, great as it was,

---

* The Chinese say on these occasions, "The emperor has fallen"
† De Statu Religionis Christ., p. 237.

could not afford them quite sufficient nourishment for that period. No one thought of ordering them any provisions, till Father Schall at last took pity on these unfortunate famishing people, and presented a petition on their behalf to the regents. He pointed out to them the sufferings of these poor Tartars, amongst whom were women and old men, incapable of enduring the fatigue of this long ceremony. He conjured the government either to allow of their returning to their own country, or to provide for their subsistence; and the regents, praising the thoughtfulness and foresight of the missionary, published an edict by which the Eight Banners were allowed to return into their encampments. The Tartars who wished to remain for the grand funeral ceremony should, it was added, be maintained at the expense of the state.

On the fourteenth day of the first moon, the oath of allegiance to the new Emperor was solemnly taken. The princes of the blood, the six supreme courts, the various tribunals, the mandarins of the first and second rank, and all the great dignitaries of the empire, were introduced into the palace, and ranged according to their due order of precedence. The coffin of the deceased Emperor was raised upon a magnificent platform, and after the company had wept, as in duty bound, one of the regents read the formula of the oath, and afterwards burnt it on the coffin in a golden urn, all the persons present prostrating themselves, and striking the ground three times with their foreheads, as if to call on the deceased Emperor to witness their fidelity. They then repaired to a pagoda within the palace, to ratify their oath in the presence of the idols. Father Schall, who could not take part in this religious act, approached the regents, and informed them that, being a worshipper of the Lord of Heaven, he was not permitted to bend the knee before idols; he therefore asked permission to perform this part of the ceremony in his own chapel. "Maffa," said the regents kindly, "if you should not take any oath, no one would ever doubt your fidelity and devotion to the Emperor; but since you desire to perform this rite, let it be in your own house or elsewhere as you please."

As soon as the ceremony of taking the oath of allegiance to young Kiang hi was concluded, that of the funeral of Chun-Tché was commenced, in a style of magnificence surpassing anything of the kind that had hitherto been witnessed. To the solemn and sumptuous pomp of the Chinese rites, were added the extraordinary and barbarous customs of the Tartars. Tragic scenes took place, in which many of the attendants of the late Emperor put themselves to death, that they might proceed to the other world, and continue their accustomed services to their master. It is stated in the annals of China, that the empress mother, perceiving a young prince who had been the intimate friend and favourite of Chun-Tché, expressed to him, with strong emotion, her grief and astonishment at finding him alive.

"Is it possible," said she, "that you are still alive? My son loved you, is doubtless now waiting for you;—hasten then to join him, and prove to him that your affection was sincere and generous! Run and bid adieu to your parents, and then have the courage to die! Your friend, my son, is stretching out his arms towards you."

According to the historian, these words, uttered in a tone at once affectionate and severe, caused great distress to the young man. He loved Chun-Tché, but he loved life also, and could not think of death without a terrible shudder. He was surrounded by his afflicted family, who were urging him to escape by flight from so frightful a sacrifice, when the empress mother sent to him a present of a box ornamented with jewels, and containing a bowstring for him to strangle himself.

The unfortunate young man still hesitated, for he was at the happiest time of life, and could not resolve to die of his own accord, as the barbarous prejudices of his nation required, but the two officers who had brought him the fatal present

Standard Catholic Publications.

ILLUSTRIOUS WOMEN OF THE BIBLE AND CHURCH HISTORY. By Mgr. Bernard O'Reilly. Full page illustrations	2 50
IRISH FIRESIDE LIBRARY. 6 vols., per set....................	6 00
" NATIONAL SONGSTER. 200 pages.......................	1 00
JAPANESE MARTYRS. By Rev. Joseph Broeckeart, S. J.........	75
JESUS IN THE TABERNACLE. Cloth, red edges...............	50
KEENAN'S DOCTRINAL CATECHISM........................	50
KEATING'S HISTORY OF IRELAND. By Rev. Geoffrey Keating, D. D. 750 pages, gilt edges...........................net	5 00
KEEPER OF THE LAZARETTO.................................	40
KEIGHLEY HALL, AND OTHER TALES.....................	40
KEY OF HEAVEN. 18 mo. (Prayerbook). Prices upward from	75
" " " 24 " " " " "	60
" " " 32 " " " " "	50
" " " 48 " " " " "	25
KERNEY'S CATECHISM OF UNITED STATES HISTORY, net	15
KING AND THE CLOISTER. By E. M. Stewart................	1 00
KIRWAN UNMASKED. Paper covers...........................	12
LATIN CLASSICS. Expurgated. Part I, net, 40 cts. Part II, net,	50
LADY AMABEL. By Miss Agnes M. Stewart.....................	40
LA FONTAINE'S FABLES. Red Line Edition. Gilt edges....	1 25
LAST OF THE CATHOLIC O'MALLEYS........................	75
LEGENDS AND FAIRY TALES OF IRELAND. Over 400 pages	2 00
LEGENDS OF ST. JOSEPH. By Mrs. James Sadlier............	75
LILY'S VOCATION, AND OTHER TALES.....................	40
LITTLE LACE-MAKER, THE; or Eva O'Beirne................	75
LITTLE FLOWERS OF PIETY (Prayerbook) Prices upwards from	25
LITTLE FOLLOWER OF JESUS, THE. By Rev. Grussi, C.PP.S.	75
LITTLE LIVES OF THE GREAT SAINTS. By J. O'Kane Murray	1 00
LOST GENOVEFFA. By Cecilia M. Caddell.....................	75
LOVER'S WORKS. 5 vols., 12 mo. Leather half-morocco, gilt tops. Per set,..net	3 50
Sold separately, single volumes, each..................net	75
Handy Andy. Rory O'More.	
Treasure Trove. Songs and Ballads.	
Legends and Stories of Ireland.	
LOUISA KIRKBRIDE. By Rev A. J. Thébaud, S. J 530 pages..	1 25
LOUAGE'S MORAL PHILOSOPHY. New Edition..........net	75
LOVE. By Lady Herbert	75
LOVE OF JESUS CHRIST. By St. Alphonsus M. Liguori. 24 mo, red edges...	50

Standard Catholic Publications.

LOST DAUGHTER, THE. By Mrs. James Sadlier	75
LOST SON, THE. By Mrs. James Sadlier	75
LIBRARY OF AMERICAN CATHOLIC HISTORY. 3 vols.,	6 00
LIBRARY OF CATHOLIC NOVELS. 6 vols., per set	7 50
" " " STORIES. 6 " " "	7 50
" " CONTROVERSY. 4 vols	3 00
LILY OF ISRAEL. New and approved edition. Illus. 380 pages.	75
LIFE OF OUR LORD AND SAVIOUR JESUS CHRIST. By St. Bonaventure. Over 400 pages and 100 engravings	1 25
LIFE OF CHRIST. By Rev. Henry Formby	80
LIFE OF ARCHBISHOP MAcHALE. By Rev. Canon Bourke.	1 00
*LIFE OF JOHN PHILPOT CURRAN. By his Son	1 00
LIFE OF FATHER MATHEW. By John Francis Maguire	2 00
LIFE OF FATHER MATHEW. Cheap and popular edition	1 00
*LIFE OF DOCTOR DIXON. Primate of all Ireland	50
LIFE OF CATHERINE McAULEY. By A Sister of Mercy	2 50
LIFE OF MOTHER McAULEY. Cheap edition	1 00
LIFE OF MOTHER SETON. Steel portrait. Red edges	1 00
LIFE OF MARY QUEEN OF SCOTS. By Donald MacLeod	1 50
LIFE OF THE GLORIOUS PATRIARCH, ST. JOSEPH	75
LIFE OF ST. PATRICK. By Rt. Rev. M. J. O'Farrell	1 00
LIFE OF ST. PATRICK. By Rev. James O'Leary, D. D.	1 00
LIFE OF ST. WINEFRIDE. 180 pages, illustrated	60
LIFE AND LABORS OF ST. VINCENT de PAUL	75
LIFE OF POPE PIUS IX. By Monsignor O'Reilly, LL.D.	2 50
LIFE OF O'CONNELL. Cloth, gilt edges. Crown 8vo.	3 50
LIFE AND TIMES OF ROBERT EMMET. 328 pages. By Madden	1 50
LIFE OF WASHINGTON IRVING. Steel portrait	75
LIFE OF WILLIAM CULLEN BRYANT. Steel portrait	75
LIFE OF ST. ALPHONSUS M. LIGUORI. By Bishop Mullock	50
LIFE AND MIRACLES OF ST. BRIDGET. Paper cover	10
LIFE OF BLESSED MARGARET MARY ALACOQUE. By Rev. George Tickell, S. J. 12mo., 500 pages. Colored frontispiece	1 25
LIFE AND TIMES OF ST. BERNARD. By M. L'Abbé Ratisbonne	1 50
LIFE OF ST. ELIZABETH OF HUNGARY. By the Count de Montalembert. 430 pages	1 50
LIFE OF ST FRANCIS OF ROME. By Lady Georgiana Fullerton	1 00
LIFE OF ST. FRANCIS de SALES. By Robert Ormsby, M. A.	1 00
LIFE OF ST. LOUIS, King of France	40
LIFE OF ST. MARY OF EGYPT. 180 pages, illustrated	90
LIFE STORIES OF DYING PENITENTS. By Rev. Edw. Price	75

Standard Catholic Publications.

LIVES OF JAPANESE MARTYRS. BLESSED CHARLES SPINOLA, Etc.	75
LIVES OF THE CATHOLIC HEROES AND HEROINES OF AMERICA. By John O'Kane Murray, LL.D.	8 00
LIVES OF THE EARLY MARTYRS. By Mrs. Hope.	1 25
LIVES OF THE FATHERS OF THE EASTERN DESERTS.	1 25
LIVES AND TIMES OF THE ROMAN PONTIFFS. From St. Peter to Pius IX. 2 volumes, octavo, leather, half morocco gilt tops, nearly 2,000 pages, steel plates, per set	10 00
LIVES OF ST. IGNATIUS AND HIS FIRST COMPANIONS	75
*LIVES OF THE SAINTS. BY REV. ALBAN BUTLER.	
4 volumes, octavo, 12 full page steel engravings. Nearly 4,000 pages; leather, half morocco, gilt tops. Per set	8 00
Half calf extra, full gilt edges net	15 00
In 12 vols. Leather, half morocco, gilt tops	15 00
" Half calf extra, full gilt edges net	25 00
LUCILLE, OR THE YOUNG FLOWER MAKER. By A.T. Sadlier	40
MARIAN ELWOOD, OR HOW GIRLS LIVE. By Miss Brownson	1 25
MARTYRS, THE. By Viscount De Chateaubriand	1 50
MARTYRS OF THE COLISEUM. By Rev. A. J. O'Reilly, D.D.	1 50
MAY BROOKE; OR, CONSCIENCE. By Mrs. Anna H. Dorsey.	1 25
MALTESE CROSS, AND OTHER STORIES	40
MAIDENS OF HALLOWED NAMES. By Rev. C. Piccirillo, S. J.	1 00
MAKING OF THE IRISH NATION. By J. A. Partridge. 8 vo.	1 00
MANNING'S WORKS, (CARDINAL). 5 vols., 12 mo., uniform edition, english cloth extra, in box. Per set net	2 25
Sold separately, single volumes, each net	50
Four Great Evils. Internal Mission of the Holy Ghost. Sin and Its Consequences. Vatican Council. Temporal Mission of the Holy Ghost.	
MANUAL OF THE CHILDREN OF MARY. Cloth, red edges	50
MANUAL OF BL. TRINITY. (Prayerbook). Prices upwards from	1 00
" " Catholic Prayers " " " "	37
" " Crucifixion " large print, " "	63
McCARTHY MORE. By Mrs. James Sadlier	1 20
MEDITATIONS ON ST. JOSEPH. By Brother Phillipe net	60
MEDITATIONS ON THE INCARNATION. By St. Liguori	75
MEMORIAL OF CHRISTIAN LIFE. By Rev. F. L. de Granada	60
MERCHANT OF ANTWERP. By Hendrik Conscience	1 25
MEN AND WOMEN OF THE FAR OFF TIME. By S. H. Burke.	50
MEMOIRS AND SELECT SPEECHES OF SHIEL & CURRAN	1 50

www.ingramcontent.com/pod-product-compliance
Lightning Source LLC
Chambersburg PA
CBHW031847220426
43663CB00006B/524